FIGHTING MONSTERS

FROM BRITISH ARMED FORCES TO REBEL FIGHTER: A FIRST-HAND ACCOUNT OF BATTLING ISIS

JIM MATTHEWS

MIRROR BOOKS

First published in hardback by Mirror Books in February 2019

This paperback edition published in June 2019

Mirror Books is part of Reach plc
10 Lower Thames Street
London EC3R 6EN
England

www.mirrorbooks.co.uk

© Jim Matthews

The rights of Jim Matthews to be identified as the author
of this book have been asserted, in accordance with the
Copyright, Designs and Patents Act 1988.

ISBN 978-1-912624-00-3

1 3 5 7 9 10 8 6 4 2

Every effort has been made to fulfil requirements with regard to
reproducing copyright material. The author and publisher will be
glad to rectify any omissions at the earliest opportunity.

Cover images by Stephen Mulcahey / Alamy

For Naomi – keep fighting

"Whoever fights monsters should see to it that in the process he does not become a monster."

Friedrich Nietzsche

"Partial knowledge can polarise opinion. Scholars insist St George didn't kill the dragon, which means either it never existed or it's still out there."

Steve Aylett

FOREWORD

In February 2016, after a year in Syria and Iraq, I left the gunfire, the bombs and the bloodshed behind; and my nightmare began. I'm not talking about PTSD, or related matters. I barely had room to consider those things, because on return to the UK I found myself in a fresh battle straight away.

Arrested on arrival, I walked free from court some two and a half years later, after the Counter Terrorism Division of the Crown Prosecution Service failed to convict me as a terrorist: for fighting *against* the Islamic State (Daesh). The case was consistently murky throughout. They never explained in detail the basis for it, and similarly refused to say why they dropped it.

The charge was that I "attended a place or places in Iraq or Syria where instruction or training was provided for purposes connected with the commission or preparation of acts of terrorism."

Terrorism here means, "the use of firearms or explosives to cause or threaten serious violence to a person or property, for the purpose of advancing a political, racial or ideological cause."

When the highly controversial Terrorism Act was first brought in, nearly two decades previously, it was argued in Parliament that the wording was too general. The example provided to illustrate the point could hardly have been more apposite to my own case: Kurds fighting Saddam Hussein in northern Iraq, and people supporting them from the UK, would technically be terrorists. The then Home Secretary retorted that the idea of the law being used in such a way was the product of a fevered imagination.

Had my case gone to trial, the prosecution would have had to explain not only how I could be a terrorist when I was fighting *against* a proscribed terrorist organisation – *alongside* an international coalition which included the UK – but also, how I could be a terrorist when the YPG (the Kurdish fighting group I joined) was not.

The prosecution's arguments continually shifted and contorted as things progressed. There is no room for detail here, but an example piece of correspondence sent to my lawyers essentially said (when boiled down and straightened out): *we aren't actually calling him a terrorist, even though we're charging him with terrorism.*

It could be argued that any journalist attending the same place of training (to report on it) would technically be guilty under the above law also. Perhaps that too is a fevered imagination at work.

I was also, originally, charged with possession of a firearm as well, but they dropped that more quickly – perhaps reconsidering that I was on the front line of a war at the time.

My day-to-day life, while this went on, was rather less droll if equally bizarre.

My passport was seized and my movements restricted. I lost my teaching job after the police announced the decision to charge me on Twitter. Terrorism law had never been used in this way before, so the press jumped on it. Then Halifax bank froze my account without warning. I couldn't access my own money and, like the prosecution, they simply refused to explain. I nearly lost my home. I could have crashed with friends, place to place, but that would have broken my bail conditions to reside at my given address. I half-expected to be remanded in custody pending trial.

"How can they accuse *you* of terrorism?" I was constantly asked. In attempting to explain the prosecution's reasoning, to baffled, exasperated people, I'd repeatedly end up putting the case against myself. It was an odd time.

I expected scrutiny, of course. I'm old and ugly enough to realise the authorities wouldn't just leave me alone altogether. But I didn't think they'd make it impossible for me to exist. Fighting the Islamic State was one thing. Fighting the British state was another.

And some have speculated that *another* state could have been mixed up in this – which may provide the key.

The Turkish state, which brutally oppresses the Kurdish people not only within its own territory but also over the Iraqi and Syrian borders, spends hundreds of millions of pounds on British-made weapons. Following the defeat of Daesh, the British government may well have been keen to restore relations with Turkey, having rankled it during several years of coalition support for the Kurds.

It has been suggested that the Turkish government may have put pressure on ours, to crack down on support for Kurdish resistance in the UK. At one of my police station visits, a Special Branch officer casually remarked to my solicitor: "Well, the YPG aren't on the proscribed list, but Turkey, which is a NATO ally, says they're terrorists, so…"

My lawyers requested disclosure from the prosecution, regarding discussions between the British and Turkish governments about British volunteers fighting for the Kurds. They also requested disclosure on discussions held within government (ours) over whether the YPG should be proscribed. We never got that material.

Notifying us of their decision to drop the charges, the prosecution wrote (unprompted): "This decision is not in response to the applications before the court for disclosure or to stay the proceedings."

The court declared that it was for the Attorney General to explain all this to Parliament. The Attorney General said it was up to the prosecution. So far, no explanations are forthcoming. Some would say I made my own bed here. I have no problem with that view, but I suggest that questions still need answering. Next time there's a terrorist attack in Britain, remember how your money was spent.

My true subject, however, is not the absurdities of British justice, so I shall keep this short. This book is about a world where – contrastingly – one finds no shortage of nobility and honour in the dirt.

London, July 2018

PROLOGUE

Rojava, northern Syria
January 2016

"We have been waiting all the day to join the battle," sighed the young Iranian-Kurdish woman, black eyes reflecting the light of the fire where hunks of fresh-slaughtered sheep were roasting, skewered on twisted, rusted wires. She was new to the war. Desperate to fight.

It was a cliché, and not a good one, that all the female fighters in Rojava were searingly beautiful; but this one was. Even in grubby winter layers and cheap combats, in this dirty, abandoned village we'd taken for a base, she looked out of place. But it was her unalloyed sadness, and not her looks, that I found so arresting. That went *all* the way down.

Her unit had been on standby all day. The firefight had finally got going in the early afternoon, and was wound up by dusk; perhaps four hours, all told.

Shots had hit the ground dead ahead as we entered the enemy village, small tuffets of white cloud spitting up a few metres away.

One casualty down immediately; blood all over the concrete, trickling like tea from her leg. A hasty bandage job behind cover and I threw her over my shoulder, light as a lamb, dashed back to my Hummer and packed her off. I was never thanked for that and didn't expect to be. If a Kurdish fighter has to turn back into danger and pull a friend out, there are no medals or back-slapping; it's just something he – or she – had to do today.

Before the Hummer had roared off I'd grabbed my machine gun from the turret and latched onto the advance group from the *salderî* (infantry), maybe seven of us altogether. As we spread out and scrambled into cover, I'd headed up an outside stairwell overlooking the enemy positions and hunkered behind a concrete wall just one block thick.

Now it was over, all I wanted to do was sleep. The barbecue was getting going but I was too tired to eat, yawning constantly, like a nervous paroxysm. The intense concentration of the fight would sap anyone's batteries, even if I hadn't spent the previous night sleeping in the same cramped steel turret, swaddled in blankets in the freezing fog, one hand resting on the machine gun.

Highlights of the violent exchange still reverberated in my tired mind.

The narrow, cluttered stairwell, suddenly lit up like a photographer's darkroom – a lurid red glare and a cinematic *vwoosh* as the rocket meant for me passed low overhead, exploding right behind me. Jarring the concrete, ringing in my ears. I'd been looking down, cramming rounds into my ammo belts, so I swung my gun up just too late as the two figures dashed back into cover.

PROLOGUE

The gaily painted suicide truck racing out of the village, down the track, on the heels of our fleeing Hummer. Replaced by a startlingly white cloud, luminous fragments arcing and spiralling outwards from the blast, trailing threads of smoke.

The bomber aircraft dipping and soaring again on a sharp angle against the setting sun, deciding the day by erasing three buildings out of four. *That's that, then…*

"And now the attack is over. And we did not do anything…" lamented the woman, bringing me back to the present moment. She looked down, rifle hanging forlornly from her shoulder, heart on the ground. I felt an ache of sympathy. Waiting on the very brink, for hours, then being made to stand down. I knew that feeling well; it ate away at you inside.

"You didn't miss much, really," I told her. She'd get her chance. And a chill ran through me as I said it.

Thinking back to last winter, and all the *friends* since.

Thinking back to someone who once said those words to me.

I wish I'd known then what I know now; I've got regrets enough to last me. Strange, that you can lose so much but still come out ahead.

1 INTRODUCTIONS

In December 2014 I'd just started a new job in Saudi Arabia: teaching English to young cadets at a military base in the country's Eastern Province. Short contract, good money, the kind of job I tend to prefer. I'd been there about a fortnight when I caught the media splash about two British men returned from "fighting" alongside Kurdish forces in northern Syria. The amount of attention they got, you could hardly miss it.

I'd heard of Kobani, of course. You could hardly miss that either: the brave, emblematic city of female freedom fighters that had defied capture by the Islamic State. But I hadn't paid it particularly close attention. For one thing, it was the latest *cause célèbre* of the radical-political circles I'd once moved in, and I was done with all that. I kept in touch with some friends from those days, but hardly outside of Facebook.

Those teenage girls armed with rifles and limited ammunition will not be able to defeat tanks and heavy artillery. Jets will. Just saying, I remember commenting on the post of a friend who'd replaced his profile picture with a black square bearing the word *KOBANI*. (People were doing it "in solidarity".)

To western eyes, the Islamic State – the new face of Islamic terror – seemed to be sweeping in all directions unchecked, like some unstoppable poison cloud. Rising from the ash and rubble of botched invasions, occupations, uprisings and civil wars, they had seized swathes of territory in ruined countries unable or unwilling to resist and were laying claim to actual statehood.

The west's plummeting enthusiasm for military intervention provided part of the backdrop to their rise – a rise accelerated by the increasingly well-equipped and veteran nature of the fighters, by their well-established outreach channels and by an entrenched and mounting worldwide sense of outrage to tap into. Their time had come. They'd boiled it down: a pure strain of holy crusade, righteous outrage and zero tolerance, then added a monthly paycheque for boots on the ground and the chance to rape and butcher in the name of God. Even al-Qaeda considered their *modus operandi* too extreme, it was said; hence the Islamic State's rift with their progenitor.

But there were many takers.

At a small Kurdish enclave in northern Syria, though, they were stopped in their tracks by what seemed the unlikeliest of adversaries.

Until the siege of Kobani, the Kurdish YPG (*Yekineyen Parastina Gel* – People's Protection Units), whose formative militias sprang up in the power vacuum of the Syrian civil war, had drawn little international attention in the context of the wider picture.

Now, the world's media took sudden notice of these units (and particularly their female element) as they resisted the siege laid by a vastly superior military force who battered them mercilessly with artillery shells, bombs and missiles.

These units also gave the war on radical Islamist terror a new, iconic face in the Middle East, however distorted: images of photogenic, enigmatic young women in combat gear reverberated around the world. Armed with the most basic weaponry, equipment and tech, outgunned and surrounded, they stood defiant, month after month, fighting from the wreckage of their city. On the one side stood religious tyranny, bloodlust and reports of massacres and sexual enslavement. On the other, brave and stunning young women with guns and ammo. It became a sensation for dubious reasons. But it was better than obscurity.

US-led air strikes had begun against Islamic State positions, though low-key and specific. Even among the usual anti-war circles at home in the UK there was a rising sense that this wasn't just another case of western interference, though the cries of "hands off" still echoed from some quarters. The Kurds, along with Arab and other local groups, slowly started to retake ground.

This was the first I'd heard about western volunteers getting directly involved in the fighting on the ground. There was no way I'd do it, though. I'd been a soldier once, but that was a decade and a half earlier.

I was no stranger to Middle Eastern conflict and tragedy either. Some years earlier, I'd been involved with human rights and "non-violent direct action" movements in Palestine, and similar things in Lebanon and Iraq, on a broad anti-war/anti-occupation basis. It had started when I left the army and went to university, aged 24, and *got involved in politics*.

At this stage in my life all that was now long behind me. A badly busted relationship in my mid-30s had been my wake-up call. Those activists I'd hung out with years before were now parents, homeowners, career people. The revolution had never happened. To get my own life on some sort of track, I'd done a postgraduate course in teaching English as a foreign language.

I may not have had ideas about changing the world any more, but the Saudi contract never sat totally easy with me, given my background. If the country's shocking human rights record wasn't enough, the provider of teachers to the Saudi military was BAE Systems – Britain's biggest arms manufacturer. Years before, I'd received a 28-day prison sentence following a London street protest against the arms trade. But I was over it. This was purely for the money. No more crusading for me.

Still, my interest in the Kurdish conflict in Syria, passive until now, had been piqued. I started reading up.

Kobani was one of three small regions, known as "cantons", along the northern Syrian border with Turkey, an area the Kurds called Rojava. Though Kurds made up the majority, the population was polyethnic, being comprised of Kurds, Arabs, Assyrians, Turkmen, Armenians, Circassians and others.

The Islamic State were known as Daesh to their enemies locally: a word I, like most people in 2014, had never heard before. Controlling large areas of ground both outside these cantons and within them, pursuant to their aspirations of state-hood along strict religious lines, they applied hard-line rule with gruesome reprisals for transgressors.

The Kurds' struggle was garnering mass appeal, then – regardless of one's politics. For the broad spectrum of a public appalled by the Islamic State's archaic spectacle-of-horror PR tactics, purveyed through modern media and technology, they were the light. Something about the photo of a grinning Daesh fighter clutching a woman's severed head by the hair, one finger raised to the camera like some kind of gang sign, struck me more deeply than I could articulate. It touched something elemental inside. It was eons since I'd last gone do-gooding in a foreign war zone and been bounced out again by the real world, idealism and certainties in fragments on the floor. But I think I was catching a wave of urgent public feeling that this *just had to be fought*.

But what did that have to do with *me*? Even in my activist days, the war on terror was hardly our remit. We already had measures for that: the military-industrialism of Uncle Sam and friends, the teeth-arms of the global capitalist behemoth causing all the *other* problems, at least ensured that al-Qaeda and the like remained small and politically negligible. We needed to change everything *else*…

Well that, in part, seemed the rub. Daesh had far outstripped any comparable organisation before them in combined terms of extremism and territorial claims, and their fantasy notions of nightmare-statehood seemed to be nudging up against reality, right before our eyes. Meanwhile, the expected response from the world police was a long time coming. Some limited assistance had been lent in Kobani, but it was tears in a bucket compared to what it could have been, what it needed to be. How much of this horror would the big powers permit before decisive action became politically expedient – before enough was enough?

The Kurds weren't waiting around. They'd pledged not only to rout Daesh from the region, but to establish an autonomous territory (*state* is a problematic term) by freeing and linking the cantons. They made gains from the air strikes, just as they made opportunity of the chaos of Syria to stake their territorial and political claims.

And on their side of the fence was more, to intrigue and entrance those with leftist or liberal political values and sympathies. What the Kurds were attempting to build *inside* these cantons was at least as inspiring as their courage in battle: a purportedly democratic, egalitarian society whose values were strongly reflected in the structure of the YPG itself, where decisions were taken collectively, where all faiths and races were welcomed, where women made up over half the numbers and rank was distributed equally between genders.

"Democratic confederalism" was the name for this social philosophy, conceived by Abdullah "Apo" Öcalan, leader of the PKK (Kurdistan Workers' Party), which for decades has fought a bitter guerrilla war against Turkey. While the PKK was proscribed, the YPG – their sister organisation in Rojava – was not, despite also looking to Apo as their founder, figurehead and mentor. This opened the door to NATO cooperation, much to the ire of Turkey.

As I read up on this, I had a growing feeling that democratic confederalism seemed almost impossibly utopian: a grassroots political system where everyone had fair and equal representation in social decision-making.

It called to mind another movement that had caught my interest years before; the parallels were unmissable. Like hundreds of thousands of other people in the 90s and 00s, I'd been swept off my feet by the Zapatista phenomenon in southern Mexico. Declaring indigenous territories autonomous through guerrilla insurgency, the Zapatista Army of National Liberation gained strength not through their (negligible) military prowess, but through mass global support for their anti-neoliberalist agenda, articulated by their poetic, wise-cracking masked leader.

In the Zapatistas' balaclava-framed eyes, it was one battle the world over: corporate greed, the military-industrial complex, erosion of rights and freedoms on the one side, and indigenous and environmental struggles and human rights in general on the other. A struggle of one *no* and many *yeses*. They took up arms so that they could one day lay them down. They wore masks so they could one day take them off. Their dreamy rhetoric held millions spellbound.

The Zapatistas, it was said, had even inspired Apo and the PKK to relinquish their dogmatic Marxist politics and agree a truce with Turkey, which had held until very recently.

Apo's new programme in Rojava smacked of experiment, I thought: of revolutionary fervour, of romanticism not seen since the days of the Zapatistas. A black-and-white struggle, then.

Well, obviously not. But closer than anything in recent memory. And while "civil society" – the activists, NGOs, liberal academics and media, and so on – was responding, as it had done to the Zapatista struggle, with messages and gestures of solidarity and support, this newly spotlighted cause had something *else*. Whispers were gathering of an international brigade, formed of volunteers trickling in to fight alongside the Kurds, Yazidis and others against Islamic "fascism". That was entirely new: at least for my lifetime.

I wished them well, and wished it had happened when I was young and idealistic enough to want to act on it.

***

That day, I sat outside the jeweller's store on the low wall of a Saudi mall's ornamental fountain, waiting for Paul (a colleague on the Saudi contract) to finish up in there. At my feet were several carrier bags. We'd just been paid, and I'd splurged on some fancy outdoors gear: a brand-new Gore-Tex jacket and a fleece that zipped inside it, with a lining of tiny metallic dots for reflecting body heat, a thin, expensive sleeping bag with the same type of lining, and some Good Boots.

The glare of the mall lights, reflected off the marble-tiled and glass-fronted stores, made my eyes squint with tiredness. I hate the glitter and glimmer of malls, and the garish opulence of Middle Eastern taste made me feel almost ill.

The manager of the jeweller's was leafing through a catalogue of watches under Paul's direction. I'd taken a mild interest at first, three shops ago. Rolex released a precious few of certain new models each year (single figures, Paul had explained), and you could make an easy few grand just by scooping one up – right place, right time – and taking it back to the UK for a client on order. Right now the fascination was beginning to wear off.

"Paul," I said. "It's nearly seven."

We were meeting three other teachers at a mall restaurant. At seven, all shop shutters would come whirring down as everything came to a temporary standstill for evening prayers. As long as you were in by then you were OK.

In the restaurant, Andy (another teacher) showed us on his phone the girl he'd been talking to. I saw a profile with Arabic script, and a lithe female figure in an expensive and revealing dress – photographed from the neck down. He swiped through several similar photos. There was a culture of young women doing this: fake names, faceless profile pics.

"It's understandable," said Andy. "You know – she's young, she's beautiful, wants to show off her body…"

We leafed through the menus, talked shop.

"Today I wrote out two questions on the whiteboard and when I turned round, half my students were fucking snoring," said one of us. "I've never seen a more ridiculous learning environment."

"I've given up. Now I just play them videos of Saudi Drift and Mr Bean, and stand on the door watching out for officers."

Every morning we caught the shuttle bus from the employ-ees' compound in darkness. Out through the multiple layers of heavy security, down a dust track in the wastes and onto the wide, immaculate roads, through the unending construction site of Saudi Arabia: shacks and slums elbowed between glass and steel grotesques, a colossal regeneration project in the dust. We'd reach the military base as it got light. First lesson was at 6am, by which time our students, the young cadets, had been up for hours, ragged up and down the drill square and bawled at by their instructors. It continued throughout the day, punishment drill in the punishing heat, relentless. Then for 50 minutes each day, groups of 20 or so cadets were packed into a stuffy classroom for a language lesson.

"Apparently the officers used to patrol the corridors and if they saw a teacher outside, they'd come up to you and ask what you were doing out of class. Sometimes they'd just wander in while you were teaching and tell you you were doing it wrong. So eventually the teachers complained and got it stopped – and since then they've been trying to sabotage the programme by knackering the lads out," someone else commented.

Conversation turned to travel plans. In a fortnight all the short-hire teachers on this contract had a week's paid break, flights included. Andy was staying here, arranging something clandestine with his mystery lady. Paul and Rich were off to Thailand.

"I've set myself a goal to spend as much money every day as I'm getting paid for that day," said Rich. "I've got to stay in a good hotel, eat a porterhouse steak for lunch at a restaurant, bottle of wine…"

"Where are you going, Jim?" one of them asked.

"Erm – Sulaymaniyah, mate. It's in northern Iraq," I said. Heads swivelled.

"Er… Aren't ISIS quite active around that area right now?"

"Well, they were recently – near Erbil, the main city, a bit further north. But now the fighting's mainly happening in a small mountain range called Shengal, near the Syrian border." I drew a map with my fingers on the table. 'So Erbil's here, Sulaymaniyah here, the border, the mountains…"

"What the *fuck* would you want to go there for?"

I told them how I'd taught at a school in that region four years before. It was my first teaching job, after passing the Certificate in English Language Teaching to Adults (CELTA) course. I'd wanted to get out of London and the UK for a while, and had taken the first thing that came along. The job had not gone well and I'd left after a month. But over the past few days, I'd emailed everyone I'd known there to say I was coming for a visit. I'd even arranged to call at another language school, with a view to teaching there after my Saudi contract. My hotel was booked and I was all ready.

We finished the last of the meal and headed outside to catch the shuttle bus back to the compound, which picked up employees from the mall at 9pm sharp. Paul sparked up a smoke, offered me one.

"Thanks, no."

"Are you actually going *camping* there, or something…?" he asked, nodding at my shopping items. I mumbled something vague in reply.

***

The two British "fighters" were featured in an exposé by the Daily Mail a few days after the media splash. The pair were never near any combat, witnesses claimed, but had managed to make money from pictures and video footage. By then, however, I'd got into talks myself with the Lions of Rojava Facebook group, helpfully mentioned in the Mail article.

I wrote them a private message, introducing myself. Presenting my credentials and expressing a polite interest, *nothing more…*

I must have checked for a reply every spare waking five minutes. Two days later I received one.

Ok you have to answer a very important question to me. The questions I did not ask you, but ypg want to know. You have to answer everything correctly and neatly. Do please a decent list on your resume. Without this information, you can not join unfortunately. Because ypg will have no criminal. And there are some who want to escape and want to find refuge.

All you need is Good Boots, thermal underwear, warm Jacket, winter clothes and the Ticket (don't bring with you military gear ok!!!!!!!!) You need visa please ask iraqi Embassy for visa Kurdistan Autonomie government Sulaymaniyah city.

We need your pictures, of your Ticket, picture of your passport and your cell phone number. Ypg picked you up From Airport Sulaymaniyah city of iraq then drive you next day to Rojava.

I wrote down what you need to do everything to you. So will ask now:

Your first name and last name. Where were you born? What is your nationality and country? Where do you live? Have you committed a crime? If yes, what? you take drugs? Have you sold drugs? You sat in jail? If yes, when and for how long and why?? Have you killed a human being? If so why? Do you have military experience? If yes, when, where and for how long?

Among my answers I mentioned having done a few short stretches in pokey for protest-related activities. *Why lie?* I thought.

Your a wonderful human being. How could arrest you the fucking cops?

came the reply. My acceptance by the unknown contact crystallised over the following days, and our exchanges became more like a distance friendship. And somewhere along the line, though I couldn't trace the exact point, it became a done deal. My trip was going to be one-way.

So, what had happened to *wishing them well* and *a polite interest, nothing more*? What about cynicism, disillusionment, wisdom?

***

Back at the compound some hours after the restaurant meal, these questions recurred, and continued to recur as I slouched out of the walk-in shower, enfeebled by the sustained pummelling of the hot water jets, grabbed a thick fresh towel from the rail and padded across the room to the soft king-sized bed made immaculate by room service.

Why?

Using the remote I turned on the overhead AC fan and, with another handset, dimmed the ambient lights. I was getting too used to this. A thin sliver of time was all that separated my world of comfort here from the dirty, dangerous one I was headed to. *Very little to eat and the smell of dead bodies of ISIS rats all around,* as a Lions Facebook post cheerily put it – to warn any dreamers expecting an enjoyable war tour.

Two weeks. Was it even real?

Come on man, you're fucking 40, said that voice inside me. *You REALLY gonna do this? Give all this up, burn your boats? Do well on this contract and you've cracked it. After years of low-paid work and unemployment. You know how these trips turn out. You'll end up on your arse again, sadder if no wiser.*

Perhaps it was because this was a chance to actually *fight*, for once. Not to protest, or campaign, or negotiate. Maybe some not-grown-up part of me, which I thought I was over, still regretted never using all that infantry training for real. I did an operational tour of Bosnia in 1996, a very different time to *be* in the military, but there was precious little real soldiering involved. And all the wars on offer since then were bad ones, as I'd seen it, so I'd protested against them instead. At university I read about the Sandinista revolution in Nicaragua, and wished it had happened in my time. In 2001 I travelled with the Zapatistas on their caravan to Mexico City: my mind-blowing introduction to the international anti-globalisation scene. But they weren't recruiting as such, and it wasn't that sort of war, anyway.

At the end of the day, you can hash reasons around in your head forever, because your mind changes all the time while the choice facing you is a binary one: go or don't go. The onlooker's insistence on clear, consistent *reasons why* perhaps demonstrates a lack of understanding and experience, to say nothing of imagination. I'd guess that major decisions have been taken throughout history by people whose minds were more or less made up at the time, give or take. Besides, I'd mixed with enough politicos and activists to know that too much certitude isn't always a great thing.

So. I could tire the moon with my agonising and contemplating – but either I was going to board that plane or I wasn't. Progressive politics, armed struggle and an open door to foreign volunteers don't often line up together. Perhaps it was the chance of a lifetime.

The perennial *why* was only one of a blizzard of questions, practical and otherwise, swarming through my mind. Where would they send me? Were internationals *actually fighting*, or was it all a big PR show? From what I'd seen on Facebook, virtually every volunteer out there was in Cizire (the eastern canton) doing little besides taking and posting photos. I was giving up a lot here. I decided to ask.

Hi there
    I read today that it is impossible to go to Kobani
from Sulaymaniyah. Is this true?

Yes it is true. But we can go to Kobani soon

OK is there fighting in Cizire canton? If I come to Rojava
I want to fight ISIS. Not take photos and do nothing like
these other two British guys. Please let me know.

You can go to Shengal

This is where the battle is, right?

It is like Kobani

Are there other volunteers at Shengal?

Yes American

Shengal (also called Sinjar) is in Iraqi Kurdistan, not Syria. It was
the same fight, essentially – just over the border. A few months
earlier, Daesh had massacred some 5,000 Yazidi men there, and
kidnapped thousands of women and girls. Tens of thousands had
fled the area. Now, Kurdish and Yazidi forces were fighting them
through the Shengal mountain range, towards the adjoining city
of the same name.

Fine, I thought. *That'll do*. Apparently it was freezing cold – hence my new gear.

In my final few days in Saudi I tried to get my head back into a soldiering frame of mind, to blow out 15 years of cobwebs. I'd probably have to justify myself to those of the intervening generation: Iraq and Afghanistan war vets, maybe Special Forces types or seasoned mercenaries on a busman's holiday. How we'd get along socially remained to be seen.

I watched YouTube videos on stripping and assembling the Kalashnikov (the standard weapon of the region). I Googled *skill at arms* and found a scan of Basic Battle Skills, the field training manual of the British army – so old it was probably deemed benign. Reading up won't make you a soldier if you've had no training, but it does wonders for a rusted memory in need of a clean and oil.

I scoured the shops for essentials: a knife, a torch, a cheap, waterproof digital watch. Leather gloves. A lighter. Whatever first-aid gear I could find. Gaffa tape, string. Thermal underwear, waterproof bags for socks and pants. Those were the things I'd need – not fingerless gloves, wraparound shades and a death-skull face mask.

Would I be any good when it came to *actually fighting*? I'd been well trained once, but so what? Ducked a bit of fire here and there, but never aimed a weapon at another human being and pulled the trigger. What would I find in the other volunteers? On the social network pages the leftist element, with their utopian rhetoric and dreams of a Spanish Civil War-style International

Brigade, talked one way, the ex-military types another. Having a bit of a foot in both camps caused me no small amount of introspection.

I stood at my living room window at night, staring across the compound's dust-field assault course that no one used, and over the low, flat-roofed buildings to the towers in the distance. The mosquito screen turned their glaring lights into beaded crosses. Kurdish forces had finally routed Daesh from Mount Shengal. As the Lions told it, the Peshmerga (the government troops of semi-autonomous Iraqi Kurdistan) had turned and fled, while the YPG stood firm and pushed them off the mountain into the city, which they still held. Daesh had rounded up and executed 100 of their own fighters immediately afterwards, for trying to leave. It was past midnight and I had to teach my first class at six. But I could barely sit still, let alone sleep. *Get me out there...*

The day drew closer.

Hi there

Can you please tell me exactly what I need to do when I arrive at the airport?

Ok will do.

When I arrive I need to know it is your guys picking me up and not some Daesh who is reading this. How will I recognise your guys?

Dont fear. We are not Daesh

No I know! But someone could pretend to be from you and I wouldn't know.

Walk outside airport and get in the white mini-bus (it's free).
   It will take you on a short journey (a couple of minutes) to a larger taxi rank outside of airport where we will pick you up. His name is Heval —

Thank you. I look forward to meeting him.

But it can change person

OK I have to be sure who I am getting in a car with. The bad guys could send somebody who pretends to be with you. How can I be sure it is the right guy?

No fear

I wished I could say that. But that was the deal. No guarantees, on either side. *Have you ever killed a human being? – NO.* But the risk was of course mine.

***

On 15 January we short-hire staff set off on our separate ways in taxis throughout the day, in ones and twos, with a cheery, "Have a good holiday, lads," and, "See you in a week!"

Not if things go as planned, I thought to myself.

The most common questions customs officials tend to ask in "hot-spot" airports are, "Why are you coming here?" and "Where are you staying?" Hence the hotel and other arrangements. It was worth $20 for an alibi.

Fingering the printouts of my hotel reservation and language school invitation, I went through the script in my mind as the plane began the descent. Since most of it was true – I *had* taught in the region before, and so on – it didn't need that much rehearsing. I had no intention of keeping my appointments, though.

Touchdown. The airport shuttle bus pulled up to some scruffy sheds to disgorge, and I scanned the crowd, rapidly, from person to person, looking for those who'd be looking for me: a lone westerner among the Kurds and Arabs. Trying to spot them first, size them up in an instant.

Him. There. Looking right at me.

Eye contact with a short, stocky guy in a velvet jacket and flowery, open-necked shirt – straight out of the 70s. Through the cracked, dirty window we nodded simultaneously to each other, and each cracked a smile. Well. He looked OK. There's not much else to go on, at that point.

Warm handshakes, and a mobile phone with my photo on it. Few words.

"*Yeh-per-geh*?" he said, with a wide, welcoming grin.

"Eh?" It took me a second. "Oh – YPG. Yeah!"

We jumped into a battered white pickup and sped away through Sulaymaniyah, Iraqi Kurdistan's second city – generally low-rise and shabby, poor cousin of the richer, smarter and prosperous Erbil.

In an unpaved alley somewhere on the outskirts, we pulled up at a one-storey house and went through the small yard.

"All right, mate?" said a young English voice, inside the house.

Lounging on the sofa of a clean and comfortable living room, with tiled floor, smoked-glass coffee tables and several armchairs, all in the typical creams, browns and beiges of the local taste, was a pale and skinny young guy in a T-shirt and jogging bottoms. Jac Holmes was the first friend I made in Kurdistan, and the last person I'd have expected to meet there – but then I hardly looked the part myself right then, standing there in my best suit, worn in the hope of getting smoothly through customs. What a pair we made, I thought, surrounded by bustling militia agents – short, dark, serious men in thin leather jackets, with no time to hang around – and the posters of Kurdish mountain guerrillas that staked out the place's identity.

We chatted about the journey we'd had getting here, and swapped what bits we knew about the road ahead. Jac looked quite at home: cheerful, unruffled.

"And you're going there to do *what* – again?" I asked.

"To fight, mate. Same as you."

"OK… Have you *been* in the military, or… anything…?"

"Nah…" Whatever his reasons, there was no doubting his commitment. "I tried to come here last year. Before I flew out, the Special Branch turned up at my house, asking me stuff like *Have you made a will?* Trying to put me off. I flew to Erbil but the British cops had already tipped them off and they wouldn't let me in. Made me pay for my own flight home and stuck me on the next plane out. *Cunts…*"

Yet here he was. He was 21, from Bournemouth, and had a fair grasp of the developing situation in Rojava. His other interest in life was rolling a blunt in his dad's shed and getting baked to a pebble. Maybe that accounted for the detached, mordant expression lent by the downward slant to his upper eyelids – an impression that shattered when he broke into a grin, as he did often, through a thin furze of blond facial hair, making deep creases round his sharp and delicate features. Words like *elvish* and *puckish* came to mind. I felt somewhat uneasy. I mean, he seemed savvy and together enough, for a kid; but… did he have *any* idea what we were getting into? I wasn't even sure *I* did.

Later on, the door opened for an older guy, white, perhaps 45. He gave us a nod and a grunt in greeting, and sat stiffly by himself in a hard-backed chair by the door. For the next hour or so we absorbed ourselves separately in laptops and phones as people came and went. Eventually the three of us gathered round the kitchen table to while away the evening. The older guy, Ronnie, was an Australian ex-soldier and trade unionist, here for his socialist convictions.

We chatted away over tea and smokes. Would the western nations recognise a Kurdish homeland in Syria? What about Turkey? Would the US put forces on the ground? The talk between us was generally analytical and speculative, touching occasionally on ethics and politics, rather than gung-ho and macho. Only one person was trying to steer it that way – a loud, big-bellied Kentuckian with an *Iraq Warrior* tattoo. He faded after a few false starts, occasionally popping his head back round the kitchen door to say things like, "Kill 'em all and let God sordidout!" and then retiring again when he found no takers. He was travelling the opposite way to us, getting out after a week in Rojava.

Young Jac was little more than half my age – and size – and at 75 kilos, I'm hardly the biggest bloke. He'd barely been out of Bournemouth, as far as I knew. Hell of a first travel destination.

"Listen, Jac," I said, as we lay on thin mattresses on the floor that night, talking low as the others snored, "you're going to meet all kinds of people in a scene like this – and some are worth listening to, and some you just need to avoid. I might not be able to stick with you, because I'm trying to go to Shengal, not Rojava. So the best thing you can do is, find someone a bit older who's got his head screwed on, and stick with that person until you know your own way round. Like Ronnie, for instance. He's sensible, he knows his stuff. If you and me get split up, try and stick with Ronnie. OK?"

"All right, mate."

Someone had to keep an eye out for him. But I had my own plan, and I wasn't changing it.

Shortly afterwards, sleep came easily, as can happen when you've finally stepped off the edge and whatever follows is out of your hands.

Early next morning we drove through the town, out into the countryside and up a mountain road, switching vehicles onto a dirt track and finally walking with our bags. A typical Middle Eastern winter day: warm enough to break sweat in the open, cool enough to freeze it on your skin in the shade, as we languished at a mountain camp of camouflaged shacks. The sharp clean air had me dozing off on the warm grass fretted with patches of snow, iced over and resisting the thaw. Against the bare blue sky, a savannah of rugged evergreens clung to the further mountains all around.

In a few days they'd start missing me in Saudi. *Gone clear.*

2 RIVER CROSSING

"Why do you come here?" said a woman's voice out of the darkness. Wary of my footing, I took a step closer to see her more clearly. We stood together on the shore of the Tigris. It was close to midnight.

With our Kurdish guides, Jac, Ronnie and I had waited at the camp till nightfall, then picked our way down the mountainside, joined by others en route. Now, around 30 of us stood pressed together in a clearing, by water flat and calm as a steel blade. The temperature had dropped sharply as darkness fell. Tiny lights glowed from the few houses dotting the surrounding hillsides. Down here, it was too dark to see anyone properly, even close up. Even so, the residual light glancing momentarily off the woman's features revealed enough of the strong, gentle good looks that seemed to match her voice.

Two of the group leaders worked deftly to unravel and inflate a rubber dinghy. Through the group's low chatter, the champing, many-limbed mass of bodies and equipment, the conjoined fog from people's breath and furtively-cupped cigarettes, hummed the muted yet charged murmur of anticipation.

"To… support the revolution in the cantons… and to *fight ISIS*," I answered. I was content with the neatness and brevity of it.

The cause. For *freedom*. Daesh, and their *atrocities*…

It sounded good. But still.

Why did you come here?

Maybe there was no clear answer. As with other ventures in the past, I was compelled, so I came.

***

It looked like the world's biggest carnival on the eve of battle. As protesters streamed into the Italian port city from all over the world, the streets buzzed with dizzying contradictions. Armoured troop carriers thundered up and down past half-naked, dancing people with body paint and bongo drums. Zones declared out of bounds were ring-fenced by tall steel barriers, festooned immediately with flowers, streamers and placards.

The G8, Genoa 2001. A meeting of the leaders of the world's eight most industrialised countries, and the site of the biggest summit protest to date – dwarfing those of Seattle and Prague. The tide was rising, we had come and we were unstoppable. We'd shut them down.

What were we protesting about? Well, everything. Capitalism. Globalisation. Neo-liberalism. Words that summed up the root of the world's ills. Immigration laws, the arms trade, environmental destruction, child labour, child soldiers, sweatshops. You name it.

Camped in the grounds of a stadium, we had spent the preceding few days constructing shields and body armour from any scrap materials available, and scouring the shops for helmets, respirators and first aid gear. We were going equipped.

On the designated "direct action day", helicopters clattered above the clouds of tear gas and flying debris as police and demonstrators fought pitched battles over makeshift barricades. A police jeep was trapped between an upturned metal dumpster and rioters battering it with rocks and bottles. A cop huddled inside as a protestor repeatedly rammed a wooden plank though a broken window. My own side was going way too far.

I ran up to the jeep, facing out at the crowd, yelling "Stop!" Their stones battered my makeshift shield and crash helmet. Then a loud bang and everyone drew back. A youth, taken down by a shot coming from inside the jeep, lay behind its wheels, blood pouring from his eye. The jeep reversed over him, bouncing horribly, and screeched away. I knelt beside him, checked for pulse and breathing, yelling for an ambulance as journalists snapped and the square emptied. A phalanx of cops stormed towards us and we scattered.

In the mass exodus from the city the following night, I was lucky to evade the snatch squads and get out.

Back in London, I and my new political "comrades" learned the wider context of the violence. Video footage showed gangs of cops jumping up and down on screaming, bloodied protesters. Amnesty and other groups published reports of torture and mass beatings of prisoners in police stations.

Over the next few years I racked up numerous arrests and minor convictions on the streets of London, protesting a different issue every other week. What happened in Italy only convinced me that after four wasted years in the army, I'd finally found the right side: the good fight.

The anti-globalisation movement, only superficially cohesive, gradually fell apart and turned largely into an anti-war movement with the invasions of Iraq and Afghanistan, and the worsening situation in Palestine. I went with it. In 2002 whole cities were under military lockdown in the West Bank and rumours circulated of a massacre at Jenin refugee camp. I was desperate to get out there.

I travelled to the West Bank and Gaza three times between 2002 and 2004, blocking tanks in the streets, riding on Red Crescent ambulances to discourage the IDF (Israel Defence Forces) from firing on them, monitoring checkpoints, negotiating, reporting. We used our international status to intervene – an uncomfortable dynamic, but it sometimes worked. I funded these trips by labouring on London building sites.

One typical day in Jenin, the IDF were shooting up the town as I took cover with several other internationals and locals. Anyone's yard or doorway was anyone's cover; it was a good way to meet people. Where an alley met the main road, a teenage boy managed to blow up a glass bottle full of gunpowder – which he'd meant to lob at a passing tank – while he was still holding it. The army were seconds away, heading towards us. Blood dribbling from his mangled hand, he was rooted to the spot, oblivious to our screams of warning.

I ran out under fire and dragged him to safety, then several other internationals took over, elbowing me out. They didn't know first aid, they were bungling it, but there was nothing I could do in the melee. They'd been there longer, was the thinking: it infected everything, hampered everything.

I'd expected to find solidarity and selflessness here, but found egotism and jealousy instead. There wasn't enough glory to go round. Which was pretty ridiculous, since none of us were doing anything that remarkable. Incidents like these, combined with a late-dawning sense of the complexity and general hopelessness of things, left me with a disaffection as strong as my original zeal had been.

It seemed to me that you had to sort of tally your accounts to yourself, in moral as well as pragmatic terms, on such ventures. Could I honestly justify my being there? I'd probably have done better by just giving all the money I'd spent to some Palestinian family. After my third trip I never went back.

My time in Palestine left me with nothing but a sense of self-loathing I wanted to forget. Perhaps I was more like the activists I'd come to regard so cynically, in not separating my own ego from the bigger picture. Some people work tirelessly in obscurity for some small change. I wasn't one of them.

***

The woman's innocuous question hardly called for any answer so searching, but maybe I wasn't the only one prompted to a moment of reflection, standing here on this shore with the water lapping as they floated the dinghy onto the surface.

Anyway, here I was. A couple of press articles and a Facebook chat was all it had taken. Perhaps it was a chance to make good on previous failures: to find purpose and self-worth in some noble cause bigger than my own small existence with its mundane concerns. To fight the good fight.

Organised into small groups, we removed our footwear and picked our way barefoot over sharp rock through shallow water, and crammed together along the dinghy's soft, tubular sides, bags and boots in our laps. It took maybe 10 minutes to shuttle each group across the 100-metre stretch, boat upended at 30 degrees to the water level, as the rowers dug and plunged with their paddles.

On the rocks and sand of the far shore we reassembled ourselves while the boatmen deflated and stashed the craft in a metal box hidden by tall weeds. We were now in Syria.

Our guides led us up to the high ground, and a road with waiting vehicles. We jumped aboard, each of us stowing whatever baggage we were carrying.

We drove up high again, to a small compound atop a ridge of hills. A scattering of concrete shacks and wooden huts, and a large open-air shelter made of badly welded scaffolding backed onto a sheer cliff that dropped away to the flat Rojava countryside below. I'd said I was supposed to be taking a different route to Shengal, but was told to sort it out further down the line.

Ronnie and I were the only two up next morning around six, checking out the view from the frosted copse of low trees along the cliff's edge – the vast, featureless flatlands; the distant towns and villages; the dormant pumpjacks of disused oil wells, hammers standing idle in pools of slick. On the nearby hilltops were other, larger buildings, a tiny graveyard, and a giant metal radio mast: Qereçox (*Ker-a-cho*), the YPG headquarters in this region.

Ronnie pulled out his cigarettes and I blagged one off him as I had the night before, wondering how long it'd take me to go from non-smoker to full-time professional on this trip. The Middle East always does it to me. We sparked up, exhaling dragon's breaths on the frozen air.

"So what does your wife think about you coming here then?" I said. "Or would you rather not be asked questions like that?"

"Aaah, probably the latter," he replied, but smiling warmly.

"Yeah, fair enough."

After a breakfast of flatbread with jam, tahini, olives and white cheese, seated at long metal tables under the outside shelter, we had our induction brief with a stout, middle-aged female general, translated by Delal, the woman I'd spoken to on the river crossing. Like the general, she was now dressed in the combats of the YPG, made of thin synthetic cloth with a predominantly dark green digital camo pattern. In the dark she'd appeared charming and friendly, eager to know us, to befriend us. Now, in the daylight, I was somewhat struck by her magnetic self-possession.

We each had to pick a codename, by which we would be known during our time there. Think of a word you like, and Delal would translate it into Kurmanji (the most widely-spoken dialect of the Kurdish language).

Jac's name was a done deal already. "I think you like Şoreş (*shoresh*)," smiled Delal. It meant revolution. They'd chatted about it on the night walk.

My mind was a winter whiteout.

"So, some people choose the name of a mountain, or river, something like that," said Delal, to help me. "Ararat is the biggest mountain here."

"OK... What's a smaller mountain?"

"You can take... Cûdî (*ju-dee*)? It is smaller mountain."

I settled for that. I'd be known as *heval* Cûdî everywhere from now on. *Heval*, the form of address for generals and footsoldiers alike, translates as friend or comrade. Everyone here was a *heval*.

Delal explained how we'd go from here to military training, and then to battle (pronounced *bat-tel*, with a slight stop between syllables, and a soft "t"). How often did a word like that sound pretty?

We walked to the cliff edge and down a little, to a natural dip in the rocks where we each sat and made a declaration, stating our names and reasons for being here, while another young woman from the YPG media section filmed from slightly above. If you're killed in the YPG, they'll use that video to prove you joined them of your own free will.

***

Weapons training, in the main room of the academy's bare, lone concrete house on the plains, was somewhat rudimentary.

"Now, this gun is called *karnas*. It is not like *kalaş* (Kalashnikov rifle); it is sniper weapon. It is use for… *murdering* –"

Polite titters rippled round the room. The 12 westerners on this intake sat on rugs lining the two long walls. It was an infectiously jovial atmosphere among the Aussies, Yanks, Brits, French and others. When Jac, Ronnie and I had arrived, the others had greeted us with real warmth: the more the merrier. At that time there were maybe 40 of us internationals in-country, all told.

The translator, a balding man in his mid-20s with a thick, neatly trimmed beard, stopped in his tracks. A look of confusion fell across his perpetually affable features. He checked the dictionary on his phone. "It is right? *Murr-dering?*"

Next to him a veteran Kurdish fighter, gnarled as a walnut, leafed back and forth through a sheaf of printouts, brows creased and mumbling as though overwhelmed by the plethora of info in his hands and the challenge of relating it to the weapon in front of him, which he knew like the inside of his own mouth. We had a few minutes each to strip and assemble each weapon, and learned some valuable random facts like when it was invented, and which countries manufactured it. Stoppage drills would have been nice.

"When we fight inside building, we do not shoot out of window. We make hole in wall, like this." He held up a hammer.

"Sometimes when you are fighting and enemy is coming very close you can want to... *toilet*, but don't be worry, this is normal."

I was dressed in the same cheap green combats as the rest, both familiar and alien. Jac, sitting opposite, looked transformed.

"OK. Before we going, anybody needs anything?" asked the translator.

"Ice-cream!" we choroused, for the umpteenth time.

"Yeah. *Nice dream*," came the proverbial response, to groans and jeers from us.

We fired 10 rounds each, out in the hills, and practised some basic assault tactics. Some had served with the French Foreign Legion and the US Marines while others, like Jac, had never touched a weapon.

The westerners slept in the same room, laying out our mattress pads, sleeping bags and blankets side by side after the communal evening meal of bean soup, rice, bread and other basics. When the laughter and banter resounded off the damp, crumbling walls at night, you could imagine yourself in a backpackers hostel, rather than a bare-arsed concrete shed on the wuthering Syrian plains, the doorstep of unknown danger. The job and the colleagues I'd left behind in Saudi, just a few days earlier, were a world away by now; all but forgotten already.

If I'd had concerns about Jac's suitability, they were blown out of the water by another young English guy of about his age, codenamed Welat, and referred to by our translator as "the schoolboy". Physically he seemed robust enough, but he had slightly rabbitlike features, whose primary expressions were bewilderment and vexation.

The first night we were treated to a slice of his life, by popular request from the others: a convoluted story of a hooker and a house fire, with random details popping up like ninjas in jelly. A bombardment of questions from every side egged him on.

"So why did you follow her back to her place?"

"Because I thought she was my girlfriend."

"What, you thought she was your girlfriend, even though you hadn't even been out on a date yet?" cackled Jac.

"I didn't know she was a hooker. I said to her I said, you're a wrong 'un…"

"And what about the bit where you nearly burned the place down?"

"Oh – I slept on the floor that night. I was so angry and – drunk… I picked up the shovel and –"

"What was the shovel for…?"

As my stomach folded into cramps with laughter, I exchanged helpless glances with Ronnie, who was faring no better, snake-jawed and agonised in the opposite corner.

Welat seemed out of sync with everything, at all times, and to have drifted into this scene by sheer inattention as much as anything. For a short while he and Jac appeared to have linked up; I saw them knocking around together, divvying up some found chocolate – the two babies of the group. But pretty soon Jac's better judgment led him to distance himself.

About 40 young Kurds were going through training there as well. We did a joint attack on a group of prefab shelters with half of them, while the rest played enemy. We used dummy weapons, rifles with their working parts removed.

Before we went out on the attack, the translator said to us, "Normally you would take weapon from prisoners, but – please don't take from these because for them it's… *shame*."

Afterwards, back in the room, we were invited to give our feedback on the operation. It was rough, but the plan was decent, and with practice… By the look of it, fighters here did most of their learning on the job.

In the evening the westerners, finished for the day, would collect on the concrete porch to smoke, chat and watch the local recruits practising their evening drill. When they knocked off we'd fraternise as much as our languages allowed, sharing cigarettes and our first Kurdish words.

What I wanted most was to get a proper rifle and sit by myself with it, stripping and assembling until I knew the thing inside out. But whenever I obtained one for a little while, people would gather round me and it became a group exercise, which was actually just what I didn't want. Call me unsociable.

I was sitting on my bed when Jac was carried into the room.

"Raise his feet," said someone, as they laid him on the mattress next to mine. I grabbed a rucksack and put it under his legs. No one really knew why he'd fainted.

"I dunno… people were just talking about blood, and injuries and things, and the next thing I just felt myself falling backwards," he said, squinting up at the light. After a lie-down and a couple of soft drinks he was fine – for now, at least.

Then, after we'd only just started, it seemed we were wrapping up there. "We hope you have enjoyed our training, and we apologise for any mistakes we have made," said the head instructor, with impressive humility, through the translator. And that was pretty much it. The last day's highlights were a giant tub of pistachio ice-cream and a standing ovation from the Kurdish recruits assembled in ranks outside, sending us off with handshakes, embraces and the customary double kiss, one on each cheek, singing and cheering ramped up by the presence of camera phones and Go-Pros as we drove out in Hiluxes at twilight. Back over to the HQ for our weapons. And then – they said – to *battle*. Just like that. Training had lasted three days for Ronnie, Jac and me. The others had been here two weeks, and we three had just been chucked in with them towards the end.

"So how does everyone else feel about this then?" I said, as we crammed magazines into webbing pouches and sorted out bayonets and other bits and pieces outside on the lit-up porch of the HQ. In the final debrief with the general, indoors, we'd had a couple of last-minute dropouts: Welat, who (with our vigorous agreement) had decided he needed "more training", and a big Texan who'd tried playing leader to us all, until his bravado had finally worn off.

"Fucking shitting myself," grinned Bruce, a former US Ranger. He didn't mind admitting it, and neither did I.

"What about you, Jac?"

"No, mate," said Jac quietly. "No. I'm ready." He looked at me steadily, with no trace of that impish little grin, nor the pale and ailing look from when he'd fainted.

A small group of YPJ women walked by. Bruce remarked that he could do with a piece of ass for the next 15 minutes.

We loaded into and onto a couple of waiting Hiluxes, and sped off down the unlit dirt track into the night. I was still asking about Shengal. Still, battle was battle…

***

At night they burned truck tyres and wooden roof beams ripped out of abandoned mudbrick houses in the surrounding area. Groups of young men and women, some very young, danced by the fire, hand in hand in rows, to strident music pumped from the stereo of a parked Hilux.

Giggling teenage girls, one hiding behind another, nudged each other to ask me, "Where are you from?" and so on. One of the young guys grabbed me and dragged me into the dance, counting out the steps in English as I stared down at his feet and clattered along two moves behind. *One, two... six.* I got applause when his patient tuition started to pay off, and brought the house down with a reference to Michael Jackson.

I crouched on the ground next to an older Turkish/Kurdish volunteer named Mansur, nibbling pumpkin seeds and spitting the shells towards the fire. It was a skill, requiring dexterity of fingertips and teeth. I could shell one to his three.

"Look at that," I pointed. He turned and looked at the fire-shadow of the dancers cast on the mudbrick wall.

"It would make good introduction for a film," he said. "With the music."

I nodded; I'd been thinking it looked more like old-school stencil graffiti, animated somehow. Mansur had studied media and communications in Germany, where he'd lived before coming here. He was tall for a Kurd, possibly six foot; 27, but older-seeming; he had the air of a political academic, accentuated by his receding hairline and thick moustache.

In my mind's eye I saw the shadow-figures disappearing, one by one, leaving gaps like missing teeth, the remaining figures dancing on regardless. But I didn't share that thought. No image so romantic would be called for in my time out here.

Zara was a bare and barren place. A few mud huts and larger buildings, on the brown dirt-plains in the back of beyond. I'd come to this village alone, of all those other new volunteers at the academy. We'd got split up on the night drive, at a base en route, into smaller groups, and packed off in different directions. I'd volunteered to be the single person required for my vehicle, since no one else wanted to go alone and since I had Shengal uppermost in my mind anyway. I'd said little about that at the academy, because I thought I'd have less chance of getting there if it became a bandwagon. Going it alone suited me fine – making friends was important, but fighting came first. So where was this battle?

The days in Zara were given over to some basic continuation training for maybe 40 young Kurds, male and female, and the other westerners here. There were two old bikers, one Dutch, one American, and a little Estonian youth with huge dreamy eyes, nicknamed Junior.

One of the bikers was a Texan who went by the name of Fat Jack. Though only five years my senior, a life of liquor and easy riding, of drugs and of "fighting and fucking everything that moved" across the Southern states, had left its mark in the deep lines and beetroot patches of his face, in his slow, aching gait, his blasted eyes.

"We were driving through this town at night an' a bunch of whores was standin' on the street corner an' I opened the door an' stuck my head out an' shouted *repent, whore a Babylon, 'n' turn from yer ways a sin!* An' this big black whore says, *motherfucker* 'n' took off her shoe 'n' come runnin' over the street an' my buddy leaned over an' jammed me in the door so I couldn't get back in 'n' slowed the truck down *real* slow. An' she started whackin' me over the head 'n' hollerin' like crazy 'n' my buddy's cryin' laughin' at me. Thought it was real funny till I started gettin' whupped upside the head with a shew…"

Junior, the Estonian, was 20 but looked about 14. He was here because his girlfriend had been kidnapped by Daesh, he said, and fighting them was the only thing he could do about it. But if the YPG wasted much more time hanging around then he was planning to try out for Assad's forces instead. I advised him to think long and hard about that. Teenage girls, revolutionary songs and dancing by firelight would *not* be the order there. I wouldn't overrate my own chances in such an outfit, never mind a delicate little guy like him.

The other biker was a Dutchman, Hans, in his 50s, probably the oldest person I'd met so far and a contender for having the most interesting past. Headhunted from a young offenders' facility and railroaded into the Dutch secret service, he'd been on every clandestine black ops Special Forces mission from Israel to Columbia and back. He had stories of unrecorded assassinations, of desperate firefights behind enemy lines from which he was the lone survivor, of murky missions which left him burnt and scarred and a prisoner to his conscience. Stories you'd need to be as howling mad as him to believe a single word of.

These guys were disinclined to join the nightly revels. Kicking our heels was all we did here, according to them. Disaffection oozed from the walls in the westerners' room. An operation to retake the city of Tal Hamis from Daesh was coming up, they'd been told. Everybody would fight. Some had been waiting months in backwater places like this. Fat Jack was considering going on hunger strike and Hans was laying plans to get himself airlifted out of there by helo. All it would take was a call to some friends in Mossad who owed him from way back…

So, this was where I'd ended up.

***

At night we did an hour of *nobet* (sentry duty). From the sentry post on the roof I could see the Shengal mountains, just 12 miles away, and could see the flashes and hear the thunder of bombs being dropped on the city by coalition forces. So near and yet so far.

In keeping with the principles of democratic confederalism, the group held a regular meeting of all *hevals* to discuss matters affecting us as a group and give everyone a say.

At one of these meetings, I explained that I was happy here, had made good friends and appreciated all the efforts they had made to accommodate westerners like us, but that I had come here as a soldier to fight. I had made sacrifices, come a long way, given up a job etc…

"There is no fighting now – anywhere. We all want to fight but we must wait and be patient," came the answer from the commander, through Mansur. "We have all given up jobs, left family, come from far away – from Turkey, Iran, Iraq… In some weeks we go to Tal Hamis and everybody will fight."

"Yes, in Cizire, OK. But I arranged to go to Shengal. Please can you send me there?"

"There is no fighting in Shengal now."

(*Yes, there is, I saw it on the news three days ago.*)

"There are no foreigners in Shengal now."

"OK." *(Yes, there are.)*

I felt a growing combination of disappointment, anxiety, and a feeling more ugly that I as yet wanted to resist. But after a week at Zara, the seed of doubt I'd had back in Saudi had sprouted and grown. Well, I hadn't come here to be political window dressing, and since it was now clear that my Facebook contact had no clout on the ground out here, it looked like I'd have to shift for myself. And looking around me, my colleagues hardly seemed battle-ready. A few days later I gave the commander an ultimatum: send me to Shengal, or send me home.

***

That night on *nobet*, Mansur came up to me to give me news that a prisoner was being held here for the night. Whether Daesh or not, he didn't know. "And by the way," he said, "tomorrow you will go." And he walked away.

I assumed they were packing me off home. It could have been shabbier, I thought. It had taken some people months to suss things out; they'd spent all their money and had nothing to go back to.

To offset the disappointment, I started setting my mind to practicalities. For perhaps the first time since I'd left, I thought of Saudi again. Maybe I could save my job with a well-coined excuse about the situation here. Though I'd come to see it as a closed chapter, in actual fact I was only a few days over the week's leave period. I'd left my gate pass on the desk in my room in the Saudi compound, since I didn't want to make my exit worse by taking it with me. Maybe try and email the company from Sulaymaniyah…

"Cûdî. You… *going?*" said Torlvadan, a fierce little Yazidi guy, coming to relieve me at my shift's end.

"Yes."

"Yes. You going to Shengal tomorrow."

What?

I ran to catch up with Mansur.

"Yes, you will go tomorrow to Shengal. Sorry, I thought you understand."

"What about the others?"

When they'd heard me asking, everyone had said they wanted to go too. But they'd been less pushy.

"For you it's different… You are *soldier*. For the others, we take them to a place like this so that − they can feel they are in a war. Because some people are not ready. But for you, the commander see you, on training, and he say, yes, this man can go to Shengal."

I won't deny I'd been deliberately angling for such a verdict since my arrival in Zara: trying to impress the head-shed in various ways, from showing off on the training to criticising their drills and tactics. I'd been downright obnoxious at some moments and I wasn't proud; but the campaign had worked. The squeaky wheel got the oil.

"Oh. OK. Yes, maybe some people need to train more."

"Yes − and, me too. I have not so much experience now."

"Well, I was watching you today and you were moving pretty well," I said.

"Thank you."

As our translator, Mansur had his work cut out. Placating dissatisfied westerners, passing on half-truths from the management. Though not physically fragile or oversensitive in nature, he was quiet, thoughtful and confrontation-averse; a man who'd come to do his time at the front before returning to the Party and a role that suited his talents. I hoped I hadn't been too hard on him in my single-minded drive to get where I wanted.

Everyone turned out to see me off, cheering and clapping. Off to Shengal, the big symbol. I turned round on my way to the truck, laden down with weapons and a rucksack I'd yet to streamline, and gave them a clumsy YPG victory sign. Just as I was getting in the truck, Shahin, the boy who taught me dancing that first night, came running out shouting my name. Nearly missed me. *Big hugs, laters kiddo. Thank you for the music.*

3 IN SHENGAL

After less than a fortnight in-country, I was finally in the war for real.

On a frozen grey morning I clambered atop a pickup which wound up the Shengal mountainside, into the highlands with their thin air and thin, mean vegetation. Every so often we'd come across a ragged shepherd kid who'd wave a stick over his sullen herd, harrying the grumbling creatures out of our way. The roads were strewn with damp, grubby clothes, twisted over into long tangled ropes by passing vehicles like worms come out after rainfall. I assumed they'd been dropped by fleeing refugees now camped in the UNHCR tents and makeshift shelters of scrap materials, scattered high up around the mountainsides. Lower down, a few moulded concrete picnic tables stood like memorials to happier times. I clung, white-skinned, to the truck's sides as it waltzered down a scribble of hairpin bends and upended me in a small, crowded yard on the city outskirts.

White plastic garden chairs scraped across the battered tiles of the small patio as a mass of Kurdish fighters stood up to greet me, according to custom. They were a variety of ages, but mostly older, veteran, gnarled and grizzled in traditional mountain dress, typically shorter than me, as Kurds usually are. In their midst, and towering above them, was a pale-skinned and shaven-headed young westerner.

In the ensuing round of handshakes and mumbled *merhabas*, he just nodded, without saying a word. Perhaps he was just an unusually large Kurd, after all, I thought; one who liked accumulating bits of western military dress. The sleeves of his thin army undershirt were rolled up to reveal powerful forearms, a sweat-rag was neatly knotted to the upper strap of his webbing, and a woolly hat sat high enough on his head to display the grade zero. All were of similar downbeat shades of green.

People seated themselves again. In the middle of the yard was a small fire: young, tangled branches smouldering reluctantly in a makeshift tray of rusted metal. Two soot-coated metal teapots, one huge, one tiny, balanced above it on a contrivance of twisted wires and bricks, heating up in no particular hurry.

It seemed the western-looking man and I ended up sitting next to each other by mere chance, but maybe the Kurds arranged it that way. I greeted him in Kurdish and then realised my first impression wasn't wrong. "Where are you from, mate?"

"Nottingham," he said.

"Oh – British." I gave him the closest I could get to a grin. "I'm from Stoke."

"Oh."

"Have you been in Shengal long?"

"Two weeks."

That was a long time, compared to my none. A lot gets learned in the first fortnight.

He could have been a boxer, maybe. Or a builder. Or both. Big. Beefy. Lots of round Bs, like his rounded face and rounded muscles, and the rounded shape his mouth made in that tight-lipped half-scowl.

So… had he been in the military?

Yes.

Maybe issue-squaddie breed, then; a tour of Iraq or Afghanistan to his name and here for the grim fun of the fight. Take it to those bloody Muslims. If he wasn't cradling an M16 rifle in his lap he'd look at home holding a flag at an English Defence League rally. Well, the scene was bound to attract all sorts.

Maybe I should ask him his views on democratic confederalism… Normally I'd have just matched his reticence and sat there smoking quietly, or practised my language with the others, if I felt up to it after that ride. But we were here, in Shengal; this guy was in with the others and he knew the ground.

He told me (speaking more to the fire) that 11 or 12 westerners in total were stationed up on the higher ground that sloped towards the mountains. He mentioned a couple of familiar names, guys I'd heard of, either through the internet or the mainstream media, or by word of mouth since my arrival. It was a very small world, and some people's names went ahead of them, for a variety of reasons.

"I've heard of that Estonian kid," he snorted. "Faints after he's run 200 metres, apparently."

For some reason I felt a little defensive. "Yeah, he's not the greatest athlete. Something to do with his blood sugar, I think. Very good shot, though."

"*Really?*" His eyes flicked directly to mine and stayed there.

"So I'm told. That's why they've given him a sniper rifle."

He shrugged and returned his attention to the fire. Flakes of ash danced like snowflakes above the logs, cresting the warm current and ducking the cold air.

A sudden crash sounded as a mortar round landed in the distance. A dry, scouring sound in the air signalled a closer mortar, on its way. This time the crash was louder. Then another, closer still, but not close enough for alarm. We both listened appraisingly – too experienced to play it *too* cool – then carried on the conversation we were barely having.

Someone got up and jammed the tall metal gate shut with a rock. Added protection from the flakes of metal skimming through the cold air out there.

It turned out we both got to Shengal pretty much the same way – pushing against the management till they gave in.

I nodded in the direction of the westerners' base. "So, have you seen much contact up there?"

"Yeah, most days."

"How do you rate the local fighters?"

"Yeah… They're quite together, like –" He scratched his forehead, grimaced slightly. "But they're *amateurs*, know what I mean…?"

His name was Kosta (codename Kemal) and he was an ex-Royal Marine. I mentioned having done the commando course myself, and we tossed a few secondhand scraps of chat back and forth, then finally into the fire.

The basic British commando training programme (in my time, at least) didn't deal in underwater shark-fighting or ninja skills. It was standard infantry stuff. Slave-driven over the moors for weeks on end, relentlessly checked and assessed, you maintained the standard without breaking or slipping or you were out. A commando was essentially defined as *a soldier who won't give up.* Most did.

Royal Marine Commandos were *brought on*, raised to a standard where they could pass the commando phase of their training. The All Arms Commando Course, which the marines ran separately for soldiers, sailors and airmen wanting to join commando forces, worked a bit differently. Weeding you out was the idea. No unwashed army *pongos* were taking that green beret home easily.

***

The thick army sleeping bag was like a cocoon I never wanted to leave. Foetal and smouldering, my body had even warmed the cold metal rifle between my legs. I pulled the drawstring on the bivvy bag (the Gore-Tex outer shell), expanding the tiny hole I'd been breathing through all night, and stuck my face out into frozen fog. As I moved, the bivvy bag crackled with frost.

"Morning, Phil," I said, to the artillery lance corporal I was buddied up with.

"Morning, Jim," he said, forcibly chipper. *"Lovely fucking wet kit to get into,"* he continued. Like either of us could possibly have any other thought in that moment.

"Yep. Don't think about it, man. Just get straight up and into it." We scrambled out of our bags, out of the dry combats we were wearing, and into the wet gear draped across our Bergens (military rucksacks). Hardened with frost, the cloth burned the skin all over. You saved your dry gear for sleeping in. Your doss-bag was your last haven. If that got wet you were fucked.

We fumbled to light a Hexi burner, crouching down around the white tablet's tiny flapping yellow flame. First light wasn't for another 20 minutes or so, but the instructors would be snoozing blissfully away. It was blag to survive on this course, no matter who said what. They cut corners and so did we. After a few minutes we guzzled down some boiling-hot ration chocolate and then pushed our way through dense, slick branches to the clearing where the other blokes had already started laying out their kit for inspection on rolled-out ponchos.

An older soldier, a foreign student from Lebanon, was all over the place. Kit in rag-order and struggling to understand the two young officers trying to help him. It was a mark of prestige to come here and do the British commando course, but this guy would be lucky to finish the first week. Lebanese Special Forces. Whatever.

"Pete, let's get in there," said one officer to the other.

As the sky started to pale we stood smart to attention, wet, cold and filthy, as the instructors made their way around. Being covered in yesterday's mud was no excuse for not having a wash and shave. A spot of surface rust on any part of your weapon was a formal warning. Mine was fucking pukka. Spotless, even in the pitch dark.

"Ah, Matthews," smiled Corporal Edwards. "Do you have your mirror handy, perchance? Thank you. Now, if you look closely, you'll see there's a little wisp of cam cream in your left eyebrow."

"Corporal."

"Pack up your kit and get on the flank…"

The flank (the row of guys picked out for punishment PT) *was about to set off; I was one of the last. I frantically shoved my gear away; if I was late it'd be an even more miserable morning.* Fucking wisp of cam cream. *If that was my partner* I'd *have got the blame for not checking him properly. Edwards had it in for me. I gave my Bergen a kick, knocking it over.*

"Matthews."

"Corporal."

"Go and throw yourself in Peter's Pool. You're on a warning."

As I jogged downhill to the icy pond I pretended not to hear Edwards say, "And you've got one minute to get back here." Which was just bloody stupid of me. Eight seconds too late; go again. I was in and out of that burning water three times, sloshing up and down the hill, before joining the flank.

OK, webbing on, rifle, off we go. Running in a gaggle up the steep, sandy track; diving down into cover. Crawl, over the red gravel. Back up, run. Down again. Crawl. Up. Run. Down. Crawl, on a vicious gradient, till your knees exploded. Then more crawling, crawling without end, through a shallow stream, through clumps of gorse, through a thick black bog. Crawl properly, get your belt buckle down. Keep your weapon out of the dirt.

Up and running, up the hill. Chest heaving, lungs full of molten metal. Double mark-time at the top, wait for the others. Covered in shit again. Pays to be a winner, gents: first one to the bottom can sit out, the rest go up again. Some guys sprint for first place, the rest too knackered in their flopping muddy rags to do any more than keep their feet moving. Sapper Daniels, well in the lead, slows as he nears the finish and I bomb on past him, rifle in one hand to pump my arms for the sprint.

"Well done, Matthews! That's what we want to see…"

I sit down, watch the others go up again. Sorry, Daniels, but I've had enough this morning.

OK guys, go and join the others.

Sat on their Bergens having a brew all this time, those who'd passed the morning inspection packed their mugs and water bottles away and everyone gathered round for orders.

3 Section will yomp to here, 4.7 miles, arrowhead formation, and harbour up. I want you in there by 0930 hours. We will attack…

And so began another jolly day.

"So, Matthews, if you're infantry-trained already, what you doing this course for?" Corporal Edwards asked me.

Most soldiers here, following their basic training, had gone onto specialise in their fields of engineering, logistics or artillery. For them, this course was a learning curve as well as a career move. I was learning little here because as a pioneer, I'd had to do the twelve-week infantry programme in Catterick, North Yorkshire, after my basic training. That had been an intense and, over the time, undeniably transformative process – demanding an unstinting adherence to standards under the baleful eyes of obsessive NCOs. Every one of them was a screaming religious nut about it, and the results were astounding. Out in the field, if they heard so much as a peep or saw a torch flash while we were packing down a harbour (bivouac site) and moving out on patrol in the middle of the night, or setting up an ambush position, then woe betide us. So we learned to move like ghosts, through pitch darkness, through dense forest, over treacherous terrain, no matter how much we were carrying or how exhausted, rain-soaked and blistered we were. It became natural.

Here, although it was far tougher physically and mentally, you could get away with murder as long as the training team weren't looking; and half the time they couldn't be arsed to (unless they had it in for you).

Here students clattered around in the dark, cussing each other out; squabbled over the sentry rota, shrugged chores onto others and just generally bitched and shirked their way through the eight weeks. Too much depended on the whim of individual instructors, which made the course such a mercurial combination of the sadistically punitive, the desultory, and the cake-and-arse. "Commando spirit" (comprising cheerfulness, unselfishness and other virtues) was sacred to all – but only while those cunts were watching. A favourite topic of barrack-room conversation was the end-of-course kicking they were all going to get.

"I thought it might be interesting," I said, in answer to Edwards' question. He shook his head.

***

When I was awarded the "coveted green beret" in a wet field at the end of the final, 30-mile yomp over Dartmoor, I felt like I'd been dragged through a toilet backwards. I still have dreams about it.

At times I could be both exhilarated and repelled by revisiting that stuff. In that moment I was neither, though I was pretty stoked to be in Shengal at last.

"What *is* a pioneer?" Kosta frowned.

"Infantry soldier with a... basic engineering role. Building defences on the front line, that sort of thing. Very good at shovelling."

"You'll be useful up there then," he grinned. "We've got tons of sandbagging to do."

From the way he talked about it, he'd washed his hands of the British military. Quit the Corps before his time was up to come and get involved with this. Apparently his commanding officer actually gave him his blessing.

It was a while since I'd left the military myself, of course.

What had I been doing since? Kosta wanted to know.

Now I was the one inclined to be guarded. *How long have you got, mate…?*

"A few different things…" I said. "Directly before this, I was in Saudi, teaching English to military cadets." I talked a bit about the twisted route that had brought me here.

"Oh. You're a *teacher*?"

"Yeah, well – ESL."

Now he was looking at me intently, but without any hint of confrontation.

I expanded a bit on that, since he seemed to genuinely want to know. It was more interesting to him than swapping chat about the Tarzan assault course and slogging over Dartmoor. As it turned out, his mum taught the CELTA course, the one I did. This led to a chat about education more generally. At 25, he wasn't far off the age I was when I quit the military to go to uni. One of the best things I ever did. Had he ever considered it himself? It was a good way to travel and get paid…

"No. I sort of see *this* as my education, really. I reckon I'll just go on doing this till I… catch it up somewhere."

We felt a jolt through the ground. The first couple of mortar bombs weren't strays. A bombardment was getting underway and they were landing much closer, one so loud it sounded like next door. People jumped up. Some darted indoors, some hugged the wall. One or two seconds and we collected ourselves.

A wiry, wizened guy, much older than the rest of us, was still crouched on the ground in a tight ball, arms wrapped round his tucked-in head. People looked at him, at each other, then respectfully away, ignoring him till he got up. If I wanted to say or do anything, it was not my place.

Kosta and I hustled indoors with everyone else, from the soot and debris of the yard onto spotless white marble tiles, most slipping shoes off on the doorstep. The spacious kitchen and hall were immaculate – maybe their way of trying to make the war stop at the door. Since my boots were slower to remove than the local fighters' trainers, I kept them on and idled in the doorway with a smoke. A huge, broken rocket lay on the step at my feet, casing split, silver powder spilling out in a heap.

The bombardment soon died down and we went out into the yard again. Someone removed the teapots from the wire grill, placing them on the floor. A tray of glasses was brought from inside and the Kurdish *çay* (tea) ceremony began. Not a formal one, of course – this wasn't feudal Japan – but there was a slightly ritualistic feel to the cleansing of each glass with scalding water from the large pot, followed by the dash of thick, red-black tea poured in from the small one, and the final topping up to the brim from the large one again, diluting the strong brew; then finally, the passing of full glasses from person to person until everybody had one. Where there were fewer glasses than people, a contest of good manners ensued. As a westerner and a newcomer I wasn't even in it. Take my tea and shut up.

Everyone sat in a large circle now, warmed by the shared tea into a convivial spirit. Kosta was obviously well liked by the locals, which was a damn good reason for my making a bit of effort with him. One of them was badgering him, in a good-natured way, about his thin shirt in the freezing winter air. The guy produced a woolly jumper from somewhere and thrust it at him. Kosta eventually put it on, laughing and playing along. When the conversation moved on he removed it again, to peals of laughter.

"Err… *germ* (hot)," he shrugged, smiling apologetically.

We were kicking around in that yard for some hours. Kosta was waiting for the commander to come and collect him for something. I was supposed to stay there the night and go up to the position the following day; Kosta reckoned there was no reason I shouldn't go up now, but that was just how things went sometimes.

"Come on," he said. "I'll show you where we are from here."

We went out the gate with the same scrupulous care as the others and he pointed up to where a berm (or bunline, as he called it – a farming term, so he was my teacher today) wound uphill, the raised ridge protecting a track, fronting a higgledy-piggledy cluster of low-rise buildings.

He must have been pretty keen on this particular scene to leave the marines for it, I ventured, as we sat back down in the yard. And we got onto reasons for being here, the way we saw this war, the situation, and so on: my position on the last couple of wars Britain had fought; the reasons I saw this one differently – thoughts that I'd have been less inclined to flag up an hour or so earlier. We agreed that this particular enemy was quite untypical – as wars go – in being *evil* in a plain and straightforward way.

"And – the YPG *are* the 'good guys'…" he added.

Eventually the commander turned up, though I barely glimpsed the guy as he stayed outside the gate, vehicle purring. Kosta gathered up his gear, relaying to me that someone would come and collect me later. He'd loosened up a bit, anyway, even if we weren't clapping one another on the shoulder and swearing undying comradeship.

There are always some who avoid their own kin when abroad, whether they're backpackers in Thailand or human shields in Palestine. I was just as guilty, really. Maybe I just didn't like having it done to me.

Kosta took off. I'd pegged him as the budding mercenary, and perhaps he'd partly confirmed it. I didn't see how else he'd go on "doing this". But there was evidently a bit more going on under that drab green carapace.

***

A few hours later I was picked up in a battered *panza* (a general term for armoured personnel carriers of all types) loaded up with potatoes, RPG rockets and other ordnance and comestibles. We crawled up the winding dirt track behind the high, crooked ridge of the berm running alongside, maybe ten or twelve feet of earth, rock and stones heaped up by bulldozer.

We got out amid crumbling, tumbledown suburban dwellings and tracks leading off in all directions, some tarmac, some just hard earth. The tracks bore the regular scars of caterpillar tracks from vehicles like ours, and every surface was littered with debris, rubble, bullet holes and mortar splashes.

"Hey. How's it going?" said a short, capable-looking Vietnamese-American, also codenamed Cûdî.

"Hi. Nice to meet you."

"OK. From here to here, keep low," he said, as we set off towards the westerners' base. "Here we run across the gap one at a time."

Mortar bombs continued to sound in the near distance, joined by occasional bursts of gunfire. We threaded a route through holes bashed in house walls, through room after room – living rooms, bedrooms, kitchens – up and down ramps and over furniture and machinery, rubble, junk and mortar fragments, climbing, dropping, moving in cover.

This suburb seemed older than the main city. The undulating ground dictated the varying levels of steps, corridors, courtyards and gardens. Uneven walkways rose and fell between buildings haphazardly crowded and conjoined; rough, uneven walls of boulders packed in concrete, cracked and crumbling, some peppered with bullet holes, some bombed to rubble.

Wild greenery was springing up in profusion in the absence of regular human society; sprouting from steps, walls, cracks in every surface, glowing in the sunlight that fell in rays and shafts. Basic ornamental features were all around – simple arches, short pillars, vaulted ceilings, tiny gardens with trees and shrubs once well tended – lending a certain charm to the devastation. People had been happy here once, I felt.

Cûdî led me through to our base, and I ended up in another enclosed yard with a dozen other western volunteers. Another round of friendly introductions.

"Come on," smiled a tall American with clean-cut, boyish looks and a goatee beard. "I'll show you round."

I recognised him instantly from numerous media features: Jordan Mattson, the first westerner to join the YPG. I'd expected a certain aloofness but found him very friendly and down to earth. Like others here, he seemed genuinely pleased to see new arrivals coming in. It contrasted sharply in my mind with the jealousy and rivalry of the Palestine solidarity activists.

A narrow track wound uphill between the sloping high ground on our left and the earthen berm piled up on my right, beyond and below which lay Shengal city.

He'd just pointed out the last of the sandbag positions along the berm when a familiar dry, scouring sound came whispering through the air.

"Mortar! Come on!"

We pelted back downhill, burying ourselves in the berm as it exploded in the near distance. In Shengal mortars were a fact of life, as constant as the weather, and less predictable.

***

We had the mountains, they had the city.

I pulled my first *nobet* that night, crouched in the bunker. Jordan took me to where I needed to be. At a break in the berm sat a darkened house, the perfect lookout point. Jordan went first, through the small yard and the doorway and through into a rear room. Glass fragments and debris cracked and crunched underfoot.

"Hey," he whispered, through a hole bashed through the wall, "we got a new guy. A Brit."

"Oh, hey man," whispered another American voice from the darkness the other side. "Come on in."

I recognised the voice – it was Matt, a young guy with long curly black hair and a handlebar moustache I'd met when I arrived earlier in the yard.

I felt the safety on my rifle and crawled through the mouse-hole and down into a roomy dugout in the ground lined with rugs and cushions. Above was a roof of corrugated metal and wooden beams, leaning against the outside wall of the house. Light from the sky filtered dimly through gaps where the roof's edge met the hard earth ground. Otherwise it was pitch dark in there. I crawled forward and looked out through a gap: a few abandoned, shot-up shells of buildings in the scrubland, and the darkened city beyond.

"*Don't look out the spy-holes for too long,*" whispered Matt. "This is mainly a listening position really, in case anyone tries to sneak up."

A third guy was also in the hole, I suddenly realised. It was unclear why. He demonstrated what Matt had just told me

– peeping through the hole, then quickly ducking back in. Then he started chattering away in Kurdish to Matt.

"Yeah, I know, I know," said Matt.

Matt's Kurdish, though better than mine, was minimal. The guy was being a nuisance.

"What's this guy doing in here apart from socialising?" I said.

"That's what I'm trying to figure out."

Finally the guy got the message that three was a crowd, and left. We sat back in the darkness and enjoyed a furtive smoke with our hands cupped around the glowing tips to hide the light. We chatted in whispers about the usual topics – why we'd come here, other places we'd been. Trips behind and before us, military and otherwise. As a committed Christian, Matt seemed to view this war in moral/spiritual terms as much as anything. After this he wanted to volunteer with a Christian charity in the Philippines. He took regular counsel from his saint on such decisions. I forget which one.

Later that night I fell asleep to the sound of small arms fire in the near distance. *Here at last.*

***

Next day dawned bright and cold, but the chill faded from the air around mid-morning. The yard made a nice sun trap to idle around in with a smoke. Behind me were two rooms, with double layers of blankets hung down over the doorways, inside and out, for blackout drapes and insulation against the elements. To my front was a corridor with an arched entrance in that plain decorative style that gave the place so much of its human character, leading out onto the track. Directly over the track was the *nobet* house. By day you darted from arched entrance to house, and occasionally the whizz of a close-passing bullet would remind you why. A thing that sounded so small and harmless, like a minute quickening of the air; gone before your senses registered it.

To my left was a wall, just over head height, on which one of the guys had written *The Chappies*. A wooden ramp with rungs nailed into it sloped up to a gap in the wall, through which was another, higher, yard like this one, with more rooms on two sides.

At the top of this ramp appeared Kosta, large as life.

"Mate – you should go see it, before it dehydrates. It's a foot an' a *half*!" he grinned.

He was talking about a shit he'd just done.

Soldiers will be soldiers, and some weeks ago they'd had a competition, apparently – shitting in the most original place. The winning entry, I learned, was a child's boot.

Some banter ensued. I'd never taken to this sort of squaddie humour when I was 20 and actually in the army. Not finding it funny, but not wanting to seem aloof. I was less inclined to agonise now. Thanks boys, but count me out…

There were seven or eight of us around now, including Kosta, Jordan and Matt, so we had a late breakfast at two small flimsy tables in the centre of the yard – bread, spicy tinned tuna, triangle cheese and jam. The usual fare. I could eat that tuna with the chilli pepper inside all day.

"Someone said there was tomatoes," said one of the men, searching hopefully around the kitchen corner of the yard, where a cabinet stacked with tins and jars and bags of onions, and sugar, boxes and gas bottles stood near a looted, temperamental gas stove. In the opposite corner was an organised clutter of rocket launchers and machine guns, and boxes and belts of rockets and rounds. Bits of random junk were littered about; a few helmets nobody wanted, a discarded water canister. A small alcove in one wall held a shovel and several other tools.

I grabbed a pack of smokes from a torn-open carton on top of the cabinet. If you wanted cigarettes anywhere in this war you just went and got them from the kitchen.

"Man, I was sitting in the back room of that fucking *nobet* house yesterday and a Dushka round came right through the fucking wall above me. We need to line that fucker with sandbags."

"Well, I'm hoping we're gonna get pulled out for Tal Hamis in the next few days."

"*Fuck* knows when that'll be."

Gunfire crackled overhead. Rounds snapped and popped around us.

"Seriously, man…?" A scowl of mock annoyance, in the direction of the fire.

"Tryin'ah eat *lunch*!"

The Shengal vets, salty as hell. Soldiers playing soldiers…

"It sounds like music!" grinned Kosta. There was a discernible rhythm in the crackle. I hummed a few bars of *Peter and the Wolf* and he joined in.

"It was some heavy shit up on the berm last night. Spent three full mags. Doubt I hit anything though," said someone.

A young English-speaking Kurd nicknamed Bucky stood up and stretched. "I think I will take my *karnas*," he said thoughtfully, "and... *shoot* at them." He picked up his sniper rifle and sauntered off.

"All this firing back and forth means nothing. We need to take buildings," said Kosta.

"If we go down into that city now, we'll get slaughtered," said Cûdî Vietnam.

From the ensuing responses, it was clear Kosta had opened a popular subject. Everyone had a bit to say.

"We could take Shengal, but we need the Peshmerga on board. Can't do it by ourselves."

"Why are we just sitting holding our dicks?"

"Because the Pesh don't want the YPG here. They want this to be *their* show."

"It's a pissing contest."

The YPG had a foothold in Shengal for their part in defending the mountains when Daesh had invaded, and subsequently clearing them off. But they ultimately belonged in Rojava, over the Syrian border, and it was taken as read that the Peshmerga and the Kurdistan Regional Government of Iraq, to whom they were allied, would far rather they were back there.

"Know what I'd like to do? I'd like to nix that fucking bunker. If a mortar lands on that you're *fucked*."

"It's a death trap."

Just then, the sound of mortars joined the gunfire, as if summoned by our chatter. Most people walked about unconcerned; the occasional closer explosion had people jumping into rooms as the noise filled the contained space, leaving it ringing.

"Don't sit here, don't sit here!" Commander Soran came striding through the arched corridor into the yard. "I tell, all-body!"

Our *tabor* (fighting unit) was the only one of the several based in Shengal to comprise Kurdish and international fighters. Soran was its somewhat maverick leader. I'd met him earlier that morning. Though on the short side, his frame and features exuded an obvious strength: a stout, energetic fireball of a man with a fierce expression framed in a black beard and tightly-curled black hair wrapped in a black, piratical headband. He looked maybe 45, but many Kurdish men look older than they are. He took his codename from his home town of Soran in Iraqi Kurdistan, and like most of the Shengal Kurds spoke mainly Sorani (the Kurdish dialect of that region) though he could speak Kurmanji too, as well as Arabic and basic English. Dark, steady eyes suggested a stable and loving relationship with death and pandemonium. The sort of bloke pirates have nightmares about.

We grabbed our weapons and headed up the ramp into the cover of the westerners' room on the right. The guys had shuffled up to give me a bed space.

"So, how was it last night with Soran? Good?" Cûdî Vietnam asked Kosta.

"Yeah. Good." He nodded.

He'd gone out into no man's land to give cover while Soran laid some *mayns* (IEDs: improvised explosive devices – pronounced *mines*) in the ground. He was still quietly charged up about it, you could tell.

"What'd be great would be to do a sneak attack. A small team with RPGs and a couple of machine guns, hammer one of their positions, maybe blow something up – and just fuck off back here. Classic commando raid…"

"Yeah…"

Pictures culled from Bibles decked the crumbling yellow plaster of our bedroom: the Crucifixion, several saints, the Annunciation. When Kosta wasn't doing a hundred other things, he'd sit quietly on his bed and read the Bible he'd brought from home. The group of westerners was probably 8/10ths Christian. Jordan had *CHRIST LORD* written over the cross on his first aid pouch.

"So – do you play chess?" Jordan asked me, with a hopeful smile.

"I've been known to… But I'm not very good."

"Doesn't matter," he said, obviously eager.

"Maybe later," I said. I wanted to think.

When the mortar storm died down we went out, back down to the lower yard again.

Two fighters appeared in the yard, one young, the other a very small, almost-old Kurdish man. He held a hand to his face.

"Friend," explained the younger man to us, pointing and miming. "*Şehid. Howen.*" (Martyr, mortar.)

One of our Dushka gunners had just been killed at a position up on the high ground by a mortar – he'd turned and faced right into a direct blast of shrapnel which covered him from head to toe. I reached out my hand to the old-looking Kurdish man as he went past; he touched my arm without stopping, eyes full of tears, and headed for the dim interior of the room beyond.

Soon after, I heard Kosta arguing with Soran in the same room.

"It's too dangerous now, *heval* Kemal!" Soran was telling him.

"I know – that's *why* I should be up there!" Kosta replied.

***

That night we had a bombardment like I'd never witnessed, a gathering concerto. Rifles and light machine guns struck up the tune, joined by heavier guns, Dushkas and 57s, rattling and battering away, jarring the room, punctuated every so often by rockets exploding right outside as the guys snoozed on. It was all around us and it was getting ridiculous. I scanned the prone shapes of the others. *Are you guys serious,* I thought, *sleeping through this?*

The bedroom's religious decor really came into its own, dimly illuminated by the low flames of a paraffin lamp and some small candles, and accentuated by the thought of what might come smashing through those walls at any moment.

Finally the big bass drum sounded, the big brother of the mortars I'd heard earlier. The floor juddered and the flame trembled in the paraffin lamp as plaster dust came showering down like someone was throwing a wardrobe against the outside wall, again and again.

"We're getting mortared!" I yelled. "Guys, stand to! Come on…!"

They scrambled into gear and out of the door in seconds, took up fighting positions.

One of the Kurds hurried up to Matt. "*Çibû?*" (What's going on?)

A rapid exchange followed in Kurdish and English.

Matt turned to me. "Those were airstrikes, dude…" He grinned.

The coalition had dropped two bombs on the enemy. I'd never heard them land so close before.

"Oh… Sorry. Sorry, everyone…"

No one gave me a cross word or look as they stood down and shuffled back to bed. New guy.

They flew over most days; sometimes bombing, sometimes not. I got used to that hollow, echoing score in surround-sound, boring its way through the air towards you like the aircraft's own sound being gradually, then more and more rapidly, turned up to the final report which loosened the bones in your head and the atoms in your surroundings. You developed a fine sense of when that diving plane noise blended with that of a bomb on its way down. *Will they drop one or not?* Sometimes you could count down to the blast, judging the when but never the where. Christ knows what it must have felt like on the other side.

***

"I never get picked to go anywhere," I whined as Kosta and I washed up the dishes from breakfast and the previous couple of meals. On the steps leading up to the roof was a water butt.

"You haven't been here long, mate," he said. I'd been kicking around in this yard two days. He tipped the water butt forward to eke the last trickle out of the bottom. "I'm going to go on a water run. Come if you want."

I walked behind him, carrying one empty 10-litre container while he carried two. He knew a yard with a water tank that was still part full.

"Can't they get you a better jacket than that?" I asked on the way, gesturing to his ragged women's woollen coat, obviously scrapped from a room somewhere, with sleeves that ended halfway up his beefy forearms.

"I'm trying to blend in with the Kurds. Wear what they wear." For the same reason he wore pumps instead of boots and was growing the thin-beard-thick-moustache combo, in the local style.

"You look like a fucking criminal."

"Yeah. Fagin! Bill Sykes!"

People's dress said something about them. Most of us had a mix of YPG, other military and civilian gear. The only guy with the full works was an ex-US marine codenamed Akif – with state-of-the-art plate carrier, chest-rig, helmet, knee pads, fingerless gloves, ballistic glasses – all of a set, always on. To an outmoded pioneer like me (from the more ignoble end of the military spectrum) he looked like some sort of cyborg-warrior prototype.

Our route took us down some narrow steps that ended by an open doorway. I briefly glimpsed a group of men and women in baggy mountain dress, sat round on cushions in a small carpeted room, chit-chatting and laughing. They seemed like a family. Kosta gave them a polite greeting.

Back at our accommodation, there ensued an argument about one of the occupants we'd seen.

"No, she's *my* imaginary girlfriend."

"No way, she's mine. *Your* imaginary girlfriend was that girl at the HQ," said a ginger Australian called Bagok (real name Ashley).

"In the market, are we, guys?" I ventured.

"Yeah," said Kosta. "I want a Kurdish wife."

He was keen on getting into an all-Kurdish unit too, to force his language along.

"He's going full Kurd."

"Doesn't the fact that you're six foot three put you off at all?" I asked.

"*Never* go full Kurd, dude…"

***

A few hours later I was in my first firefight. It was nothing special, really.

The ambient gunfire was growing more intense as the evening grew darker. By dusk it was in full swing and three of us were sent up to man positions on the berm.

I lay flat on the cold soil, head up over the ridge to face down into the darkened city. All across my front, muzzle flashes of enemy fire flowered on and off, illuminating tiny details of distant buildings. Gunfire rattled away and rounds whooshed and snapped above us, occasionally thumping into the berm and pranging off two metal water-towers behind and above us, silhouetted cuboids on skeletal steel legs, perforated like colanders. The reason they took so much flak was that the Peshmergas' Dushka guns were close by. As we lay there they hammered out long salvos in return, red glowing tracer arcing over our heads down into the city.

"This is a shit fire position," I said to a guy called California Pat, lying next to me. The soil and rock surface was so loose and uneven that I felt myself constantly sliding down. I scrabbled with my feet, digging footholds to stop myself slipping, and heaped up the earth around my front to prop my elbows into and steady the weapon.

We pressed ourselves down into the dirt as two rounds, among the countless swarm, snapped in the air low above us, fired from one of the nearer buildings, perhaps 200 metres out. Possibly aimed at this position, if it was known, or maybe just strays. I clicked off the safety and stared over my weapon at the muzzle flash fading like a camera bulb. My rifle's iron sights were virtually invisible in the darkness and I still hadn't had the chance to zero the thing. (Zeroing: firing shots at a target from a specific distance, and adjusting weapon sights to the individual user.)

"Any reason not to open up?" I asked, lining up as best as possible.

"Nope."

The flash flared again. I fired off two return shots, on single setting, just as another round snapped overhead as if in answer.

Instinctively I shifted a couple of metres to my left and started building up my position again.

I got utterly absorbed. Spot targets within range and return fire. Shift position, count your rounds. Chew dirt when the really low rounds come. Training clicked in as if from the day before, not 17 years ago.

The muzzle flash I'd been mostly engaging had stopped appearing there, but that meant nothing.

Soon the fire on both sides started to die down.

"*Hey.* He says, don't fire any more," said Pat, translating for Agît, one of the Kurds in our group. I hadn't noticed him on the track behind me. "The enemy's too far away. We gotta go down."

"Really?"

"Yeah, they don't like you firing unless you can actually *see* the enemy, at like 50 metres or less."

We got down off the berm and followed Agît back to the accommodation.

"Ah well. I was just getting into that."

"Yeah."

We had one form of contact or other most days, as Kosta had said, standing to on the berm or in the upper rooms of the front-facing buildings. If you thought a target was worth engaging, you might try. Usually you just conserved ammo and waited it out. The main thing was just to be up there when things were in full swing, in case the enemy tried to approach under cover of the maelstrom. The YPG were amateurs, but not, as a rule, trigger-happy ones.

When we weren't caught up in these exchanges, we divided our time between the security routine, our household chores and personal admin, and just plain idling around waiting for something to happen.

By day, our only light source in the bedroom was the doorway, so we pinned back the blackout drape and put up with the chill. I was sitting up against a couple of cushions, half in, half out of my sleeping bag.

The house backed straight onto the main track. A heap of scrapped machinery and white goods made a flimsy barricade in the gap between it and the wall to our right.

I sparked up my ninth or 10th cigarette of the morning. As predicted, my nicotine habit was proceeding apace. Tea without a cigarette seemed a waste now. The Australian, Bagok, didn't smoke, but didn't mind me doing it. He didn't mind much, apparently.

"And then she says, 'Well, where does that leave *us*?'" He kicked off his boots and sprawled across his thin, worn-out mattress pad. "And I'm like, I've told you: I'm in Syria, I'm volunteering with a militia, I just don't know what's gonna happen. I might even go to jail when I come back." His look of exasperation faded quickly from his clean-cut but grubby features, leaving the trace of a smile. It was hard to imagine him staying irked about anything for long.

Cûdî Vietnam nodded earnestly, as if grappling with another of the unfathomable mysteries of the universe. I retreated into my corner, only half listening. If Kosta's default mode was brooding intensity, Bagok's was a wide grin – displaying a mouthful of great teeth, housed in a jaw as well defined as his overall physique. He could have looked belligerent if he hadn't been so obviously geared to warmth and mirth. He often sported wraparound shades, and the whole ensemble – sleeve tattoo and a black wristband on his left arm, a pistol on his hip that someone had given him – made him look like a private-military type, perhaps, or a film star playing one. He carried these trappings as lightly as he carried everything else.

He was thinking of trying to get into the Special Forces back in Oz, if he avoided jail. But he was far from a knuckle-dragger. He'd loaned me a copy of Öcalan's Democratic Confederalism, and he wanted it back to reread it. I don't think he was deeply into the politics though; he wasn't one of those volunteers who went on about it endlessly. No one in the Shengal group was.

Bagok, Kosta and Cûdî Vietnam conscientiously kept up their fitness: press-ups, pull-ups, dips and some weightlifting with various improvised heavy objects. They'd asked me to join them but so far I'd put it off. My fitness was always there when I needed it, training or not. Thousands of cigarettes later, I'd be forced to revise that attitude.

Physique aside, however, Bagok's general appearance didn't seem a concern for him. A patina of built-up dirt disappeared down the neck of his T-shirt and reappeared on his forearms. It had been there for so long it had actually worn clean again in patches.

The conversation moved on to another of Bagok's women. Cûdî Vietnam was trying to understand why he saw no real

future with this one either. From what I gathered, she was too…
different… Something to do with her being so concerned about
whether things were going OK that she couldn't just chill out
and enjoy stuff…

Cûdî Vietnam's brow creased. "So you mean she was like…
too nice…?"

"I wouldn't say too…" Bagok's expression switched from
reflective to baffled. "What does that *mean*, anyway?"

"It means you're a cunt!" I said – then remembered I barely
knew the guy. He turned slowly towards me, his shoulders vibrat-
ing with silent laughter.

Good-looking and easy to like, I had no trouble believing
he was popular with the ladies. He wasn't a boaster though; he
just liked talking about girls. It was equally easy to imagine that
exasperation and bafflement weren't rare in Bagok's affairs of the
heart. He reminded me of a Facebook meme that went, *behind every
angry woman… is a guy who has absolutely no idea what he did wrong.*

Directly opposite ours, maybe seven metres away, were two
more rooms. The rightmost accommodated two more foreigners.
The metal door of the other was kept shut with twisted wire
when not in use. That was the pissing room, as Bagok put it.

"What, so you just go up there and piss anywhere?" I'd asked,
down in the yard.

"As long as it's the pissing *room*. Not just on some poor
dude…" he chuckled.

You had to go further out for a shit, through a gap in a
crumbling wall, over mounds of rubble and under a tree's low

branches, into another tiny bombed-out and overgrown yard strewn with rubble and household possessions. Further out lay more abandoned dwellings and yards like these. Everywhere was trashed in this quarter, indoors and out; floors strewn with furniture, clothes, VCR cassettes, family photos. Trashed lives. I assumed Daesh had done it, before the YPG reclaimed the area.

From this devastation we scrapped and scavenged everything we needed. Paraffin heaters, cooking equipment, blankets, rugs; a crate of soft drinks or maybe a useful tool if you were lucky. At first I couldn't bring myself to rummage among the heartbreaking wreckage, but when I eventually needed practical things – a waistcoat with pockets, a lamp, a child's schoolbook for writing paper – I got over it pretty quickly.

4 CHARACTERS AND CHEMISTRIES

Peter wanted to see us all in the bedroom.

He'd turned up a couple of days before, a stranger, older – early 40s, say – and had come across as just a friendly, all-American guy, joshing with Jordan and a couple of the other long-termers about this and that. Perhaps there was something a bit stretched about that jollity of his.

"Yeah, I was up on the berm last night. They were telling me to get down, and I'm like, no, I'm having too much *fun* up here…!"

"Yeah, Apo… Well, if anyone asks, I just tell 'em straight: I'm a *capitalist*. Sorry. There it is!" he chuckled. I pictured him with bubblegum and a baseball cap; maybe a sleeveless bodywarmer or one of those campus-jock football jackets from the 80s movies.

Physically he looked the model soldier: close-cropped hair, a slim, athletic build, visible through close-fitting American fatigues. His M16 never left his side, hanging from one shoulder, muzzle pointing upwards.

I'd introduced myself and, when he didn't volunteer his name, asked it.

"Peter," he said. "Fought from Tal Tamir to Haseke last year, been out here since September…"

"Nice to meet you."

Enough said.

The following morning he and someone else planned to go to a disused sports ground to zero weapons. I asked if I could go along. My urgency to zero mine wasn't shared by the command at any base I'd passed through, and it still wasn't done. The absurdity of being in an actual firefight before even zeroing didn't register round here. Sure, said Peter, come along. But next day I woke to find they'd left without me.

I said a few sharp words when I saw him next.

"Well, we were gonna come get you, but you were sleeping," he said.

"Why didn't you wake me? Zeroing's important!"

His eyebrows lowered into sharp zags above his dark eyes. You might say a shadow fell across his face, and looked right at home there. Jordan was going later on, he said. I could go with him.

Shortly after, Soran appointed Peter to take over all the *Emeriki* (westerners/foreigners).

***

Today, as soon as Peter came in, the change was visible. He moved in a measured, almost stiff manner and the bubblegum smile was gone.

"Have any of you attended a *tekmîl* before?" he asked the room, in a low voice.

I thought I had, but didn't say anything. Neither did anyone else.

"Well, the first thing to do is to stand up."

We looked at one another, then stood in a circle around him. No one was to smoke; people were to speak one at a time, in turn.

"So a *tekmîl* is a group meeting, where everyone discusses and reflects on issues affecting the group. Now I've been told to take charge of this group. I didn't ask for it, but there it is." That dour expression, with the slightly curled upper lip and bottom teeth bared, fell in naturally like the remembered creases in a leather boot, as he looked downwards at no one in particular and continued to speak. "OK. So we begin by asking if anyone has any points to raise."

Someone was keen to get on with lining the *nobet* house with sandbags and reinforcing the bunker roof. Several had concerns about the laxity of some of the younger Kurds regarding *nobet* and other safety practices.

Now the ice was broken, I suggested staggering the rotation times of the doubled-up night-guard, so that one sentry switched halfway through the other's shift, instead of both at the same time. That way the person just coming on, night-blind and disorientated, paired up with someone fully awake with their night-vision attuned. *Old eyes, new eyes*, it was called.

"Kemal – anything to raise?" said Peter, turning to Kosta.

"No, not really – except, I don't know why you feel you've *got* to be in charge of us, Peter," Kosta began. Not only was he proudly independent, but for him the thought of being a burden – especially on someone he held in such obviously high regard – would be intolerable. I hastened to agree; I mean, we valued Peter's experience, but –

"One at a time," said Peter, cutting me dead.

We focused on logistics again. Reinforcing the *nobet* position did need to happen, and Peter would speak to logistics about getting sandbags. Also, there were numerous weak points along our lines where the enemy could break through and attack. It had happened before and would again, so we might want to think about having our weapons to hand at all times.

No one questioned Peter's sudden appointment over us, or would have thought to. His experience dwarfed ours, hence the implicit deference from the likes of Kosta and others, and the mutual respect he shared with Soran. And something more: he *looked the part*. If that impression had come somewhat belatedly to me personally, any doubts were dispelled by his words – both their content and delivery.

"Sooner or later the Tal Hamis operation will begin, and we will actually start attacking. This isn't like a NATO military, with good intel, good equipment, good tech… They don't have the capacity to fight that way. And they probably never will. But they've got initiative. They're resourceful, good at improvising with what they do have.

"Discipline is low, tactics *are* basic – and you can't change it. But what you *can* do is set an example. If you're up at six every morning, cleaning your weapon, they will see it, and they'll take it on. If you're up at 7.30, if you're sitting outside when there's *howens* (mortars) flying – enjoying the sunshine – who's gonna listen to you…? *I* wouldn't."

He didn't even look at me when he said that; he didn't need to. My sunbathing hadn't gone unnoticed.

"A lot of what you know, from your own military backgrounds, won't mean anything to them. But you *can* apply your training at a personal level. Keep your drills tight, think for yourself. If they tell you to run to somewhere and *you* don't think it's safe – don't go there. You're all good soldiers, you can use your own judgment.

"If they take you with them on an attack, it won't be like what you're used to – with a plan A, a plan B, a plan C. They'll just say, we're going to fight Daesh. Tag along, watch how they do things – and be happy that you're going to fight."

The effect of this potted speech on our group was palpable. Not only because we now felt far more clued up about this scene than we had just an hour before, but because this guy was from our world (sort of) and he *got* it, when it came to our questions and uncertainties, our concerns, doubts and misgivings. It's hard to put a value on so much pertinent, condensed common sense, for people who'd hitherto been scrabbling around in a fog of scant information and mistranslations, trying to join the dots and figure things out for themselves.

That afternoon I overheard Peter asking if anyone had any spare thermals. I took out the extra set I'd bought in Saudi for $50 a pop, and left them on the bed space he'd taken in our room.

Later, as we sat in the yard, I got a dreadful feeling I'd stitched myself up again. I'd asked Kosta if we could chat a bit about battlefield first aid, refresh my memory, since he was fresh from service and had been a section medic in the Corps.

"And you apply the tourniquet as high up the thigh as you can get it," he was telling me. "Make sure you're not trapping the guy's testicles in when you tighten it – it actually says that in the book…"

As he spieled away enthusiastically, pointing at his notebook, Peter appeared in the yard. In the background again.

"You might want to write some of this down," Kosta went on, as Peter walked through.

Great. As if sitting sunbathing in a mortar storm (and snoozing when I should have been zeroing) hadn't impressed him enough, now I looked like I needed remedial schooling in things that should be second nature to any soldier. Whether Kosta was looking for brownie points or not, everyone wanted to shine and this was hardly my moment. Karma, maybe, for my cockiness at Zara.

***

"You're going out on the ambush tonight," said Peter, appearing in the bedroom doorway. He was looking at me.

"OK," I said, sitting up, trying not to look too pleased. Cûdî Vietnam turned to me with a bright smile. *Good for you,* it said. *Getting to do something at last.*

Peter turned to go.

"Is there a brief for it?" I asked.

"Get your brief off one of the guys who did it yesterday."

"Right."

The word for ambush is *kamîn*. I was paired up with Mason, a greying, rotund little Canadian in his 50s, warden of his local church.

Carrying a canvas bag full of *bizfink* (RPG) rockets, I followed the others uphill. Depending on moonlight and cloud cover, visibility could be superb or close to zero. Tonight the guy five metres ahead of me was striding along with zest as I picked my way gingerly over hidden rocks and craters, tripping and cursing under my breath. I've never known anyone like the Kurds for night vision. It's uncanny.

At the top of the track was a concrete bunker covered with earth. Inside were bunk beds, a small seating area and a bunch of bare wires to set off two *mayns* (IEDs) in the ground and one in an empty house a short distance forward of our territory. We didn't expect to ambush anyone, particularly; this was a permanent position. The duty was basically *nobet*, with the capacity to replace an intruder with a cloud of soil and blood.

The bedding was twice its own weight in dust, the silt of dried winter mud trodden in over the months. It flew up your nose and down your throat, built up on your chest, made you cough up clumps of crap. But without blankets you just froze, and to stay alert on shift you needed your sleep in between.

Mason and I rotated with a young Kurd called Efrin and a shifty-eyed little Arab kid of about 20 called Hamza.

It was coming up to 2am. Mason was in the bunker, with the controls; I was out on the berm at one of two sangars (sandbagged sentry positions). The moon was lurid. A steady orange light glowed from a burning building in no man's land. A firefight had flared up, briefly, earlier in the night and someone had *bizfink*ed the building from our side, setting it alight. Now all was silent.

Crunching footsteps behind me. Hamza was climbing up to my position. He smiled at me, then without saying anything picked up a handful of stones from the berm and threw them past me, down at the nearer buildings of the city.

Then he climbed higher up the berm, with half his body exposed over the ridge, and waved his arms over his head. After that he headed in, leaving me to it.

Knowing the game better than we did, Hamza and Efrin stitched us up like mackerel. The minutes they shaved off their shifts onto ours added up to nearly two hours by the end. On their off-time, instead of sleeping they stood outside the bunker talking and playing music on their phones, which glowed a mile away. They went to bed about an hour before their graveyard shift and I had to literally boot them awake after Mason, a shy and retiring type, came to me at a total loss.

"I told them it's their shift but they just kept saying, *10 more minutes…*"

"Right. Take over here, mate. Soon fucking sort this."

***

Two nights later, I sat in the underground bunker at the *nobet* house, on regular *nobet* by myself. Instead of doubling the night guard they now just had the *sûbay* come and check on you every now and then. A *sûbay*'s job was to take care of any problems the sentries might have, to run messages if necessary (for those without radios) and to basically make sure they stayed awake on shift. When he approached the bunker, he was supposed to call ahead quietly so you'd know who was coming, saying, "*Heval?*" to which the answer was the same word repeated. Hardly foolproof, but better than nothing.

As I sat in the darkness, someone appeared in the mousehole in the wall, filling it right up and expunging all light. I waited for whoever it was to initiate things. Not a word.

"*Heval?*" I said eventually, ending my dilemma – I'd been as invisible as them, before I spoke.

I waited. Slowly I reached out for the rifle beside me.

"*Heval…?*" I repeated.

I brought it up into the shoulder, pointing at the mousehole. Was there a weapon trained on me, right now? Could I release the safety – which would make an obvious sound – and get a shot off in time?

The figure turned and walked away without a word. I got up and followed with my weapon. There in the middle of the track, where the rounds sailed merrily downstream during the day, was Hamza, pulling up a chair – on *sûbay*. Dumb fucker.

I brought it up over tea with Masiha, an Iranian ex-Special Forces guy, in the room he shared with Mason.

"This, normal in YPG," he said. "Discipline *very* low. One night I go with Soran and two YPG to put down *mayns*. Everyone very quiet – security – look, listen. After 20 minutes I look, and one – " He mimed a texting action on a mobile phone.

Masiha was 35, a veteran fighter and a Christian, hence his chosen codename (Messiah, in English). If he went back to Iran from here he was likely to be arrested, and God knew what else.

Was I married? No. Was he?

"No. I think, 40-45 is good time for be married. For now, good travel, good fighting… But this, not good fighting." He pointed in the direction of the city. "This – *game*. Baby game."

***

I made no bones about it at the next *tekmîl*, because Jordan had his own beef about Hamza and Efrin, and because I didn't know how much I was in the doghouse with Peter still. I merely reiterated Jordan's view: "Different offences, same general theme," I said. "Those two are a liability in my estimation."

Once the *tekmîl* was over, Bagok, as ever, had an eye to the funny side.

"Fucking *Hamza*, mate…" He broke into a grin, remembering something. "Once, I found this photo in a wedding album – this woman in a really low-cut wedding dress, showing a bit of boob. I showed it to Hamza and he grabbed it off me, shoved it in his pocket and walked off," he laughed.

Since Peter had moved in to the room, even our downtime took on a different mood, the banter more guarded, when the big cheese was around. However, he had other business that took him in and out of Shengal. As time went on, he spent more of it away than here.

We were doing not much one morning when Matt appeared in the doorway, talking like the house was on fire. "Oh my *God*. You won't fucking believe it."

I sat up. "What?" After a couple of weeks here, there was precious little I wouldn't believe.

"I just heard that fag *Brandon* is coming here."

Like several of us, Matt's contradictions were right on the surface. A conservative Christian with Woodstock-era long straggly hair and moustache, he threw the word "fag" around quite casually and was thinking of getting an Apo tattoo.

I knew Brandon from the training academy. I'd had a go at him myself, once, for larking around with Welat (another great specimen) on the live-firing range, but we'd sorted it out.

"Is he that fucking truck driver?" someone asked.

"Yeah. Told everyone he was infantry," said Matt.

Apparently he had a bit of a rep. The conversation went over "Walts" we'd known or heard about – liars of Rojava. Some names popped up wherever you went.

"Remember that guy Max, at the training camp? Told everyone he was in the French Foreign Legion for 10 years. Till this real ex-Legionnaire turned up and asked him what unit he was in – and he said he *couldn't remember*!"

"What the fuck?"

"What was that other guy's name – total fruitcake, American?"

"David." Bagok affected a voice somewhere between Truman Capote and Andy Warhol: "I'm not sure how I should *feel* right now. I mean, I want to feel like a *man*; but I don't know *how…*" His voice broke up towards the end, joining the volley of guffaws.

"Did you hear what he did? Walked off base in the middle of the night. Went up to a checkpoint and tried to bribe his way to the front with a carton of Arden cigarettes."

"But they're free!"

"Yeah. They just arrested him and brought him back."

"*Vital info for people interested in coming here to help the Kurdish people: I spent seven years in my country's army reserve (rifleman and section-level combat medic).*"

Bagok was reading out loud from the screen of his phone. My phone had been taken off me at the academy; I might have been able to get it back if I'd really insisted, but so far I was getting used to not having it.

"*I only deployed on peacekeeping operations,*" Bagok read on, "*and though I enjoyed my time in the army it was mostly pretty uneventful.*"

"*I am writing this because in my short time here so far I am absolutely disgusted by the number of Westerners that feel the need to either inflate or completely bullshit their resume.*"

I recognised the text, because I'd seen it on Facebook a month or so earlier.

"*There are a good number of people here with actual military experience from all over the globe that can and will immediately spot you as a fake. All the* Call of Duty *in the world won't hide your complete lack of basic soldiering.*

"If you have no military experience, yet have skills that can be utilised and the right attitude, then don't worry. Be honest and the guys here will gladly get you up to speed as best they can. Lying about yourself over here is not only selfish but incredibly stupid.

"The Kurdish people are some of the most kind and trusting people I've ever met and your lies will get people killed. This isn't a playground to live some fantasy or play soldier. It's a fucking war-torn region with countless people suffering, dying and being displaced.

"Coming here full of bullshit and for selfish reasons is a waste of everyone's time, effort and money, and will simply get you a kick in the arse back to the airport."

"Bloody hell," I said, "I read that! That was you?"

"Yeah. And afterwards I got all these people saying, *You're only a fucking reservist, what do you know?* and all this kind of shit. It's like, you've totally missed the point. I'm bagging out my *own* military career in order to say, you don't have to pretend to be something you're not. Just be fucking honest."

For Kosta, such characters were no laughing matter. Which brought the conversation back to *That Fucking Brandon.*

"If I meet him he won't *want* to stay," he said.

"Well, let's give him a chance," I said. I had little more sympathy than Kosta, but perhaps the group was being a bit too keen to judge on the basis of rumour.

"I can't be arsed with dramas like that," said Kosta, taking a shaving brush from a webbing pouch and starting to brush down the outside of his rifle. He brushed it down so often the dust rarely built up there to any degree. *Squared away.* "If they shouldn't be here, we should make them leave."

Bagok muttered something about "closed door meetings"; he and Kosta exchanged grins. I didn't smile, because I was in an army unit called Deepcut in the 90s, a place that saw a shocking number of suicides among young soldiers fresh out of training. No one sees it coming till it's too late. Neither Kosta nor Bagok were malicious guys, however; we had a decent group and we wanted to keep it that way. This was a war, not a social club.

Several other stars of Rojava's international volunteer scene were discussed by us: including a junkie, clucking his nuts off at the training camp till they sent him home, and a guy claiming to be a combat medic, until one fine day when they actually needed one and he turned out to be clueless. A scene like this was obviously going to attract a few sketchy types, but there were many, many more than that.

"I thought you knew I was a chocco," said Bagok, looking across to me.

"Sorry?" I'd faded out of the conversation for a moment. "A chocco?"

"Reservist," he shrugged.

"I couldn't care less, mate. You know your stuff."

As with most of us, the YPG was Bagok's second army, if it could be called an army, and he'd clearly done his time. But while Cûdî Vietnam's experiences here and with the US infantry in Afghanistan had made him a textbook soldier, cautious and sensible at every turn and naturally averse to unnecessary risk, Bagok remained resolutely lighthearted in a heavy gig. He had a streak of the Aussie beach bum about him, did Bagok: a bit *too* cool, on occasion.

His bravery wasn't in doubt; if anything, he could be called fearless to a fault. A few days ago, I'd been stood-to in the upstairs room of a house with Cûdî Vietnam during a salvo of incoming fire, crouched below the upstairs windows, peeping out occasionally. It seemed like intuition told you when to put your head up and when not to. Doubtless plenty of dead soldiers have thought similarly.

Bagok strolled in suddenly, right across the room, and leaned his back against the wall, looking at us like we were worrying about nothing. I must have looked daggers at him because his mouth dropped a good couple of degrees, from cocky to slightly embarrassed. Later I overheard him saying something like, *I need to start treating the danger more seriously…*

A couple of weeks before I arrived in Shengal, he and Cûdî Vietnam had been buried under rubble when a suicide truck blew up immediately outside a house where they were on sentry duty. The Kurds had taken their time dragging them out because they thought they were dead, and they'd spent several days in hospital. A third guy, Richard, was still there now, in a coma. But Bagok wore that lightly too – still here, still fighting and laughing. Though there were times when I got little more than a nod by way of greeting, I never once saw him properly angry or pissed off.

A scarecrow beard was sprouting up to join that sharp sprig of ginger hair, gone lank just lately beneath the baggy woollen hat, like a huge, filthy old sock, that he wore in preference to the more traditional *keffi* headdress.

"I'm trying to look as homeless as possible," he claimed. Either this was related to his Special Forces aspirations, or it was Kosta's influence. He'd turn them all into wandering ascetics, Kosta would.

Bagok and Cûdî Vietnam seemed to be here for decent enough reasons. The desire to fight was a given, but not every fighter would trouble to observe, as Bagok did, that this theatre presented the most legitimate case for foreign intervention in the last couple of decades. Some cared more than others about such things; some didn't care at all. Conventional codes and mores were of limited application here, I felt, when it came to someone's character. Instinct was a better guide.

The experience of being bombed out had cemented the bond between the two of them. I'd once asked Cûdî Vietnam how long he planned to stay in Shengal, and whether he'd cross into Rojava for the Tal Hamis op. "Well I'm just gonna go wherever this guy goes," he grinned, indicating his friend.

Like the rest of us, Bagok was keen to get on the fabled Tal Hamis operation, to get on with some "*real* fighting", but he was at home in Shengal. What united our disparate characters, it seemed to me, was that we were all fulfilling something very deep-rooted simply by being here. We were drawn to the thing itself. Kosta once said, "My reasons for being here change all the time."

Reasons, like battle plans, rarely survive the first contact.

5 HARD ROUTINE

We decided to get off our arses about the *nobet* house, finally, and make the desperately needed reinforcements. We had two shovels and a stack of outsized sandbags scored by Peter, so we rotated the labour between the five to eight of us in attendance at any one time as the morning dragged on.

"Hey, a lot of my friends are gay, you know," I said. Jordan and Matt were making liberal use of the word "fag" as we worked away, and I decided if I didn't say anything at all I'd be reproaching myself for it.

"I don't *cayyrre...*!" laughed Jordan in that geeky comedy voice of his, like a right-wing Jim Carey.

Thereafter I did my best to drop as many references to Jordan's latent gayness as I could. At least, until it got too boring. Hardly the most robust of confrontations, but then it hardly seemed the place for robust confrontations.

Kosta was behind this effort, as he was with so many such things. I've known few people in my life so relentlessly motivated, always pushing himself in one way or another, demanding the highest standards of himself. Any work, any danger. When they advised recruits in training to pick a role model and try to emulate that person, they meant people like Kosta. Sandbagging, cooking, fetching water; if none of us had volunteered he'd have done it by himself even if it took him all day.

No way was I letting that happen, so I was first up after him.

"Don't take from the berm," said Jordan, as we clumsily shovelled the earth, loose rock, random clumps of vegetation and bits of litter into the giant hessian sacks.

Even in winter the late morning sun could be fierce. Soil spilled and the air filled with dust; grime stuck to fresh sweat, layered on old sweat (and grime), in our depleted hygiene. Ablutions generally consisted of going off somewhere private and washing from a water bottle or other plastic container – when you had water to do so. We must have stunk.

Kosta wasn't joining in with the "fag" banter. We'd discussed Apo's democratic confederalism project a couple of times, in no great depth, with its emphasis on gender equality, plurality of faiths, races and cultures and so on. I remarked that he never seemed to touch on the gay issue, and wondered if gays were supposed to get as fair a deal as everyone else.

"Dunno," shrugged Kosta. "Hope so."

In some ways he slotted in with that strain of conservative Christianity the other ex-soldiers exhibited, in other ways not.

Jordan made some lame quip about me and Kosta stopping

for tea with the Queen. I was surprised by Kosta's response when I said something like, "Thanks, but I'll pass…"

"You *don't* love the royal family…?" said Kosta, aghast.

"No. I don't."

"Why?"

"Well – what do they actually do?"

"They represent us, man!"

I searched his exasperated face for any trace of irony. *Nope…*

It took two, even three of us to carry a full sandbag, laid out on a stretcher improvised from a blanket (though Kosta did manage a couple by himself, just for pride's sake). We manhandled them through the narrow gate, out of the bright glare and into the cool gloom of the *nobet* house. Rays from outside fell from the bullet holes high up in the yellow plaster, lighting the dust.

No one used the underground bunker any more, since a tracer round had set the roof on fire a couple of days before. Matt, who'd suggested we "nix" it, had got his wish. To save the whole house from burning down, Bagok and I, with sweat pouring off us and streaked with soot, had dragged the bunker's wooden roof beams away, even as they burned, and repeatedly tried to tamp out the burning hessian bags which simply reignited in the gentle breeze like trick candles. We were working all the while in the direct line of fire that had lit the place up to begin with, and only too aware of the fact – but the job needed doing and timidity wasn't going to help. It's everyone's job to stash the fear away, if you feel it, and get on with things.

Now we did our *nobet* in this room and the room behind. In a room on the right was a gaping, man-sized hole in the wall and floor, straight onto no man's land. That whole room was blackened and trashed, the floor littered with burnt debris and plastic bottles, which I would add to and spread about just for some form of night alarm. They'd crunch loudly if anyone stepped on them while trying to sneak up. Better than nothing.

The whole house was lethal, shot up and crumbling. Every couple of days the Dushkas and mortars battered it a bit more.

On the count of three we boosted the dead weight up onto the ever-growing wall of sacks against the crazed and shattered concrete. Lifting higher every time – as the challenge increased, our strength decreased.

A shot resounded, fired from inside the house.

"*Malaka!*" (Wanker!) growled Kosta, as the walls rang. When it's been a while since the last one, it makes you jump, no matter how accustomed you are.

On the other side of the right-hand wall, in a nest of blankets under the stairwell, Bucky was shooting with his *karnas* (sniper rifle), just for something to do. He wouldn't hit anything. The enemy shooters were well concealed inside buildings, shooting out through holes in walls like us, sometimes two walls back. If he wanted to draw fire on himself, that was his choice, but he could have waited till we'd knocked off.

Bucky (actual codename Khalil) was our interpreter: 21, with thick round glasses, he came across like a first-year undergraduate crossed with a slightly potty grandad. He was friendly and convivial, and loved to talk. He was knowledgeable and often worth listening to, provided you seasoned his unfiltered discourse with a generous measure of salt. To cut a dash he carried a series of (completely unnecessary) walking sticks, found in houses wherever he went. In a carefully chosen moment he'd refer to himself as our captain, though I never heard him actually try and give an order to anyone. Good thing too.

At the end of the day they were amateurs, like Kosta said, and there were worse than Bucky among us.

"Incidentally," I said, "where's that fucking Hamza these days?" It was a few days since I'd seen him.

"In jail, apparently, mate. They reckon he was an agent for Daesh."

"What!"

"Yeah, I know."

Efrin wasn't around either. According to someone, who heard it from someone else, he'd only been here to spy on Hamza, who was spying on us.

We knocked off around midday, when the sandbags were one above head height.

Back in the bedroom, we listened as Bucky's *karnas* continued to resound from over at the *nobet* house. Kosta exhaled audibly, scowling and shaking his head.

"Shooting at nothing," snorted Peter.

Agît came and called us to Soran's room, where lunch was being served up. There were about 15 of us, Kurds and westerners. Plates of salad, bags of flat bread, and a stew of boiled-up chicken and potatoes, divided into two communal pots at either end of a strip of lino laid out across the rugs. We went at it with a vengeance after the morning's work. Kosta ate modestly, however, finishing first.

Following the meal, as the first round of tea was over and I made for a second, I turned to Bagok and said, haltingly, "*Heval, tu dexwazi batr çay?*" (*Heval*, would you like some more tea?)

"All *right!* Excellent…" he smiled. I'd been borrowing Kosta and Cûdî Vietnam's notes. They saw language as part of soldiering. *Be functional*, Kosta said.

"Cûdî, one day you and me and *heval* Kemal all go London together. When war finish!" said Soran, from the other end of the room. His bonhomie was genuine, but there was something slightly mask-like about his genial smile. A blind man on a galloping horse could see the darkness below the surface.

Agît was another young veteran of the mountains, always in the traditional baggy dress. He was picking up crumbs from the floor, the tiniest, microscopic specks of bread. He explained to me that when he'd fought under siege in Turkey, they'd hunted for crumbs like rats for months. He threw them onto the lino. I wondered if he picked them up now for cleanliness, or whether the habit had just been stamped on him by that experience.

Soran picked up his rifle. "I love you so much," he said, kissing the stock. "I want kill Daesh one by one…" Good thing he loved westerners.

"Leave one for me," I joked.

"Only one…?"

Conversation turned to everyone's favourite topic: the fabled operation at Tal Hamis. The when, the how.

I got up. Sometimes I was happy to socialise; today I wanted to read. I'd stay to help clear up, though.

As I carried a stack of pots outside to the water butt, I noticed Kosta was discreetly eating from a tin of tuna. He'd been as hungry as anyone else for the hot food, but was being a Samurai about it. Seeing me start the washing-up, he came and joined me. A flake of soap and a scrap of scourer against a mountainside of congealed crap. We got every pot and plate spotless, then I left; the others stayed talking.

***

Peter had us out sandbagging again a couple of days later, in a garden further downhill. I didn't really think to ask why at first, as we dug up the soil and stacked maybe 20 full bags in a row out of view.

Kosta was posing on some steps for a photo with a child's plastic doll he'd found. He'd filled it with water, bored a hole in the plastic, and held it up so it was pissing in his open grinning mouth.

"You know he *actually* pissed in his own mouth once?" said Bagok.

"You did *what*?" said Peter, eyebrows knitted.

"Yeah, I pissed in me mouth!" grinned Kosta.

"What *for*…?"

"Just for a bit of banter, for the lads, like."

Several witnesses swore it was true.

That night Peter, Bagok, Matt and I made our way back to the spot and lugged the sandbags, under cover of dark, up the stairs of a house and out onto a flat roof surrounded by a low wall. It only dawned on me then that we weren't really supposed to be doing this. It was a warm night and dirty sweat rolled down into my eyes as Bagok passed me one after another through a hole in the wall.

Arched, recessed holes cut into the balcony wall at intervals looked out onto the city in two directions. Under Peter's direction we stacked the sandbags round a hole and made a platform to lie on from mattresses and doors.

I crawled into position and took the M16 Peter passed me, looking through the night scope at the city turned grainy green. Good arcs, muzzle clearance, a good spot.

We headed back.

"Take the front," said Peter to me. "I want to see you lead."

"I'm sorry – I'm not too sure of the route back," I said. "I haven't been out this way before." It was true, but I also have a pretty rotten sense of direction.

"It's OK," said Peter.

The clandestine nature of the outing became apparent when we were stopped and questioned on the way back. Peter made excuses as we made ourselves scarce.

"If anyone asks, just say you went to the toilet," he said, when we got back.

"What, all four of us?"

"Yes. Honestly, it's such a taboo subject, they won't press it."

***

I was sitting in the house's front room on the left. Another bright, cold, late morning; another *nobet*. Blades of grass poked up through the weave in the sandbag position the other side of the exit-hole in the left wall. *Green shoots*, I thought, randomly. I shivered in the chair, hoping someone would bring me a glass of hot, sweet *çay*. For movement's sake I walked through to the back room and picked up the binoculars. Scanning…

The quiet "empty" city. Flat-roofed, low-rise, sandy-coloured blocks for the most part; the occasional modern, taller structure thumbed in among them with no sense of overall composition. Daesh flags fluttering in the cold bright air. Mosque, with dome and minaret (from which no call to prayer sounded nowadays). Water tower. Memorising reference points. Vehicles on the back roads to Mosul, coming and going, way too far to engage. Two cars appeared on a short stretch of track much nearer, running left-right, out of sight behind a building; didn't reappear on the longer stretch. Stopped behind there. A lot of activity in that area lately. Constant.

A trickling sound. Plaster and concrete dust. Part of the wall had crumbled onto my webbing. Probably standing too close to the spy hole for too long.

I sat back down in the front room. Footsteps on the track, out of sight. Two YPJ (female YPG) girls appeared round the corner, running and stopping, running and stopping, chatting and giggling. Seeing me watching them through the exit-hole, one shouted something I didn't catch. I flipped my hand over – come again? She made a shooting sound – *"Tooh-tooh!"* – pointing in the enemy direction with a questioning expression. *Any shooting?*

"*Na*," I smiled, shaking my head.

They ran around the exposed part of track on the corner, under the arch and on into the corridor.

***

"There seems to be continuous activity in the town lately," I said, settling onto my mattress back in the bedroom.

"Where?" said Cûdî Vietnam.

"You know where the mosque is, with the dome and the minaret?"

"The mosque on the left? The closer one?"

"Yeah. You go down and left of that, just a couple of fingers, and there's two grey walls in an 'L' shape with a bit of track behind. Just there."

"Wait," said Peter, turning to me. "You mean where a blue wall meets a grey wall at a right angle?"

"Erm – I think so. I'm a bit fuzzy around the blue/green part of the spectrum but yeah, must be the same place. Just in front of the left-hand mosque."

"That's where he meant," said Bagok, nodding to Cûdî Vietnam.

"Yeah, that's the place I was talking about," said Cûdî V. A few days earlier, he'd come into the yard with a hand-drawn map, looking for anyone who could get word to the mortar men up top, call in a strike. He might as well have asked for a set of skis. "In the US infantry it's simple, you relay the coordinates and the strike happens almost instantly. But here they just don't have that whole system… *down*."

"Do they even *use* maps in this –"

A sudden, deafening series of bangs cut my question short; the whole yard resounded like the inside of a massive balloon as it burst, again and again, leaving us momentarily stunned. A volley of low-flying Dushka rounds, ripping through our pitiful defences of scrap, smashed straight into the upper courtyard.

As others scrambled into the bedroom a single larger round smashed into the lintel above the door of the room opposite, spraying fragments of concrete over the yard.

"Mason's in there!" shouted someone. I was on my feet and out the door without thinking, dashing across the nine metres of yard and tearing back the plastic rug covering the doorway as more rounds smashed in overhead.

"Mason!"

Mason sat up groggily on his mattress; eyes stretching wide, mouth a small, pursed round hole. He looked like a startled woodland creature.

"Get out!" I yelled. I grabbed him as he leaned towards me, dragged him to his feet and we stumbled, doubled over across the bare open space, my feet clopping and flapping in my half-on boots.

In the bedroom they checked him over – under his shirt, in his eyes; gave him some sweets and tea while he gasped and I gabbled and Peter called us all to calm. Someone dashed out to go check on the sentry. We looked out across the yard at a large round hole burnt into the plastic blackout rug.

"What's made that?"

"That's the heat-signature of the round. Big round."

The room was declared off-limits from now on, as was the pissing room next to it.

For Cûdî Vietnam that wasn't enough; he was visibly spooked. "We got to go look for other accommodation. We can't stay here. I'm going. Anyone want to come with?"

Through the right corridor, up over the ramp and down the concrete steps was an open space with several gardens and houses further out. Cûdî and I moved through, checking one house after another.

"What about this one?" He nodded towards a bare concrete shell of a room. A battered wooden door with a rusted metal latch, like you'd see on an old barn. The building was shielded by other houses from the line of fire we'd taken that morning, but completely exposed to the city from another side, though at greater distance. *Worth a try*, we decided.

"Hmm. Still dunno if the blokes will want to move though," I said.

"Well it's stupid staying up there," said Cûdî. He looked back in the direction of our current room, mouth turned down, eyes wide. "Just waiting to die…" His voice trailed off. Being dug out of the rubble once was plenty.

***

Over the next few days, we moved into the "new" room – and then, one by one, everyone moved back up to the old one again, as it became apparent that no room was safer than any other. One morning it was only me and Kosta left, and just as we were getting up out of bed, two Dushka rounds slammed into the wall, sending us diving back down again.

"Morning, Kosta," I said, as we both hit the deck. He didn't answer. Wrong side of bed maybe.

Kosta moved back with the others. I stayed.

I sandbagged the windows and strung up a sniper screen in the tiny front garden, made from a large piece of canvas I'd found in a workshop full of rusty old tools and machine parts.

The switch was pointless in terms of safety, but I was as happy by myself as in company. I was 40, not 20, and often missed having my own room. The convivial excitement of youth hostels was long behind me. Here I could savour the solitude, and could still walk across and socialise when I felt inclined to. I scrapped a paraffin heater and worked out a system of heating water in a large pan and giving myself an all-over body wash with the rugs rolled back in the chill winter room, hurriedly drying myself and dressing and guzzling down boiling sugary tea afterwards. For a toilet I used a 10-litre plastic container with the top cut off. I'd shovel in a bit of soil, use it in the outhouse next to my room, then dig it into my small front garden.

I had everything I needed. Solitude or company, as I chose, and proper soldiering to do while waiting for the Tal Hamis op to start.

I sat on the steps of my "own" place, taking in the view beyond the series of sniper screens receding downhill like banners of protest or celebration, to which I'd just added my own. The sun was just pleasant. A light spattering of small-arms fire sounded from far away – nothing to concern anyone.

The sound of a bouncing football came from near the home of the guerrilla group. They were quite sharply downhill, though only a few houses' distance away. Kosta's imaginary girlfriend and another woman were playing in the narrow ally running along the other side.

A young man appeared on the doorstep with a glass of tea in his hand. We exchanged neighbourly waves. With his other hand he gestured to it, then to me and the open door behind him. An invitation. I was slightly torn: I'd borrowed Cûdî Vietnam's Kurmanji language notes for a few hours, and wanted to copy out as much as possible before giving them back.

I held up a hand of polite refusal, gesturing at my book. He waved and went in.

That was an immediate regret, even for me.

I mentioned it to Kosta later, referring to them as "that family" without thinking about it.

"What family?"

"That group down the hill. The guerrillas. Well. I dunno. They *seem* like a family."

"I think they've been together a long time," he said.

"I should have accepted."

"Yeah." He nodded. *You should.*

***

We were huddled in the arched corridor. A direct mortar hit had nearly brought the room next to Soran's down on top of us as we ate lunch in there. Peering out the arch, through the dust, we saw that the cinder-block shack on the roof was riven with a huge crack.

"I've been here 21 days," said California Pat, through gritted teeth. "And all we've done… is get *mortared*."

The following day he, Matt and Akif left for home.

"I'm gutted they're leaving," said Kosta. "Gutted…"

***

A spot of friction had started to chafe between Kosta and me, small but recurrent, like grit in a boot. Finally it got too sore to ignore.

The big guns were tuning up one afternoon, so I headed for our secret spot to pick targets. I was sat on the mattresses, having a last unhurried cigarette before getting into position, when Kosta appeared at the top of the rooftop steps.

"What are *you* doing here?" he scowled.

"What do you mean?"

"I need that fire position."

I thought about that for a second.

"All right, have it." I rolled off and moved to crouch by another hole in the side-facing wall. The guns were going off all over the city; it was a big one. "I'll use this one." It was just as worth watching out this side, if less comfortable.

"I mean, are you engaging the enemy?" he pursued. "Because you look like you're having a tab to me."

If he had a problem with people smoking in a fire position, he'd come to the wrong war. That wasn't what he meant anyway. *What are YOU doing here...* Well, I helped build the thing. Frankly I didn't give a fuck if Kosta thought I wasn't in with the in-crowd, or resented my not caring enough about it.

"Don't fucking tell me what to do, Kemal," I said, as he crawled into prone position, facing out and away from me. Rounds zipped and cracked overhead.

"I wasn't tel – *what* did you just say?"

"You heard."

He snapped on the safety on his M16 and turned to look at me. "Did you just call me a cunt?"

"No, I didn't call you a cunt. I said don't tell me what to do."

"I didn't *tell you what to do*. I was asking a *question*."

"Well, it's your *tone*."

We sat out the attack, neither of us firing for lack of effective targets within range. When the fire started to die down he got up and moved off.

"Just be careful, yeah?" he said as he headed out. "We've been returning fire from down in the yard."

"OK."

There's an in-crowd wherever you go. I felt I'd been half-invited, and I'd half-accepted: a comfortable enough arrangement for me. But one that doesn't always go down well with military minds.

In the regular military there's such an emphasis on the *group*, in and out of work, that the lone spirit actually offends some people. For them you *can't* be half and half. You're either in, or you're an outsider. I'd often struggled with that obligatory aspect to the fraternity. But I wasn't going to agonise over it now. At my age, I was who I was.

The funny thing was, Kosta seemed to consider himself a bit of a lone wolf too, at times, in quite a different way from me. Besides his recurrent idea of splitting to go to an all-Kurdish *tabor*, he had a strong independent mind and generally kept his own counsel. But the sanctity of *the lads* was for him non-negotiable, a position I didn't share.

That attitude stood him well out there, not only among the internationals but the Kurds too, with their romantic, "guerrilla" *heval* spirit. It took me longer to see that the convivial way was how you got on, in all respects. Kosta had understood that from the beginning.

At a guess, that was part of the reason this had come about. Or maybe it was closer to the surface: some tedious marine/ army hostility. He said he was past all that and I was pretty sure I was. Perhaps he didn't like the fact I considered myself his equal. We'd both been through the same thing to get the green beret, give or take, but the fact is your average army commando just does the course and then spends the rest of his career dining out on it. I did a little more, but didn't feel inclined to go into it.

***

FIGHTING MONSTERS

After months of asking I got myself posted to a commando unit, namely the Commando Logistics Regiment Royal Marines. Another disappointment, for various reasons. Commando soldiers generally weren't up to the standard of marines and that gave the army lads an inflated and prickly sense of having something to prove. Not having a logistics trade, I worked in the stores sheds and with the petroleum operators, maintaining vehicles and lugging gear around. It could have been deathly boring, but the action-man culture there emphasised PT and training at least as much as the daily work, and every so often you got to do something like helicopter-abseiling, which reminded me why I'd volunteered for this stuff in the first place.

My best moment of the 18 months or so I spent there was the Cambrian Patrol: a long-range reconnaissance patrolling competition, testing all aspects of infantry soldiering skills, open to all NATO countries. The patrol itself was two days long; we trained two months leading up to it, up and down the Brecon Beacons, the Black Mountains, the Cambrians. Over that time they whittled down the applicants to a team of eight: six marines and two soldiers. Somehow I made the cut.

I ended up battle buddies and drinking buddies with Tug, a marine my age from Leeds. We'd got off to a shaky start. Like most marines he gave short shrift to the perse (army) lads and on one drunken outing with the group, he and I had been separated by the Swansea police.

Shortly before the team was picked, we were in some remote Welsh pub, recovering after another gruelling few days in the hulu (the wilderness). At this stage there was no shame in anyone saying he was knackered. Talk drifted over army/marine differences again, but with no edge to it; we were all past that now.

"Just to say, Jim, we don't mean you, mate," said Tug. "You've done everything we have, you've proved y'self with us. You're just one o' lads."

It meant quite a lot for him to say it, and it was half-true.

On the commando course itself, I hadn't found the physical punishment the hardest thing, nor even the mental pressure from above, but the social side, odd though it might sound. I went down there alone, not as part of a group, like the gunners, the sappers and the loggies on the course with me. Little differences widened as the course intensified and the one real friend I made there dropped out midway through, so when things toughened up I didn't even have a group to huddle in.

I remember sharply a moment from the final field exercise. I was lying in the wet grass, thinking hard. I'd been late getting to my sentry position, and got no more than a gentle rebuke off the guy I was relieving. If he'd had a go at me I may have felt better. None of us had any time for the things we needed to do. We'd been ragged around for weeks; nothing was up to scratch. The worst bunch they'd ever seen. When he'd gone I lay there just feeling so bleak and alone, feeling everything crumble. It stripped you down to the bone like corrosive acid, this programme, ate through the fond illusions you held up to feel good about yourself, and at that age I had plenty. I felt vulnerable, exposed, worthless.

If I'd tried to explain this to my new anarchist tribe a few years later, they'd have said, "So what? Those guys are fascists – no wonder you hardly connected with anyone." They'd miss the point.

We scored a gold award on the Cambrian patrol, made Marine Corps history and had our walk in the sun. Corps rag, local press, toast of the town around camp. Tug was going on his SBS acquaint (the first phase of selection) after this. So was another of the marines, nicknamed "Youth", a hefty Sheffield lad who'd only made our reserve team because he was more of a plodder than a racing snake.

"You never thought of having a crack at two-two (22 SAS) then, mate?" Tug asked me. I.e. enough of this Mickey Mouse "commando" crap, go do something real.

"Ah, I dunno about that," I laughed. *"Cambrian Patrol's one thing…"*

Half the team had their sights set on it; Bob Wilson, the team 2ic (second in command), had already passed SBS selection but had been kept back here in limbo over some confusion about his terms of engagement. *"The thing is,"* he said, *"you build it up to be this great big thing, but then you just go and do it."*

Lieutenant Muddiman, the marines officer who'd led us to gold on the Patrol (and treated it like a quest for the grail), said, in his last words to me: *"I think, Private Matthews, that in a couple of years – not now, but when you've got a bit more experience – you should really think about going for SF (Special Forces). I think that would suit you down to the ground."*

Maybe he was right: the SF were full of misfits, apparently. I did give it serious thought. They did things differently there – the travel, languages, skills, a healthy disrespect for officiousness and authoritarianism. Grow your hair how you want, walk around looking like a bum, no one cares…

"And they might just ask you to go and kill someone," said my dad, in one of the few conversations where we'd seen eye to eye.

"I'd say give it a go," Bob Wilson had told me, *"because if you don't, you'll always wonder."*

Part of me always has. But it was a choice I could live with.

***

Kosta didn't know about any of that; and I had no reason to tell him.

Anyway, maybe I was overthinking this. Maybe it was just his two weeks' seniority in Shengal, or a basic personality clash. Hopefully we'd sort it, but there were bigger things to worry about. It wasn't essential for us to like one another.

I sat in the lower yard a day or so later. I couldn't be bothered to go visit the westerners' room since I'd argued with Kosta.

He came down the ramp into the yard and made his way over to the stove where a kettle was boiling.

"Do you want a cup of tea, Jim?" he said.

"Yeah, love one. Thanks."

We didn't talk about why we'd fallen out; we just moved on. He was a complex man, more highly educated than he'd first let on, and there were plenty of potential flashpoints between us. Maybe it was a rivalry between the only two Brits in the group; it was certainly resolved in a very British way, anyway.

We sat in the yard, enjoying our tea.

"See that?" said Kosta, pointing up at some buildings in the near distance. A bird, off-white and solitary, was perched on a ledge below an overhanging rooftop.

"It's the last pigeon in Shengal – all the others have fucked off!"

***

"Hey mate. I think you're going to be happy," I said, peering through the bedroom doorway one day. "Matt's back."

"Ah, I'm *made up* about that, mate," said Kosta, sitting up.

"Oh. By the way. Here you go." I chucked over a couple of empty cigarette packets I'd saved. He kept his spare rounds in them. We had tons of 7.62 for the Kalashnikovs, but you had to hoard your 5.56 rounds if you had an M16. "Those things'll kill you," I said.

"Nice one."

Matt had had a chat with his mum, and another with his saint, and done a U-turn. His return gave our group morale a shot in the arm. Shengal was becoming a bit of a grind for everyone, and people leaving didn't make us feel better.

I checked the duties list, scribbled on the page of a notebook taped to the wall. *Kamîn – Cûdî Britannia.* Bollocks.

First time I got chosen for this I'd been stoked. But you can have too much of a good thing.

Agît reminded me for the umpteenth time, with a pantomime demonstration, not to fire unless I could see Daesh sneaking up on top of me like a tiptoeing cartoon character.

"Yeah, yeah…" I rolled my eyes at the time-honoured caution. Whatever. *Some of us can hit a target past 50 metres, mate.* Anyway, whatever.

The Peshmerga had started sending blokes to join us on *kamîn* duty. They treated it as one big knees-up: music, tea and interminable yabber, punctuated by raucous laughter, into the small hours. At least it solved the mystery of the voices I'd heard on night *nobet*, drifting, distorted, towards me on the wind. It was these guys, up at the Dushka point, having a laugh.

"You can't mistake the ambush site: it's always full of noise and light!" I said.

"Nice one," said Kosta, mustering a half-smile.

Out on the berm, I scrambled up the loose, sliding soil and rock, loaded the *bizfink* and rockets into the covered sandbag position, cleared and tidied the outside area and shook and straightened the blankets to lie on. A little Peshmerga fellow stood watching me from the track, looking like he'd been dressed by his mum. A single shot winged overhead from down in the city and he scurried off into the bunker. *Good to have you with us, guys…*

***

Down in the city, two dim searchlights roamed the gloom above for circling aircraft. Low cloud, lurking menace. Freezing cold *kamîn*. I had my thermals on, plus every layer of gear I'd bought in Saudi, and a blanket thrown over the lot like a shroud. The damp was softening my bones. But I didn't like having my hood up, even when it was freezing. I could never get used to the reduced peripheral vision, and the rustle of Gore-Tex in my ears as I turned my head could be the whisper of a mortar, an approaching plane or feet through grass.

Every now and then the Dushkas piped up, jarring my nerves, making them vibrate like a tuning fork. Three-week point in Shengal. Maybe it was just the temperature.

Later, off shift, I lay on the steel bed inside the bunker, encased in my webbing, boots, gloves and *keffi* (headscarf). When there's fire all around, the weight of ammo, bayonet and grenades is curiously reassuring.

I woke at around two in the morning.

People were pounding up and down, in and out of the bunker; the firefight was well underway. Everyone was spending money tonight. A body slid down the berm from the sangar to the track. Agît got to him before me. "*Hawar, hawar!*" (Help!) he yelled, standing over the grounded figure.

"Matt! Have you been shot, mate?"

"Aaaagh! Yeah…"

"Where?"

A dark patch was spreading across the cloth above his left knee. I had a basic travel first aid kit, but had never managed to source any proper field dressings or tourniquets between Saudi and here. I took off my *keffi* and tied it round his leg – YPG first aid. The problem is, you can't use it as a compress *and* get sufficient tension on it to staunch the blood flow. My attempt was a bit rubbish.

"Let's get him into the bunker," Agît and I said simultaneously, each in our own language.

"Just don't grab my left leg," Matt groaned.

We bundled him up the track into the bunker, falling arse over teakettle when my feet disappeared into a dip, taking the other two down with me. Matt's reaction still rings in my ears; it's never going to let me off the hook. Sorry, mate…

"*Hawar, hawar!*" Agît shouted again, at the bunker door. "Peshmerga! Peshmerga!"

Not one of them came out as I grabbed Matt round the waist from behind and swung him through, but they helped stretch him out on the deck once we were inside. I told them to elevate his leg and put a cushion under his head; they just did their own thing.

"*Cûdî!*" said Agît. "*Biksî! Biksî!*" (PKM machine gun.)

He didn't need to elaborate. Go and get onto Matt's machine gun and get into the fight.

I ran up to the berm under a rain of crossfire. The machine gun position was outside the sangar, where one of the Kurds crouched at the ready with an RPG. The gun itself had toppled halfway down the slope, ammunition belt covered in loose dirt. Diving into prone on the cold soil, I righted it and started hammering three-to-five-round bursts back at the closer muzzle flashes.

Rounds slammed into the bank, snapped overhead and banged through the long-suffering water towers. I'd spatted a few rounds off the berm before, ducked a few coming back, but this was the first time I felt myself properly fighting in a war. Getting straight down where another man had just been shot, and picking up where he'd left off.

Fear can't have been far away but I was barely aware of it. That was something I'd found in Palestine, crouched in cover as bullets rattled through market stalls a few feet away, showering me with splinters and grit. I got into a remote mindset, aware of the danger but somehow blanking it out. It didn't feel like bravery, more like a conjuring trick. But it got me through. Battle felt like an exam I'd prepared for. *Judge distance… adjust sights… control rate of fire… shift position…*

Any doubts or misgivings still swarming around down there could stay down – there was nothing for it now but sheer, unalloyed concentration. It's a precarious state to be in: a slip too far towards the cavalier, and it could all end bloody…

The gun jammed, full of dirt probably, and the incoming fire was intense, so I continued with my Kalashnikov. Eventually the fight died down. Matt was brought out of the bunker by Peter and Jordan and taken away to hospital. Agît came to relieve me.

Matt was going to be fine, he said. I pointed at my own thigh and made a snapping motion with my hands, before pointing the way Matt had gone. *Is his bone broken?* He wagged his finger from side to side, smiling. *No.*

"Go inside," he said. "I'll take over."

"No," I said, "I'm staying here."

"Cûdî, go inside. There's a system."

"Nope. Staying." I was in a mental ice-tunnel – perhaps a less vulnerable place (emotionally at least) than in floods of anguish over a wounded friend and a pit of dread at sitting exactly where he'd just been hit.

"OK," he smiled. "If *tak-tak* (firing) starts up again, you can come back out and fight."

I settled for that and got up.

Back in the bunker, I got a bit of ribbing off the older Pesh blokes. "*Heval* Cûdî, smoking, smoking!" as I lit one after another. *Fucking right I'm smoking, mate.*

Matt had been shot in the thigh. The Pesh up at the Dushka point were pretty quick to say that he'd been standing up on the berm, which is highly unlikely. He'd been lying there, facing forward, with the enemy in front of and below him, and the Pesh behind and above.

There was no enquiry, of course, but from then on, whenever the Pesh started revving up, any of us out on the berm took immediate cover.

Until now I'd felt like an outsider, a visitor here. After that night with Matt, I felt I'd become – in however miniscule a way – part of this scene, this fight.

This time Matt was out for good anyway.

"I had to carry the fat bastard," said Kosta, the next day.

I could just imagine him, picking his way efficiently over the rocks and craters with Matt in a textbook fireman's lift, where I'd made a hash of carrying half the bloke.

6 TRAVELLING ROADSHOW

There was a slow creeping tension in Shengal, punctuated by the odd incident here and there, but I found myself generally unaffected by it. Or so I thought, until I blew up at a lad called Qandil over a triviality – borrowing my rifle-cleaning kit without asking – the morning after Matt got shot. I was irritated with him and a couple of his mates anyway; they'd recently moved into this accommodation from further away, and brought with them the most almighty racket day and night.

Qandil stopped momentarily with my cleaning brush, pull-through and other bits in his hand and a look of utter bafflement on his tough and slightly battered young features. He and Cûdî Vietnam exchanged a few Kurdish words.

"Ah. OK. He's saying that in the party there's no mine and yours, it's all one," Cûdî V told me. Well, that explained a lot: put something down for five minutes and you lose it to the party.

"Tell him I'm not in the bloody party," I said, getting wry smiles from a few of the others. Mason broke out into a guffaw.

Weeks earlier, at Zara, Mason had publicly complained in *tekmîl* that someone had been going through his journal and other possessions. At the time I'd been mortified with embarrassment by his behaviour and sought to distance myself. I'd since apologised to him.

The next time Qandil was about to use something he scrupulously asked me, "*Yen te?*" (Is this yours?)

I felt suffused with shame. As at so many other times, my frustration had built up and up and then found expression in the wrong way. And in this case I had particular reason for regret because Qandil, though a rough-edged youth with a bit of growing up to do, was a highly seasoned fighter with his feet firmly on the ground and had many admirable qualities, which became clear when I got to know him better.

"How did you get this?" I asked him one day, pointing to the small but deep star-shaped scar just millimetres from his left eye.

His eyes narrowed with attention for a second, then widened, round as pool balls. "*Bomba!*" he said, spreading his hands out like an explosion.

Shrapnel from a grenade in the face. He had scars all over his torso from the same explosion and several others. He'd been wounded 14 separate times.

"He's been in three armies, apparently," Bagok told me. "Yeah, he's not just one of the rowdy kids, mate."

A few nights after my little tizz over the cleaning kit, Qandil and I were up on the berm together in a typical firework show. The enemy were firing from positions unusually close, and we had our eye on a house in the foreground.

The incoming grew so fierce and low that we were forced down, chewing dirt, unable to even peer over. Rocket after rocket and a ton of accurate *biksî* fire. Qandil asked me to go into the sangar, pass the *bizfink* out to him and stay there, in cover. I fetched the *bizfink*, but came back out with it and rejoined him on the berm. He balked at first, then relented.

"OK, OK," he said. "The next time we get a lull in the *tak-tak* (the shooting), you *bizfink*, me *biksî*."

"Got it."

Unfortunately the incoming fire remained at such sustained intensity we had no chance to get in amongst it. Then, all at once, it cut out completely, as if by mutual accord, and the chance was gone. I was a bit disappointed, but Qandil didn't seem to be. I guessed that for him, the magic had probably worn off a bit by now.

***

Nobet, sûbay, kamîn. Rinse and repeat.

A still night on the *kamîn* berm. Over the city hung a loaded silence – the only kind, in Shengal.

Downhill at our position, out of the dark and quiet came a solitary voice: raucous, incensed. Some Kurdish words, some Arabic. Soran's voice.

Then *biksî* fire, from the same spot. A long volley. Then Soran's voice again, cutting through the night air like an angle grinder. You could almost see sparks.

It continued on for some 20 minutes before starting to ebb.

Commander Soran, amusing himself up on the berm. Chucking out a tirade of catcalls and abuse at the enemy city, in a variety of languages, pausing only to fire the machine gun.

Other voices, English ones, joined in.

"You pack of wankers!" Australian, possibly. Some laughter.

"Can't shoot for shit!" Definitely American.

Soran found his second wind and switched to English himself. "Wang*kerr*! Wang-kerr!"

Biksî fire.

"Yo-o-o-u muzzafuckaz! Mu-zza fuckaaaz!"

More fire.

His ranting grew increasingly random. "Happy birz-day do you! Haappy birz-day do you!" (Fire.)

When his words ran dry he just produced an odd array of vowels and ramped up the volume to compensate. "OOOH – weh, ooeh oooweh! Yah yah yah!" (More gunfire.)

All the enemy had was their "God is great" over there. The fun was all on this side. *(That's our commander, that is. Ain't he fine...?)*

***

The following night I was on *sûbay*, sat on a chair in the arched corridor. Pitch dark.

I was waiting for the kettle on the stove to boil so I could take some tea in to the guard, when the *nobet* house seemed to erupt, filling with smoke in an instant.

"Bucky!" I bolted over the track and in through the gateway. No answer from inside, and from the looks of things I didn't expect one. The cloud was too thick to see through. Inside it seemed warm, like the inside of a duvet.

Bucky emerged from the side room, dazed and spluttering with his little round glasses fogged up and, I swear – unless my memory's playing tricks on me – clutching that stupid bloody walking stick. I grabbed him and walked him through the corridor to the bedroom and started checking him over. No obvious wounds, no rips, burns in clothing, eyes normal, how many fingers?

In came Soran and sized things up.

"OK, listen to me now, Cûdî. You *sûbay*. Never go in dangerous situation like that again. You send somebody else. Even if only you, do not go."

The plan falls down if the guard and the *sûbay* end up in the same shit together.

All of 20 minutes later Bucky was back on duty, sitting in the sandbags outside the house this time. Fair play to him. I took him his tea, finally.

"Yesterday," he said, "when we were shouting and singing they say on the radio, 'YPG are crazy. We are going to mortar them tomorrow.' But nobody told me before now."

You never knew what to believe with that guy, but listening to radio Daesh was a favourite traditional pastime.

In the daylight we found a crumpled tailfin from either a small mortar or a grenade (or *something*) next to a permanent splash in the tiles, an exploded cushion and a shrapnel splatter all up the thin low wall partitioning the yard from the room Bucky had been sitting in.

"Kosta told me this wall probably saved my life," he said.

***

2am. Quiet night, and another heartwarming *nobet* shift concluded. After I was relieved I walked through the corridor, through the yard to Soran's room, hoping there was tea on. I lifted the double layer of blankets pinned either side of the doorway and went in. The paraffin heater glowed a dim red, the only light in the room. Soran was lying on red rugs and cushions, with several radios on charge near his head.

I said a quiet greeting, not knowing if he was awake or asleep. He mumbled a few words in reply; he didn't want tea but I was of course welcome. His eyes were dull, half-open; his voice low, slowed-down, like an old tape player running on low battery.

The only sound as I made my tea was the quiet, intermittent crackle of speech from those radios. Like them, Soran was on charge.

I got my tea and left.

***

The Pesh had been trying to kick it off all day. Starting with a tentative volley of Dushka rounds, they'd got frustrated at being ignored and let loose volley after volley of unbridled resentment.

"Pesh*merr*ga," spat the Irish kid, like he was tasting mould in his mouth, waving a contemptuous hand at the high ground.

He was actually Kurdish, but we called him the Irish kid for his flame-red hair, pale, freckly skin and flat cap pulled way down low. He always spoke a bit too loud, and seemed slightly dazed or drunk. I'd had to tell him to do his jacket up and put his gloves on when he was close to going down with cold.

"He's off buying some guns in the back of a pub," Kosta said once, when someone came looking for him. "Then he's gonna go and rob an Irish bank."

Towards nightfall the enemy had finally taken the bait. *Stand to, stand to, let's go…* We were getting bored of it.

"I hope they stop soon," said Kosta, as we headed on out.

"Me too. I was in a firefight the other day and all I could think about was getting back to my teapots." (I'd scavenged two very nice teapots for my room and was cleaning them when the fight kicked off.)

"I know…"

Though we were happy to be here at the sharp end while everyone else was kicking their heels in Rojava, this futile stasis was taking its toll.

We took up positions – upstairs in the top room, under the *nobet* house stairs, out on the berm. Mason and I were together in the open sandbag position right outside the house. Aras, the old Kurdish fighter with sad watery eyes whose friend had been killed on my second day here, was indulging his favourite pastime somewhere indoors, singing one of his repertoire of traditional folk songs, a feature-length epic lament.

"Does that guy have any idea how bad he sounds?"

"I know! Gives me nightmares! I'm gonna need therapy after this!"

Mason and I cackled and howled as we crouched in the sandbags, weapons at the ready. All fighting positions were manned.

"I think they come tonight," Soran had said, not for the first time.

A rocket slammed into the berm between our sangar and the next one along. A flare shot up overhead and slowly descended, switching on the sky with a cheap yellow light. We huddled down among the floating, wavering shadows. Aras continued wailing throughout. In fairness, he could hold a note.

***

"Come, come, get ready – we go!" said Soran, appearing in my doorway. It was just after lunchtime, one of those days when my soul batteries were just too low to match his animated spirit.

"Ready for what?"

"Come, take everything, we go now."

"Where?"

"Tal Hamis. Rojava. Fighting."

"I don't believe it."

How many times had we heard this? Never from Soran, mind. I had a sinking feeling we were getting pulled back to Rojava to kick around in some nowhere village again, thanks to a change of policy, up top, on foreigners at the sharp end. We'd all been the lucky few to make it here. As Peter had said, this is *it*. They're shooting at you, you're shooting back at them – it's something. There was no fighting in Rojava.

I glanced around. The battered barn door, the bare, soot-smudged walls. Suddenly, it wasn't my room any more.

"You want to stay?"

There was something special about Shengal. No one who'd been here during this time would forget it. It was a grind, but the group spirit was upbeat and friendly among Kurds and westerners alike. A place of singing, kicking footballs around in the narrow alleys behind the barricades and sniper screens, and endless rounds of communal tea-drinking and socialising in crumbling rooms to the sound of gunfire. It was a warm place, a place of spirit, however little I'd cared for that side of things.

It was with mixed feelings that we pulled out, but it was starting to look more and more real.

Loaded up with rucksacks and weapons, we trudged out through the yards, climbing and ducking through the Shengal assault course for perhaps the last time. When we reached the track I veered off, clambered atop a heap of rubble, and fired two shots down into the city. *Laters…* Then we ran downhill, laughing and chattering, to the waiting trucks.

We were going on the road: to Tal Hamis, to battle.

Finally.

***

We hit the road in force – a motley convoy of civilian and military vehicles that swelled in number and variety as we rolled on through night and day: tanks, *panzas*, Humvees, motorbikes, crudely up-armoured bulldozers, a flatbed with a 57-calibre gun, a smaller truck with a double-barrelled anti-aircraft gun fitted with a seat, one with a recoilless rifle; a score of Hiluxes crammed with troops, others with Dushkas fitted and their gunners standing on the footpads, and a motley and wonderful assortment of homemade armoured fighting vehicles: angular, misshapen things, all rough-weld and spray paint; one shaped vaguely like a bell-jar, one with the slight profile of an origami mouse on caterpillar tracks. Yellow and green YPG/YPJ flags fluttered from every vehicle and battle music blared from scores of stereos, a cacophony of traditional ethnic and modern dancebeat tracks, overlaid with the singing and ululating of a thousand-odd cheering, charged-up warriors – male and female, most in their teens or early 20s. A load of great people off to do something big.

"*Em biçin şer! Em biçin şer!*" sang Jordan, a little ditty of his own, every time we passed him on the wet roads in his winter trenchcoat over his body armour and webbing. *We are going to war.*

From place to place we set up battle-camp in abandoned villages and on the open plains, like messy travelling festival sites.

In one village they were riding a donkey and a borrowed motorbike, round and round. In an abandoned town the shops were being stripped and looted, fighters scrambling madly over Adidas pumps dumped in a pile on a flatbed: this season's fashion. In another village Soran, ever the showman, jumped out of a Hilux as it skidded to a halt and released a snow-white bird into the air.

There were fires and music, laughter, camaraderie and anticipation, meetings and reunions. Spirits were sky-high at that point.

7 MARTYRS, AND OTHER REGRETS

"Where did you sleep last night?" said Kosta one freezing cold morning, making his way through some of the higgledy-piggledy sprawl of vehicles from our convoy, scattered on the plains. It had been every man for himself the night before. The lucky ones found a cab with a heater.

"In that fucking ditch, out of the wind. Half on top of my rucksack," I said. In the early hours I'd felt the damp seeping into my sleeping bag, which now hung on a fence with a wet sheen on the fabric as the sun inched upwards. Oh for a bivvy bag…

Our moods weren't dampened so easily though.

Kosta's plan to do as the Romans do was getting out of hand. He took off his flimsy trainer to show us a hole straight through the sole. This topped even the unravelling woollen gloves which covered less and less of his hands every time I saw them. I'd offered him my spares, and got a polite *no thanks*. Once, he told me, he'd walked from London to Greece to volunteer for his national service (he was half Greek on his mother's side) with no waterproofs, sleeping rough by the roadside. I had a hunch all this might be related to his Christian beliefs. *Wandering about in sheepskins and goatskins, of whom the world was not worthy...*

"Are you seriously telling me you've come to war in *that*?" I cackled, snatching the shoe off him and peering at the daylight through the bottom. I made a bodge repair with a strip of metal cut from a tin can and a roll of gaffer I'd brought with me. Black and shiny, the result looked like half a Doc Marten.

"Thanks mate – I've almost got a boot!" he laughed, as I handed it back.

Mason left that morning. Gone to attend his daughter's graduation; his trip here was over.

Unlike in an orthodox army, where troops deploy in fixed groups and are held together by contractual obligation, there was a sense that every international volunteer was here by himself, ultimately. People made their own way to the YPG and left when they chose, with few restrictions outside of the sheer logistical practicalities and the nature and attitude of the local commander. Bonds between us were looser, developing organically, or not.

Now it was me, Kosta, Bagok, Cûdî Vietnam, Jordan and Masiha.

Kosta had been to Israel, I'd recently learnt, on a sort of pilgrimage. I'd found it easier than anticipated to broach my own experiences in Palestine and it turned out he was genuinely curious.

"I'm not slagging the Israelis," I said, suddenly cautious.

"I slag 'em all the time," he grinned.

"Well, if you ever decide you want to see it from the other side, I can hook you up with some cool people," I said. "It doesn't matter what your position is, they'll welcome Israelis and anyone."

"Could you? I think I'd be interested."

Small groups continued to trickle into the area, as others broke off and moved on.

"That David's just turned up here," said Bagok, coming over. "Have you seen him?"

"No. And when I do he won't want to be here anymore," said Kosta.

"Look Kosta, don't go bashing him, mate," I said.

He reiterated his view on unsuitable types being here.

"I know, but don't go kicking his head in or anything. I've seen enough suicides and attempted suicides in the British army; I don't want to see one out here."

A week or so ago, in Shengal, I'd have been more careful how I said that to Kosta. But I felt a newly rediscovered sense of belonging to this group again after days of drifting apart from them, partly due to the reinvigorated spirit now we'd broken the stasis of Shengal, and maybe partly because of the presence of other western groups. The night we pulled out of Shengal all the *Emeriki* in Rojava (as far as we knew) were brought together in an old school building where we billeted for the night – some 40 of us. Among them, we had a definite group identity: the lads from Shengal. Some of the few who'd actually fought out here.

Later Kosta's trainer was back to normal. *It came off*, he said. My foot, Kosta. He just wanted to eschew any and all luxury, that bloke. Talk about Gawain sleeping in his armour.

***

Across a broad sweep of open ground with several receding, parallel berms, vehicles began moving forward in formation. Lining out along a berm, waiting, discussing, rearranging, moving forward to the next. Hours and hours. Heavy weapons and armoured vehicles went first, followed by the Hiluxes.

At this point I got split up from Kosta, Bagok and Cûdî Vietnam. Soran had put them forward to make up crew on two *panzas*. I had half a suspicion I might be missing out, but only half. Who wants to fight from inside a metal box? Better to be out on the ground, on your feet, with 360 vision and able to pick your own cover.

Before taking off, Bagok came walking back towards me. "There's one of those Kurmanji books in my bag," he said, pointing at a row of rucksacks on the ground.

A few nights before, Peter had printed off several copies of Kurmanji for the Beginners in a city somewhere and brought them back to Shengal for us. I'd been on *kamîn* that night and next morning the copies had all gone out, so I never got one.

"You can take it," he said. There's no room in a *panza* for anything except crew, weapons and ammo. "I don't know if I'll see you again."

I thought little of that at the time; my only concern was the imminent battle and my (as yet undetermined) part in it. Kosta, Cûdî V and Bagok were sorted out. What was I going to do?

As things unfolded, I ended up part of a Dushka crew, on the left flank with Jordan. The gunners fired into the enemy village a klick away – quiet, no response. Masiha took a turn; Soran stopped by our position, blatted a few rounds off, then took off again.

As we worked the carrot-sized rounds into the ammunition belts with a rubber hammer, taking turns, I had an awful feeling we'd been stuck on the reserve benches.

"Gotta make the best of it, man," said Jordan, as I drained one cigarette after another, mood as black as my lungs.

Things got going for real after dark. The *panzas* raced to and fro, gunfire erupted all over like angry dogs let loose. Tracer scrawled over the night sky, a haywire of red lines on black as the hand-held walkie-talkies at our point screeched and crackled battle orders and confusion. "*Erîş! Erîş!!!*" (Attack!)

We watched from inside a half-collapsed mudbrick house with walls short enough to see over and rest a rifle on. Soran reappeared at about 9pm. He said something to Jordan behind me, while I kept watch to our front.

"...then I will come back and you and me and Cûdî Britannia will..." The rest of it was lost in the ambient soundtrack. Then he was gone again.

"What was that?" I asked Jordan.

"We're gonna go fight." He grinned from ear to ear.

The vehicles pulled back from the fight as unseen aircraft scoured the clouds. Our vehicles used the lights on just one side for night-time identification. The town shook in the din and glare of bombs and the *panzas* raced back in.

One of the *panzas* was having problems down there, limping and veering left and right. More radio screech and the armoured bulldozer went in, rounds sparking off its sides, and dragged it out.

Where the hell was Soran? As the battle ebbed to dribs and spats a sinking feeling grew and grew...

By 3am it was all but done. The temperature was close to freezing and the Dushka gunners all cried off *nobet*, hiding in their warm cabs. Jordan and I had decided to split the full night's *nobet* between us, taking an hour each in the one spare seat in a Dushka truck's heated cab.

A Kurd called Bejna looked close to hypothermic. He was crying aloud, on the verge of hysteria, and he felt like a block of ice. So we gave him the spot and resigned ourselves to a long night of shivering. All our warm gear was in our bags, on Soran's truck, God knew where.

"Don't start sweating," said Jordan, as I ran up and down on the spot, shadow-boxed and did warm-up exercises to fend off the vicious cold.

Soran did not return. We waited the night out and entered the newly taken village early next morning.

***

Kosta was stood up out of the hatch of his *panza*, pale green hat
and shirt almost matching its battered paintwork. His eyes were
pinned open and cracked like the ragged end of an amphetamine
high. Flecks of blood spattered his cheek.

"That's from where rounds have been hitting here," he said,
indicating the open hatch lid behind him.

I hadn't missed much really, he said. But he did so out of
kindness: every man thinks meanly of himself for missing a
battle. If he'd ever had anything to prove, it wasn't showing now.
Any hostility between us had vanished.

Their driver had been shot in the head and the *hevals* had
pronounced him dead, until Kosta found a pulse and got him
medevacked out. So he saved at least one person's life that night.

"By the way, you've heard about Bagok, have you? Do you
know, do you know about Bagok?" He held my eye suddenly.

My stomach lurched. Kosta had a habit of rapidly repeating
his words when nervous; which wasn't often.

"No. What about Bagok?" *Don't say that's another one of us wounded.*

"He's dead. He's a *şehid*."

No, wait, hang on. This is Bagok we're talking about here.

"Sorry mate," he said. "Not a very good way to tell you."

It was Bagok's *panza* that had broken down. He'd got out
to cover the others as they debussed, apparently, and then had
assaulted further into the village. Firing rocket after rocket at an
enemy position, while Cûdî Vietnam gave suppressing fire, he
had been picked off by a sharpshooter. Kosta had had to go in
and retrieve his body.

I said, "I'm sorry you had to do that, mate. They should have sent someone else."

"No, it's all right," he answered rapidly. "I mean, it's just a body, isn't it? It'd be worse if he was wounded…"

Kosta had used the local word for martyr: *şehid*. One who dies at the enemy's hands. A term used by Kurds, Arabs and others all over the Middle East, and loaded with a particular reverence. In a sense, there is no higher accolade for a Kurdish fighter. Perhaps Kosta's use of the term indicated the depth of his own cultural immersion, ever-deepening since the night before. An experience like his can either bounce you out, or draw you further in.

Cûdî Vietnam had gone too – gone to accompany Bagok's body to Australia. *I'm just gonna go wherever this guy goes…*

"I had half a mind to just walk across the fucking battlefield and join you last night," I said.

"You should have, mate. We were ferrying crews to and fro all night."

Us westerners needed to stick together, he said. There was no fixed *panza* crew, people came and went. He'd get me on there with him.

He got out the *panza* and we walked slowly through the town together.

"Cû-deee!" A female voice, from inside a parked Hilux.

Delal, from the night crossing and Qereçox. It had been a while. Her smile was the only good thing about that morning.

"How are you, Cûdî?"

"I'm OK," I said. I introduced Kosta. "Our friend," I said. "*Şehid.*"

She nodded, wrinkling her nose and pursing her mouth. Regret without surprise. People here didn't go in for a lot of emotion over such matters, and that suited me fine. I'd bank that for later, if at all. "I'm sorry," she said. "Are you OK?"

"Yeah, *I'm* OK…" That was the problem.

I walked full circle with Kosta; he got back on the *panza* and while I was doing something round one of the sides it suddenly drove off, rattling and squealing away. Kosta, standing up, raised his arms apologetically. So much for us all sticking together.

We caught up with them less than a klick away. I'd assumed the worst but it was routine to load up on a vehicle and not know if you were going 200 metres up the road or driving all day.

"Sorry mate, I gave you a bit of a dirty look there," I said.

"Don't worry mate. Everything's forgiven today."

***

Next time I saw Soran I mobbed him. "I must fight in the next one. You let me go on the *panza* with Kosta. OK?"

"OK," he nodded. Vehicles were rolling out past us, off to the next position.

"Fighting. OK?"

"*OK*," he repeated, with a slight smile.

I went and sat on the *panza*'s bench, back to the cold bare metal, determined not to budge.

"At least there's one of those Kurmanji books free," said Kosta.

"Christ. That actually *did* cross my mind, just after you told me about him. I thought, *you cunt*. Myself, I mean. For thinking it…"

He cut my rambling short. "Don't, mate. It's all right. We'll go through his kit, and anything we can use we'll divide among ourselves." Determined, as with everything, to do it *right*. It was what soldiers did, and therefore what we would do.

Mîrza, another of the Shengal Kurds, appeared at the open back door, looking in, looking miserable in the grey-washed winter surroundings.

"*Karem bike, heval* (welcome, friend)," said the driver, like inviting someone into your living room. A small gesture of human warmth. Come and sit in the *panza* out of the cold.

Masiha joined us next. We shuffled up in the close interior. The *panza* commander turned up an hour later with his crew and, seeing us all, told us to get out. The crew piled in and off it drove.

"I'm going back to London!" I shouted to Kosta as he receded from view, for good this time.

Bagok – Ashley Johnston, 29 – was the first westerner to die in this war. And where was I? *Safe. Out of it.*

In all honesty I don't know what was more devastating: the sheer ice-bucket of grief and loss, the shame of being spared the battle – or a feeling even more shameful in itself, harder to admit to: *jealousy*. Jealousy of Kosta and those who'd cut their teeth in a proper set-to at last. Disappointment at missing the first battle, edged with ugly resentment. And anxiety: how many more could there be? Where I'd been eager to fight before, now I was desperate. It became a gnawing torment.

I stood in the middle of the track feeling wretched. I blamed Soran. I was damned if I'd miss another.

A couple of Hiluxes crawled past across the open plain with Jac, Ronnie and some other friends from the academy, as well as Fat Jack and Junior, crammed on the back. *Fuck it*, I thought, and ran towards the rear one. Going through a ditch it slowed down and I jumped onto the footpad; Ronnie leaned forward and grabbed hold of my webbing belt to steady me. Some of these guys had been in the attack, just about. Maybe I'd have better luck in their group. I'd take a punt.

***

The rain made rushing streams through the mud, outside the abandoned, anonymous house in the remote village on the Rojava plains where my new *tabor* and my old one were holed up.

As soon as we set foot in that mud, our boots became two kilos heavier. I'd spent the first part of the day mooching round the yards, rummaging through scrap, salvaging a rusty Karabiner and cleaning it with diesel – *mazoht*, the fuel of this particular revolution – whenever we could lay our hands on some. We cleaned our guns and powered our vehicles with it, and it kept us from freezing. The smell of it belched from the ancient stove heater in the centre of the room, which wobbled dangerously whenever the kettle was removed from or replaced on it.

"OK, Cûdî," Soran said, as glasses of tea were passed round the room. "We have something today. Everybody will sing a song. Me, and then after *heval* Aras and after *heval* Delal, and after you, and… OK? Everybody sing…"

Earlier on he'd come looking for me to guard the Dushka again and I'd told him I'd had enough; I wanted to move to another unit. Delal – who, it turned out, was a junior commander in this *tabor* – had taken over the discussion when he disagreed, and the switch was settled amicably enough. When he turned away, I asked her what had been said.

"Nothing. He was think that you belong to him, but I tell him you are with us now."

Soran kicked off the entertainment with a stirring battle song, what else? Fire and the sword. Aras followed with one of his laments, then Delal sang a slow and haunting mountain song.

Put on the spot, I sang 'Bella Ciao', badly, in Italian. I'd learned it during those heady protest days in Genoa. Then Qandil, who I saw as a slightly brutish kid, turned out a ballad with surprising depth of feeling, and expressions I never thought to see the guy make.

There are phone videos somewhere of us singing in that room, out of the rain, and I'd give my right eye to have them now.

Soon afterwards the phones themselves started to circulate, as photos were scrutinised and new ones taken. People shifted and shuffled around, banging into the rickety stove, rearranging themselves for group portraits.

You had to factor in time for photo ops during every YPG manoeuvre. Everyone worshipped the camera, especially the blokes, who were as proud of their looks as all Middle Eastern men, despite the organisation's insistence on modesty. They vetoed tooth-brushing, shaving or otherwise grooming oneself in public – and particularly within view of a woman. Nevertheless, one young lad produced a comb and set about tidying up his appearance. I mimed admiring myself in an imaginary mirror, and complimented him on his exquisite features. "Most handsome. Ladies and gentlemen, the face of the revolution!"

"Yes… like… *Tom Cruise!*" laughed Delal. She was only a couple of years younger than me, and if Cruise was her most immediate idea of cinematic good looks, perhaps it showed. "But he is… very… *short*," she added quickly. A vertical crease appeared between her sharp brows. She glanced down at her feet and muttered, "I don't like… *short* men…"

A loud guffaw from me ended what was hanging, somewhat muddled, in the air: she didn't find Tom Cruise *so* handsome…

I recognised myself first in the photo on the phone that had just been handed to me. Mountains in the background, on the way out of Shengal. Who was that next to me? It took a second to register, then it hit me. Bagok, grinning heartily, making me look dour and wrinkled by comparison. Forever young. I looked a moment longer, then passed it on and turned away.

Lips slightly pursed and mouth downturned, Delal asked me if I was all right. I forced a smile and nodded.

When the rain stopped, she followed me outside. We sat on a low wall. "Are you OK, Cûdî?" she asked again.

For the third or fourth time I said I was.

She asked me for the words to 'Bella Ciao'. I recited them slowly as she wrote them in a small notebook. We had to guess the spellings. She'd grown up in Turkey but had actually spent some years living in Italy, working as a geneticist before returning home to join the struggle. She spoke five languages. Political conviction as much as ethnicity had driven her to change her life so drastically, and her status in this fighting unit reflected her status in the party. Her commitment was markedly different from the typical YPG/J village kid whose fierce devotion could seem more to do with brainwashing than independence.

In a still photo she could look severe – straight brown hair, tied straight back; sharp and definite eyebrows, her mouth somewhat pursed and set in a slight down-turn. She was taller than the average YPJ woman, and bigger, with a strong but well-proportioned frame. She could have seemed imposing. But her tendency to round those shoulders and lean forward attentively in conversation, the gentle mobility of her head and neck in the flow of words softened that effect. Then her full lips seemed to barely suppress a smile, and her rounded cheeks and large brown eyes conveyed a gentleness backed up by strength. The calm of a mountain.

Our exchange grew less formal and more personal. I usually brushed questions of family aside with one or two white lies, especially in the Middle East, where it is sacrosanct. But with her, for some reason, I was candid about having cut virtually all ties with mine. In return, she allowed me a glimpse of her own background. "My father was drink-*king* whisky a lot, and shout-*ting*. Now I *hate*... drinking."

A handful of the simplest words, signalling formative years of domestic misery and who knew what else. Quite suddenly, we were a man and a woman sitting alone together, getting to know each other. But it couldn't last.

A moment of increasing closeness is always special, and more than welcome in a harsh environment. But constantly buzzing in my mind was Bagok's death and the thing I'd come here to do: *fight*. I was sitting on hot coals with it, all the time, couldn't truly relax for a moment.

"Delal," I said. "Please tell our *tabor* commander this: if we aren't in the next battle, I will walk across the battlefield by myself and join in."

"No, come on," she smiled. "This is the army. We have rules."

"This is *not* the army, Delal; believe me..."

I left it at that, not wanting to break the spell. What *did* I want to do anyway – impress her?

As a junior commander, she had a little more licence than most. However, sitting like this – one guy with one woman (let alone a foreigner with a Kurdish woman) – was pushing the boundaries of propriety. A young YPJ girl soon came to accompany us. Someone must have sent her over, deciding that we'd gone far enough without a chaperone.

And that was pretty much as far as it went in the YPG. There was very little room for privacy, anywhere, and we were constantly under scrutiny. Now and then you heard of things going a little further, and being quickly thwarted. Considering the youth of most fighters, it was obvious why. Cultural barriers aside, the last thing a shoestring militia needed was teen pregnancy.

"What age do you think this girl is?" Delal asked me. I looked at our new arrival; a youthfully chubby, smiling kid.

"Erm – 16?"

"Yes," she nodded. "Some are very young here."

***

In my first few days in Delal's *tabor*, she and I spent an unusual amount of time together nonetheless, discussing war and morality and politics, our own lives, the people around us; and sharing a wealth of moments that come back to me now as fragments of a developing friendship.

At five the following morning she padded shoeless through the door and knelt at my side to wake me for my guard shift. It was unusual for a female to enter the men's sleeping quarters, of course. Hearing my name spoken, I sat bolt upright, muttering the word *nobet* before my eyes were even open. This rather flew in the face of the local tradition, which was to turn over and mumble and snore while the person repeated your name a dozen times and everyone else cursed the pair of you. My discipline had never been as sketchy as your average YPG fighter, but my month in Shengal had sharpened it up anyway. Later, I heard Delal telling the others about it, with, I thought, perhaps a hint of pride.

In many parts of the Middle East, every other person you meet knows functional English, and plenty are fluent. I thought it would be like that in Rojava and the YPG too; but I was wrong. In our group, Delal was the only Kurd who understood more than a handful of words, which afforded us room for a hint of the illicit. In full sight and hearing of the others, she could, with that furtive smile, pronounce me "quite romantic" while I sat sketching in the yard. And occasionally, she got bolder still.

"You smoke a lot." She grinned. "People say that if you kiss a man who smokes, it's like…" she mimed the word she was searching for, "… *lick-king*… an ashtray."

"Oh dear." I smiled, and toyed with the thought of saying, *You shouldn't kiss me then.*

"But men *are* dirty," she laughed. "Isn't it true? Men. Are. *Dirty.*"

I laughed too. "I don't think you know what you're saying…"

"I *do*!" Her eyes twinkled.

It was the look I'd once seen on the faces of some female students in a class I taught in northern Iraq years before: one girl had described, with a series of gasps, the sights that had assailed her on entering a London nightclub while on holiday. The others had affected a worldliness they did not possess. I'd found it quite endearing.

***

Mooching around another abandoned village with Fat Jack and Junior, I took advantage of the lack of Kurdish presence in our immediate vicinity to grab a shower in an empty house. I actually *was* dirty then, had been for days.

I gritted my teeth and rapidly scrubbed myself down, as the iron-cold water from the wintry ground burnt my skin and shrivelled my ball-sack to nothing.

"Don't go in there," I heard Fat Jack saying, when I was halfway through. "Someone's taking a shower…"

"Who is take-*king* a shower?" Delal's voice.

"Cûdî."

"Cûdî…?" she called through the door.

"Yes?"

"Are you take-*king* a shower?"

"Yes."

"OK."

She couldn't actually see me naked, but I obviously was, just the other side of the door. I doubt she would have gone so far as to talk to me had there been anyone around other than westerners. In the all-pervading context of local custom, our countless little exchanges were as highly charged as they would have been in a 19th-century period drama. Like Jane Austen, only with more guns.

Our rapport nudged towards intimacy, for a time, but neither of us stepped across the line. Speculation at this distance is fruitless, of course, but that doesn't stop me wondering where things *might* have gone, had we met under other circumstances

– circumstances in which we never would have met anyway – and if I'd valued it as much at the time as my cherished, burning need to get into battle.

***

The *tabor* moved from village to village, establishing quarters, setting out sentry positions. We wandered about, cleaned weapons, tinkered with bits of junk, filled in the days. We hadn't seen Soran or his *tabor* for days now, since that afternoon of heavy rainfall several villages ago. Groups went their separate ways, and increasingly I began to wonder if my switch, made in a moment of haste, had been a good move after all.

A tall Iraqi-Kurdish lad called Aso was barracking, entreating, begging and threatening two other lads who'd found several sets of Muslim prayer beads in one village and were going to destroy them. He made a grab at the beads, and the guy holding them snatched them away while the other pushed Aso back. They all looked to be around 20, at most, and a mixture of angry insistence and laughter was flitting across all three faces alternately. Aso was also waxing mortified, on and off; something he did well. Finally the two lads threw him one set and destroyed the other two, stretching the strings till they snapped and the beads, green and brown, bounced over the ground and sank into damp mud.

Aso was a character. On *nobet* one night he'd recounted to me, in hushed tones with widening eyes, how he'd been captured by Daesh and rescued by guerrillas who'd suicided themselves to break others out of an enemy encirclement. If I understood his Kurdish well enough, it had all the elements of a cracking story. He'd also claimed, on seeing me practising some Muay Thai with a French marine, to be an experienced martial artist. So Delal, with her pursed smile, had said, "Show us then." Aso hadn't a clue.

He was handsome in a coarse way, with a crow's nose and crow's feet round his black eyes, and a black fringe like crow's feathers, easily adapted to merriment or abject woe, but rarely sober equanimity. Taller than the average Kurd, he had an athletic build perhaps, but little besides dancing would have had him straining it.

"No one wants him," Delal smiled as we boarded up for a night drive, watching as he stalked from one vehicle to another, looking to her, to the commander, all around, with a mix of bewilderment and indignation. All full. Sorry Aso, you'll have to run behind.

He could exhibit a fine sensitivity and bone ignorance at almost the same moment; switching from heartfelt anguish to raucous laughter, both of which were genuine. The polar reactions from others perhaps matched his moods. I had a soft spot for him, but some of the Kurds had no time for him at all. Unreliable bullshitter.

The looting *was* an issue, however Delal tried to explain it away. Entire homes were turned over, sometimes for legitimate search or intelligence gathering, but at least as often for theft, or boredom-induced vandalism, or perhaps something more darkly motivated. But you rarely, if ever, saw a Qur'an moved from its place. It could seem like a whirlwind had beset a whole house, but the holy book remained untouched on a shelf.

***

The campaign was now well underway. Every other night the flash and thunder of battle continued on the horizon, just out of reach, less than a mile away. Bagok was dead; Kosta and Jordan were somewhere up ahead, probably in the thick of it. And here I was, left behind with a weapon standing idle as if in mockery.

I became more and more withdrawn. The shame of safety ate away at me. I resented those around me for not minding it.

After several more weeks (and several more villages), I had come to view my move as a definite mistake. The young *hevals'* casual unruliness day and night, besides making sleep impossible, affected *nobet* and other duties. Every few days the count of dead and injured came through. It was worse than being under fire. My threat to walk into the next battle by myself, repeated in a moment of petulance, earned me nothing but a spell under close observation.

Tal Hamis city, the operational objective, fell without a fight. The enemy fled.

"Yes, it's good..." said Delal, as we discussed this news one morning at breakfast. "I am only sorry that I did not – *kill* any man..."

In one of our previous conversations, I'd argued that killing wasn't actually a goal in itself.

"What do you mean?" she'd asked, looking at me with that crease between her brows.

"Well, if you can take ground without killing then it's better, isn't it? I mean, if you have to kill, you kill. But the *ground's* the objective, isn't it?"

"*Hm…*"

The YPG pushed on past Tal Hamis, west through the territory.

***

"*Çawa ye?*" (How are you?) I asked Alîn, a slight and elegant YPJ woman of 25. She'd come to sit next to me in the shade, calling a female friend over to accompany us, according to propriety. "*Başi?*" (Good?)

"*Mm. Boş, na boş.*" She made a 50-50 gesture.

"*Duşev: Gomm!… tak-tak!… Em raze, nobet, çay…*" (Last night: bombs… gunfire… We just sleep, do sentry, drink tea…) she explained. She squinted up at the sun, then turned the same grim smile on me. The small mole on her upper cheek slanted inwards, following the creases from eyes like twin black lacerations. Her changing moods could resemble a widow in mourning or a fruit machine paying out the big win. A range of expression similar to that of Aso, perhaps, though the two were not similar in any other respect. She'd been in Bagok's *panza* the night he was killed, and seemed a fighter through and through. On *nobet* late one night, she'd tried hard to recount the exact details to me but my Kurdish wasn't up to it.

Earlier in the day, Delal had put her arm round her and dragged her into a small garden to pick herbs for our evening meal, to take her mind off things. A big sister.

***

In the chicken yard of yet another mud village I told Delal: "I can't do this any more."

"What?"

"Sit around while other people fight and die."

"No. We are going to conflict. Very soon."

"Don't say that again." I turned my back and stalked away through the crumbling mud bricks and rusted junk and chicken shit.

"It's not in my head!" she shouted after me.

***

I sat in the yard of the gutted school, away from everyone else. It was how I preferred to spend my time these days. Sun was setting on another empty day. I felt the molten glow spreading across the sky softening my bitterness, and resisted the feeling. I *wanted* to be bitter. If I couldn't fight, I could at least feel terrible about it. If I had come here seeking purpose and self-worth, I'd been barking up the wrong tree. Here was only disgrace and idleness. Every hour that passed was like being held against a fire.

Inside, several classrooms had been cleared for sleeping quarters. Mattresses had been put down, weapons leaned against the walls. The playground was littered with the metal skeletons of school desks smashed up for firewood. The others were variously occupied in cleaning weapons, chatting in small groups or building a fire to cook on. The Kurds had killed, plucked and gutted a couple of chickens, but I wouldn't join the communal meal of stew and rice. I'd sit and smell it, hungry and scowling, and later grab some bread, tinned tuna and processed cheese to eat by myself.

After four days here, I'd had my fill of wandering bare corridors and trashed classrooms, kicking through books, files and papers strewn across the floors, poring over the Arabic graffiti scrawled on the blackboard.

Delal came to ask me what was wrong. "You don't eat, with the others… you are sit alone all the time…"

I'd thought long and hard about this. I told her I wanted to leave.

"Leave – to where?"

"Home," I said.

"*Home?*" She recoiled like she'd just walked into a glass door. Her feet stopped their idle shifting and shuffling on the tarmac. She bent towards me, eyes widening, an almost childlike expression on her face. After uttering that single word, her mouth remained slightly open. I was surprised by her surprise; I felt like I'd just punched her.

Such an unexpected response deserved at least some reflection, on my part, upon the course I was starting on here. Especially as my saner side told me they could no more bring the battle to me than they could drive back the sea with a volley of Dushka rounds.

My emotions were as tangled as ever. Days of frustration, bad sleep, half-truths, discomfort, uncertainty – and humiliation – had done their worst. Endless sitting on the benches watching the main game. Delal spun the web of disinformation like the other commanders, kept us hanging, jerked us around. *When are we moving? Soon. Tomorrow…* And I'd noticed a slight *edge* in the cheery way she'd say, "Where are you going, Cûdî?" whenever I walked off somewhere. Like the toilet. I could always grin and say, "Do you really want to know?" – at which she'd laugh and demur any mention of the unmentionable – but still. More than once I'd felt, and resisted, a momentary twinge of disappointment, a suspicion that what I'd taken for simple friendship might not be so simple. Maybe there was something behind it.

Delal didn't have to put up with the same as us: young vandals plaguing her every attempt to sleep. She was quite easy with their woeful standards of professionalism on *nobet* and other things, too. And I'd expressed concern – more than once – about the way they went through village houses, smashing furniture for firewood and helping themselves to things. *These houses are abandoned*, she'd say. *Nobody loots. Nobody trashes homes… We don't use westerners for propaganda purposes…*

Party lies are not a higher truth, I'd felt like saying, but I was wary of voicing a direct insult. My resentment boiled up, though, and perhaps now, where I saw a weakness, I chose to press home.

Bluntly, I reaffirmed my request and asked, would she please tell the command to make the necessary arrangements? It was in the open now, and I was too proud to take it back.

She turned away quickly, nodding to me over her shoulder – just long enough for me to see that surprise had given way to something like grief – and started walking. A few steps further on, she raised her head and tidied up her stride.

Jac, Ronnie and the others I'd linked up with again were frustrated with the situation, too. Maybe they just dealt with it better. Most people were on the same track, one way or another. It started with making that first decision to come here and fight – from feeling unable to sit by and do nothing, as most people explained it. Then, the leap into the unknown, halfway across the world, perhaps: a step not to be underestimated. And then the slow-dawning anticlimax, the fear that you might not, after all that, get to fight at all. A cavalier disregard for safety and even life itself followed, as one got more and more drawn in.

It becomes a toxic emotional swirl. Ego. Pride. Jealousy of others. Loss of comrades, grief, shame and guilt. You sit around in the shadow of dead men. You're on a dangerous path, once you start envying them.

***

Several days passed at that school, with nothing more said about my leaving. If I didn't push it, I suspected, they'd let it blow over. The side of me that was secretly relieved about that lost out to the one that wanted to show them that when *I* said something, I meant it.

A couple of afternoons later, as we loitered about as usual, some higher-ranking commanders came to visit. Taking scant notice of us foreigners, they bustled inside the main building. Catching Delal as she went to join them I reminded her of my request. Perhaps now might be a good time to ask…?

That gutted look again; full lips turned down further than I'd ever seen them. Again a quick, silent nod, and she stepped indoors. After they left, she came and told me that a vehicle would take me to Derik at the next opportunity. I thanked her curtly as a voice inside me screamed, *What are you doing...?*

Finally we were leaving that bloody school building. Early dawn, the sun just breaking through the chill mist. A steaming scramble of bags and bodies piled on the trucks; food, weapons, ammo, troops in the usual random pile. *Thank God. Fuck this place.*

During the melee someone tried to hand me a fistful of Syrian money, maybe $100 worth. The other five or six westerners were counting through similar wads. There were rumours that those units with foreigners received money for them, but this was the first time anyone had actually tried to give me any.

I don't know why I took it this way, but it felt like a spark to tinder. Now my honour was really being trampled on.

"I'm a volunteer, not a mercenary," I proclaimed, when Delal came over.

Calmly she explained it was not pay, just a small allowance for basic needs. But I'd started now. Pulled along by my own momentum, I reiterated, growing louder and angrier, that I'd come here to fight and was being prevented; my friend had been killed; others were dying every day, and *now they were trying to give me money*? Where was the vehicle to take me to Derik? I asked for the umpteenth time. It had become my little protest song.

After maybe an hour in convoy, we pulled over at a way station – a group of yellow buildings in a town, the largest one a replica of the school we'd just left.

"Cûdî, take your bags," said Delal, getting out of the cab.

I think I was slightly surprised. There had been no mention of my request to leave for days and I'd got used to it, had stopped going on about it until this morning. That last tantrum at the school, in front of everyone, must have decided her.

Half of me *did* want to leave, by now – but only half. So maybe the wiser thing to do would have been to eat humble pie in front of everyone and apologise for my mistake. Unfortunately I wasn't big enough, so I stuck to my guns. Not the first time I've clung to my pride till it's all that remained, and then discovered what shitty company it turned out to be.

Some troops from another *tabor* were to-ing and fro-ing in the road and the grounds of the main building, visible through the smashed perimeter wall. Delal spoke to a general, and gestured towards me. He looked at me for a few seconds, then said, "*Temam.*" (OK.)

I grabbed my gear, saturated from head to toe with a deserter's shame.

"Well…" Delal began. There we were, suddenly, finally. Facing each other, in the road, about to say goodbye. How had it come to this?

She shrugged, looking me full in the face. In hers was no anxiety, just a calm regret – and she seemed half over that already. I'd really pushed it, this last time. Pissed her off.

She held out her hand to shake mine.

I was wearing gloves for the morning chill.

"This breaks my heart," I told her.

"What... *me?*"

"Everything. All of it."

After that it seemed we'd both run out of words. I don't remember which of us turned away first. I didn't even wave goodbye to Jac, Ronnie and the others, as the convoy rolled away.

A vehicle was on its way to ship me out of the war. I held my nerve for at least 10 minutes after they'd gone. Then, close to panic, I asked the general, could I join his unit? Sorry, he told me, but no – only certain *tabors* were able to accept westerners.

"You are a friend of Kemal, the British man who was killed," he said.

No, I told him. He must be mistaken. I'd seen Kosta myself – just a few weeks ago...

"Yes, British," he said. "The big man. Boxer."

He filled out the description until it became unmistakeable.

I reckon I'll just go on doing this till I... catch it up somewhere.

Did Delal know? If so, why hadn't she told me?

8 DIRECTIONAL PROBLEMS

Shortly after Delal's group left, while I was still dithering in the road, another *tabor* drove slowly by in convoy. By sheer luck, it was another westerner-friendly unit, containing some of the volunteers I'd met briefly at the beginning of the op. I signalled to the commander in the lead vehicle – a non-verbal request to jump in with them. He gave me a bright smile and nodded towards a Hilux.

I hopped aboard and sparked up a cigarette. Sighing with relief, I watched as the smoke trailed out behind me, down the tapering strip of road.

On my second day in this unit it got split. Half of us were sent one way and half another, and I paired up with a guy called Harry as we were shunted from base to base in the region of Tal Barak over the next fortnight: a high lookout tower with tiny sleeping alcoves arranged star-like around the centre, entered by a 100-metre crawl through a subterranean concrete pipe; a lone house at the top of a grassy hill; other locations whose features merged and blurred, half-forgotten almost immediately. We caught the tail end of several small skirmishes as we travelled from place to place, loosed off a few rounds.

Six foot two, slim and bespectacled, Harry (codenamed Baran, which means rain) was an obvious public-school type with a gentle, almost delicate manner in greeting. This initial suggestion of a shy fragility was beguiling, however; he was tough enough in every way once you got to know him. Before all this he'd been a currency trader in the City, and a Tory party activist to boot. He had a certain charisma – charm, some might call it – and perhaps the bearing of a junior officer; something like guards or cavalry. His hero was Gordon of Khartoum. His training was slim – odd days with the Territorial Army – but it was something.

Sitting in a vengeful downpour, watching, through the dark mist, the dim shape of the enemy town on the blurred horizon. The rain looked almost too thick to shoot through. Daesh liked the rain; we didn't. They could do little sneak-attacks using the low visibility. They only had to harry us; we were the ones trying to take ground. And attacking in that slippery mess, you'd be lucky to hit the ground before you were dead.

Off-shift, we slept in holes dug horizontally into the earth of the berm, lined inside with rugs. Two men to a hole, so narrow it was impossible to lie flat together – you were both jammed in next to each other, at an angle against the sides. Lying there on the lumpy ground with my clothes full of soaking wet mud, after making intense effort to relax I'd be just on the brink of dropping into a hazy, degraded half-sleep, full of sounds and images, busy as flies – but still better than no sleep – and the Kurdish fighter lying pressed against me would fidget and roll around violently, jolting me fully awake with a battery of elbows and knees. Again and again. Three hours of that, then three back on the berm. A long night. Thank God for cigarettes.

While I was there, I learned that the commander at Zara, the guy who'd sent me to Shengal, had been killed. No longer a commander, he'd been bust down to the ranks for some reason. We'd had a brief, awkward meeting on the road a few days earlier. Now he was a martyr – no one could demote him from that.

Though chalk and cheese politically, Harry and I formed a quick bond, as two sensible characters in an unruly group always will. In this unit were two Americans, ex-marines allegedly, named Bob and Levi. Like one or two others, they'd acquired a reputation by walking off base in search of action and getting arrested.

They seemed like twins: both tall and pale, in their early 20s, and seemingly of one mind. They sat on the concrete porch, hogging the small, barrel-drum fire, and performed full-length, duet recitals of Monty Python and the Holy Grail and Full Metal Jacket, accents included, all sniggers and giggles, oblivious to the frowns of the onlooking Kurdish fighters.

"I can't believe they're marines," said Harry, taking the words from my mouth. The Beavis and Butthead of the Marine Corps.

Another arrival was a bearded young Australian doctor, overweight and overwrought all day long. Permanently furious at having ended up in a combat unit instead of being taken straight to work in a hospital, he kept saying, "These fucking people are dumb. Dumb as dogshit." And, riding high on his own macho wittiness, he'd go on, "But I'm confident that with persistence I'll eventually find the one guy in this outfit not related to dogshit who can understand me and sort things out."

When the pale marines were rebuked in the most gentle way imaginable, *sans* reprisals, for falling asleep on *nobet*, Levi took it very badly and started to fall in with the Aussie's brand of racial contempt: "It's because I'm not fucking Kurdish. That's all it is. And we come here to help these people..." The accusations, however, cropped up too frequently from one place to another to be groundless. Combined with a profusion of cranky military clichés and macho chatter, it all formed quite an unappealing picture.

Levi wore some kind of traditional military fatigues with a cap, both olive-drab. On the back of the shirt he'd drawn some kind of crest with the words *ISIS Killer – Blood Spiller – Grave Filler*, but that fatigue cap was one of his most distinctive features. On him it looked more like some odd ceremonial peak cap, since it was much wider at the octagonal top, so the flat oblong panels all the way round leaned outwards, tapering down and in towards his brow where the peak jutted out atop his vexed, glaring eyes. With a prominent overbite and frequent scowl, he could look like a pissed-off duck.

It took me some time to see that his whole act was just that.

The only guy I liked of the new set, apart from Harry, was a white-haired 67-year-old Canadian called Zinar. He was big and well built, and impressively fit and strong for his age. His face bore a likeness to Clint Eastwood's – and an inky-blue jailhouse tattoo of an *r* below the eye. I didn't think to ask what it meant.

Paired up on the berm, the first time we'd really talked, we'd hit it off on various topics and enjoyed disagreeing on others. He was a staunch Republican and I was quite the other thing; and in such circumstances, that makes ample grist for a good natter. Conversation roamed from politics to various authors and literary traditions, along with poets like Baudelaire and Rilke.

"*For beauty is nothing but the beginning of a terror we are just about able to bear, because it disdains to destroy us,*" paraphrased Zinar.

I went to get us some *çay* from the fire on the porch, pleased to find someone I could have an interesting discussion with.

"I've been serving tea to Republicans all my life..." I joked, coming back to the trench with two full glasses. We passed the afternoon with tea and fine conversation.

That bit of bonding went south one afternoon when we got taken to a house in the village for a shower. Inside the yard, a Spanish lad called Jorge kicked off the proceedings by rifling through the rooms looking for stuff to loot, until I told him to pack it in. For some reason Zinar took Jorge's side, gainsaying my every word an irrational and continual manner.

A little while later, as several of us were handwashing clothes in the yard, Zinar decided to strip down naked and walk around. I looked up in disbelief.

"Er – that might not go down very well here," I said.

Our escort came back, and was almost speechless. "This not OK. We can go to jail for this."

Then, to make things worse, an old Arab man who was looking after the place came back as well, saw the upturned rooms and started locking all the doors, shouting into his phone.

"Were you aware," said Zinar later, glaring with indignation, "that in German washrooms men undress and shower together?"

I didn't know where to begin. How about, *so what?*

***

"Hello! What are you do-*ing*…?"

I had run into Delal and her guileless face lit up, though it had plenty of reason not to. Despite her hardboiled, party-member demeanour, she had an openness I don't think she could have hidden if she'd tried.

Our *tabors* had converged at Tal Tamir, the "cowshed": a giant disused farming compound with vast concrete cowsheds, milk pasteurisation plants, milking and other hi-tech equipment, all overgrown and war damaged. A transit hub for the YPG in the region, a place to pull back to.

Sitting on a concrete block at the foot of a pillar, I took the cigarette from my mouth and shrugged, feeling stupid.

"I'm sorry about the other day…"

Someone called her away before she could answer.

The cowshed's population varied; at certain times it was like a ghost town. At others, like now, it was overrun with hundreds of troops on their way to somewhere or other. There were endless reunions like ours along the route of the travelling roadshow. Delal and I chatted away in separate groups that eventually came together. Just before leaving with her *tabor*, she turned from the person she was talking to in Kurdish and switched languages. "I. *Fight*," she said, eyeballing me with a bitter grin.

"What – after I left…?"

"Yes. We killed 16 Daesh."

After she left I realised I'd forgotten to ask if she knew about Kosta.

***

The next day Ronnie, Bruce, Fat Jack, Junior and some of the others rolled up at the cowshed. I pulled a Belgian-English lad called Nathan aside. He was an ex-Legionnaire and one of the stronger characters, part of another group originally, but there had been a bit of mixing and switching with several people lately, besides myself. Keeping track of who was where could get quite confusing. We needed to discuss these new guys, pronto, I told him. But he had somewhat bigger news for me.

They, and two other westerners – seven in total – were on the verge of quitting. They'd just come out of a five-day battle for a nearby village called Tal Nasir. It had gone disastrously. Young Jac was in hospital with a bullet wound.

I went to talk to the others. Their accounts came thick and fast.

"We entered from the left side, and after two days we had more than half the village – but then they stop! The next day

Daesh throw more grenades than I have ever seen in my life. I thought, I'm gonna die here…"

"I was in the sniper position, picking a target. Keeping silent, not moving. Two YPJ girls came in behind me and covered my eyes, joking and laughing. They wouldn't go away."

"I took a knee by the corner of a building, and the kids are all just standing milling around laughing at me. Then when the fight kicks off they panic and scatter, banging into each other and yelling and getting shot. One was so pumped up he was running up and down on the spot, weapon pointed straight down like this – shot himself straight through the fucking foot."

Corridors left wide open for enemy movement, friendly groups cut off and encircled, casualties taken because the unit stopped to rest and get some tea on instead of pushing the advantage. Wounded soldiers left bleeding on the ground, no first aid gear apart from what the westerners had, no ambulance vehicle until they could flag down a passing truck.

The guys said they wanted to start an all-westerners unit, under Kurdish leadership, and if they couldn't then they were going straight home.

Later that day a general came to meet them and talk. Though at pains to persuade them to stay he gave no clear answer on what they were asking for. Lots of talk, very little said. Which, everyone had long learned, meant no.

"Well, I'm gutted you blokes are leaving," I said that night in the bedroom. They were acting up, graffiti and knob gags, letting their hair down finally. I was even more gutted I'd talked myself out of a battle – but if I'd been there, I might now be feeling the same way they did. "But since you're definite, I just want it to happen quickly so I can get on."

Please try and get word to Jac, I asked them. He should know they were leaving before deciding what to do next himself.

"It's been an adventure," said Ronnie, shaking my hand.

"Move fast, stay low," grinned Nathan – not a man for sentimental farewells. He'd been calling me the "black cat" just lately, since my friends tended to keep dying. "What kind of flowers do you want at your funeral? Got any hot cousins…?"

If you don't like gallows humour, stay away from a bloke who's done seven years in 2 REP (*2e Régiment Étranger de Parachutistes*) of the French Foreign Legion. As mentioned, the death of friends rarely gave rise to public shows of feeling in the YPG. Perhaps in a rare and private moment, alone in an abandoned room, a quiet corner, I might let out a few tears; but ordinarily it took no great effort to just blank those feelings out. Gallows humour was fine by me.

I got a bunch of first aid gear and other bits from the guys, as well as a *biksî* machine gun. Time here had taught me that longer-range weapons got used more. I was stripping and cleaning it when they drove away, looking like soldiers.

I felt like I'd gone and dumped myself in the delinquents' *tabor*. It seemed like an age since Shengal but it had been less than a month. I kept thinking back to that group, which didn't exist anymore. I wished I'd appreciated it more at the time.

***

A few nights later, we attacked Tal Nasir again. I got a taste of what the others had been saying.

We waited up till well after midnight for *heval* Obama to open proceedings by bombing the town. He never showed, but our commanders had obviously decided to give it a go anyway. Weaving in a straggled line through yards, through holes in walls, over a stream, we finally lined up crouched in shadow along a wall.

We were tense, subdued, but at the same time it was hard to believe it was really going to *happen* this time, after all the let-downs, the empty village clearances, the broken promises.

We advanced in stops and starts over the lumpy no man's land, towards a grumbling engine sound which turned out to be a tank. We stopped behind it, waiting for further orders. Someone tapped my shoulder – it was Alîn, eyes and smile sparkling in the dark. *At last*, they said.

"*Nobet khallas,*" she grinned. No more guard duty. She nodded at my machine gun. "Cûdî, *biksî?*"

"Yep," I said, with a twinge of childish pride. I'd stripped, cleaned, debugged and zeroed it. It was mine.

Delal came along next, leading some of her youngsters. They'd brought a few *tabors* together for this one, presumably taking it quite seriously since the previous defeat.

As we stood chatting 100 metres from the enemy village, another rumbling hulk drove up and past us, a square silhouette devoid of detail. A makeshift armoured bulldozer, a great rusted iron box on tracks with the blade down, smoke chugging out of a small pipe-chimney in the roof. Its lights cut in and out, alternately illuminating it and plunging me into night-blindness.

"Move back, move back!"

A shell from the tank smashed into the village and a few *bizfink* rockets followed it up. Violent flashes and crashes returning to dark. The bulldozer crawled unsteadily forwards and stopped, tilted sideways where the ground rose up, looking stuck.

Our lines edged forward, people looking around, unsure, hunching over as incoming rounds from numerous directions snapped low overhead. Yellow sparks spat from the bulldozer's armour where they hit home. Even now, there was something unserious about it all. The way the kids were shrugging, looking round, bumbling along, lent a sense of unreality to the idea that those little whines and cracks in the air, unseen and gone before you heard them, could end the life of anyone here at any moment.

Peter had tried to clue us in about this. *It won't be like what you're used to – with a plan A…*

By British army standards it was ludicrous. But at least we were fighting. So I bumbled along with the others. *Tag along…*

I was already some way along a well-trodden track. Being merely *willing* to fight was far, far behind me. At this point I was so ready to grab any chance that came, so fearful of never getting in, that I'd make almost any compromise. Why? To avenge my friends? No. At that time it seemed irrational to want revenge for others who'd consciously chosen to fight. At that time, rationality still played quite a big part.

Knowing it was wrong, knowing better, still I allowed myself to *draw* on that group complacency and fearlessness. To tell myself it was safe.

We scrambled into a ditch and the young fighters around me shouted excitedly as I propped my gun on the rocks and soil.

"*Legher?*" (Fire?) I asked.

"Yes!" they chorused, like a clamouring classroom.

I rattled off a series of short bursts with no specific targets, moving from one likely building to another. No enemy muzzle flashes were visible despite the fire we were taking.

The bulldozer pressed on, crunching away through the town's surrounding wall and wrecking part of the building beyond. Flames grew up and a soft smoke held the orange light. Then without warning it reversed, hammering through us at full speed. Our lines disintegrated as people scrambled out of its path. We were in retreat, suddenly, jogging back over the ground, climbing over broken walls, jumping ditches and holes.

I got separated from my group in the darkness and chaos. I had walked towards a fire burning by a wall, following the person in front, and only then realised by its light that none of my lot were there. I found Delal and her *hevals* sat by a wall, and, somewhat sheepishly, latched onto them for the time being.

We milled about in the unpaved lanes of the village, emptied of anyone but YPG troops, waiting out the night. As the prospect of renewing our night attack gradually faded, colour drained from the paling sky, rendering the world washed-out and bedraggled. The fire was all but burned down. Grey embers on a grey dawn.

Radio in hand, Delal told me to wait there for my commander; her group were moving off shortly.

Her manner had shifted perceptibly over time – duller eyes, a touch of brashness about her laugh, her posture, as she bantered with a bunch of her *hevals* in the road. Not the shy vivacity tinged with mischief I knew, from when I'd travelled with her from the river to Qereçox, having no idea she'd be down here with us in the dirt. I waited patiently to ask her a question. She turned to me.

"Delal, did you know my friend Kemal (Kosta) was killed, before?" I asked.

"Yes. Yes, I knew."

She looked down, sad and feminine suddenly, as though the war-hardened shell had melted away for a moment.

"Why didn't you tell me?"

"Because of… how you were like, after Bagok. We thought you would be even more – passion…" She groped for the words.

"You should have told me."

"Yes," she said. "I should have told you."

I went to say something else but she turned to answer a question from behind: three other people needed her attention and I'd lost her again. How to get back to those days at Tal Hamis, that subdued rapport, that spark in her eyes?

They moved off, leaving me alone. Flakes of ash drifted over and settled on the ground.

I sat for four hours by that fire, stoking it up with scraps of wood, cleaning my gun, drinking tea with small groups who came and passed on.

We hadn't always seen eye to eye, Kosta and me, but I like to think we'd become real friends by the end. Of course, I'll never really know.

I'd been deliberately inflexible when we fell out. *Bigger things to worry about*. Finally it was him who held out the olive branch. Maybe he was the bigger person there. Ironies assumed, what did any Samurai or Gawain possess that he hadn't? Goodbye, you big bastard. Wish we'd had more time.

I thought of Cûdî Vietnam, the last of the three. Just before we left Shengal they'd all talked about going to Oakland together to become police officers. Whether they'd have done it or not it was neither here nor there. Kosta had lots of ideas. I saw them, lying on their mattresses in that tumbledown room in Shengal, cracking jokes, hatching plans against the backdrop of gunfire and crumbling walls. Three young men on the threshold of adventure, of the wider world. After all our feverish impatience to get out on operations, Bagok had lasted a day, Kosta a week, and I'd barely got a look in. Now Cûdî Vietnam, refused entry to Australia, was going home – alone and heartbroken.

Finally someone sat down to talk and, with some effort, gave me to understand my *tabor* was based just over there – he pointed – a couple of hundred metres away. *But run*, he said. *Snipers*. I gathered up my gear and jogged, keeping low over the open ground. This war had not improved my sense of direction.

9 NOBET AD NAUSEUM

The scruffy figure raised its head and torso above the short wall surrounding the flat roof, then clumsily ducked down again.

The second time the head went up, the crack and – *toom!* – of a weapon sounded and the figure seemed to flinch, jolting back an inch or so as the bullet smacked into it and passed on through. The air returned to stillness.

It was almost lifelike – from the waist up, seen from 200 metres away – which was the idea.

Harry worked the dummy, fashioned from looted clothes and a wooden pole, while Bob spotted and returned fire with his *karnas*: a game made to while away the hours as the chill spring was barged out by a sudden sweltering heat, and we remained static in the village.

Sniper fire was perennial. Walk too far past that wall without ducking or sprinting and you were asking for it. But all that meant, after we'd exhausted our initial thirst for exploration, was that you rarely did unless you had to. Our little bubble comprised the outside porch, our accommodation rooms and the *nobet* positions – two on the berm, and two in separate houses. Within the bubble, you could forget, for hours and sometimes whole days, that the enemy was two football pitches' length away. A shrunken world, which was driving us stir crazy. We felt as much use as that dummy. If only we were as insensible.

Besides the sniper fire, we had the familiar mortar bombardments, and every so often someone would sneak up in the night and spray our positions with *biksî* fire. Some might consider themselves at the sharp end of things and be content, but we were on the doorstep of ferocious battles that flared on and off night and day, a few klicks away. To our far left, bombs and heavy gunfire reverberated off the Abdul Aziz mountains, like a barrel drum full of stones being shaken and beaten. Half left and half right, the cities of Haseke and Serekaniye sat under cannons, bombs, and the industrial farting noise of an aircraft chain gun, stretching on through the days and weeks in interminable stalemate.

And we sat in the shade of the concrete porch. Smoking, waiting, scratching our nuts.

Harry was talking again about our aborted attack. It had clearly left an impression.

"We took 20% casualties. I mean there was just *no bloody plan*. I was lying on an open track, totally lit up, with rounds smacking off the concrete by my head. I thought fucking hell, I'm going to die here for nothing."

"Well," said Zinar. "You and Cûdî can draw up a new plan of attack… We'll go and sit down with the commander and say this time, it's my way or the highway…"

Of course, our chat was as empty as the days that dragged on by.

***

Crammed into a small darkened room, we waited for the nod: more than 20 of us, sitting hunched in our webbing, cradling weapons, feet drawn up in the cramped space. It was one of the posher houses, though it hadn't taken us long to bring it down with dirt, cigarette ash and other debris on the plush furniture and carpeted floor. A young Kurd showed me a *bizfink* rocket wrapped around with a thick layer of sellotape. He shook it, swishing liquid inside. "Benzine," he said, grinning warmly. Outside the battle was underway, barrages of fire rising and falling like a storm blowing closer.

"We will go 75, maybe 100 metres from enemy village," a young Kurd named Kendal Kobani with a decent level of English had told me. "And wait for the drone. Fire *biksî*, *bizfink*, and then look and shoot who we see."

The glowing ends of cigarettes swarmed through the dark like fireflies. Like them, I smoked one after another as we waited. *Pace yourself…*

When we had light to see by, Kendal was dum-dumming his rounds by cutting into the copper tips of the heads with my knife, exposing the steel core. There were no rules of engagement here, no carry-cards to inform us if and when we were cleared to fire. It was what it was.

The dry-brushfire crackle of small arms sounded like it was on top of us. Our tank, parked in the alley outside, had gone out into it already. *Any moment now.* Our chatter had been relaxed but upbeat. Finally we were getting to do it. Now, people had less to say. The room was more subdued.

We stayed in that state for over an hour. And gradually, almost imperceptibly, the mood shifted again, the last-seconds tension lifted and a more familiar anxiety edged its way in. The rise and fall of battle noise settled into a more constant soundtrack.

Time wore on. A few people snoozed. We were allowed some low light. I pulled out a notebook, did a bit of doodling. Anything to distract from the slow creeping fear.

For the umpteenth time Kendal Kobani said, *"Heval* Cûdî give me one cigarette please."

As I reached into my waistcoat pocket, he swiped my pen.

I let him keep it and unclicked the waist buckle on my webbing, letting it hang to the sides, heavy with ammo and grenades. I tugged at my combat shirt, flapping it to unstick the sweat-soaked patches under the webbing straps from my skin. We were cheek by jowl and our collective body heat exacerbated the sultriness of the evening.

Kendal, smiling broadly, showed me the note he'd written:

Cûdî is ferind from Beritanya and he helping us whis faithing agist Daes

"Very good, Kendal," I nodded, folding it up and stowing it between the pages of my notebook. A keeper. If I ever made the transition to a normal life I'd frame things like that and put them on the walls to hang for decades, remnants of a life I no longer led.

I should have brought out more cigarettes. Kendal hardly ever smoked normally, but when he did, for some reason he tended to get them from me. Which was fine, but I was down to half a pack and supplies were on the other side of the village. Just 20 minutes later, he wanted another one.

"Why didn't you bring some yourself?" I said, tutting as he made his request with that impudent imperative, once again.

"In *our culture...*" he began. I knew his expression, even in the dark. The sternness he so often projected – accentuated by heavy black brows under the forage cap he favoured over the *keffi* – was undermined by slightly chubby, puppy cheeks and the hint of impish laughter hovering round the corners of his mouth and bright, dark eyes.

"Oh, not this again. *Here.*"

Kendal was many things, for his 21 years (or 22 – "I'm not exactly sure"): a veteran of the mountains, and of the siege of Kobani, his home town. A skilled player of the *saz* (a long-necked lute), though he hardly ever touched it. A rigid soldier who sometimes made daft mistakes, like burning his hand on the *biksî* barrel after firing hundreds of rounds through it. A true exponent of the cause, an affectionate kid, a moody, bratty youth and a man with too much on his plate.

Like Mansur, he had some authority over us by dint of speaking English.

He was pretty tough, and looked it. Strongly built, with a compact frame and the economical movements of the natural soldier, characterised by a sleeveless jacket and that forage cap. I could see him rising inevitably through the ranks, and perhaps making the switch to political life later; a man of rhetoric and persuasion, as that baby face slimmed and hardened into a wise and well-chiselled profile. "Just a soldier," was how he described himself.

The hours ticked by, and the sounds of battle began to die down. People slept fully, in ones and twos.

Kendal produced his music box, a model ubiquitous in the YPG. Cigarette-pack size (some even had cigarette logos on them), it comprised a speaker, a track display and a USB port. Cheap and popular. The same five or six songs were equally ubiquitous, everywhere you went: Apo, The Mountains, The Party...

"Play this song for me when I will be *şehid*," said Kendal, as tinny music emanated on low volume. I rolled my eyes. The martyr's glory, the big cliché. *If I should fall, to rise no more/As many comrades did before...*

If we were being allowed music now, there was little chance of him realising *that* morbid goal tonight. The fearful suspicion had grown to all but certainty.

Our planned "short attack" got pulled at about 5am. Back to your quarters.

Not the first time, not the last. Kendal Kobani was trying hard to hide the hurt all over his face. I recognised the look from the last time we went through this. "Daesh knows we're coming," he'd said, and had slunk away, as if to lick his wounds.

We fastened our webbing, gathered up weapons and emerged blinking into the oncoming daylight. A sullen, wordless dejection hung over all as we drifted separate ways: the mixed flavours of a mock execution and a cancelled Christmas.

There was still a bit of spatting back and forth out there, the ebbtide of battle. Mansur was jogging across the yard with a bag full of ammo. Straight on *nobet* for me, he said. *Great…*

My *biksî* was on the roof, in the support-fire position, so I had my rifle. I'd been in position less than a minute when an exploding round hit the bottom of the berm right in front of me, chucking up shrapnel and loose earth.

I fired two shots straight off towards the enemy village where the *crack!* of shot was coming from, then scanned the dim scenery for shapes, movement, snapping out of the haze of overtiredness staved off by now-stale caffeine and nicotine. *Wake up.*

Mansur came round the corner of our accommodation house, staring wildly, bug-eyed after a whole night running around.

"Stop firing, Cûdî!" he shouted. "Why you fire?"

"Because I was fired *on*," I replied.

"Can you *see* enemy?"

"No, but I took accurate fire, so –"

"Do you think you can – with *kalaş* (Kalashnikov)…?" he hissed.

There was no way round that intense glare; he was high as a kite after his night of action, going from one position to another, ferrying ammo and whatever else. Tea, probably. Sometimes you couldn't know whether he was conveying orders from above or making them up himself. I turned back to the terrain I was supposed to be watching. Nothing.

After a few minutes I tried to explain the principle of REEF (Reaction to Effective Enemy Fire) to him, but I might as well have been talking to the berm. For good or ill, he'd come a long way from the shy, self-doubting trainee at Zara.

Mansur was in some ways the opposite of Kendal, in others similar. A party member of over a decade – as he liked to tell me at times like this – his dogmatism would have been better suited to political communiqués, but he was determined to do his bit on the front. And he had the insistence of the meek, like a starfish opening a clam.

We got into one of countless bitchy arguments that brought out the worst in both of us.

***

Nevertheless, throughout this unending frustrating stasis, Kendal and others continued to insist that we were merely on rotation, like all *tabors*, and that our day was coming.

And until then, there was *nobet*. *Nobet ad nauseum*. Five hours at night, five and a half in the day.

Still, sweltering days with the sun in your eyes and flies in your face. Bleak, overcast days with the wind blowing, the grass waving, grey skies; plastic sheets flapping in the rubbish and rubble, those same sheets that floated like a pinned ghost at night in the fritzing and sparking of a lone outbuilding's nerveshot electric lights. Everything else moved; just not us and the enemy.

Graveyard shift. 4am. Straining to see through the dark. The eyes drifted naturally to points of light at night, especially when the mind began to wander; but the enemy wouldn't be in front of a white wall, or a reflection on glass or water. He'd be crouched at the base of a dark tree, hunkered in the rubble or crawling along a hedgerow.

And when the mind wanders…what a torment. You close your eyelids for a second's relief, like putting down heavy shopping. Then your mind follows whatever comes up behind those eyelids, the images and movement, fooling you it's more real. Snapping to again is a physical wrench and drives you mad, because it only repeats and worsens.

One hour to go. That point when solid things seem insubstantial – trees, buildings – it all gets a bit floaty, submerged in waves of tiredness. Literally a nightmare when you're trying to detect movement.

What you do is, you close one eye and hold your finger up in front, next to the object you're unsure about. So my infantry instructor told me. *If it's really moving it'll keep moving, while your finger stays still next to it. If it's just an illusion it will go still.* But it's the effort of a few seconds just to shift focus from finger to object and back again in that light. It's impossible to look at both at once.

Jarred into alert mode suddenly. *Sounds of crunching feet. Up ahead on the right-hand track.*

Four silhouetted figures emerge from the darkened trees – a route our *hevals* never take. *Shit.*

Tonight, anybody that side of the berm is enemy, I'd been told.

I fumbled with my rifle. It's easy to be quick and slick when it doesn't matter.

Fire, or don't fire?

"*Heval, were-were* (come here)!" I hissed urgently, to someone behind me near the porch.

"Hmmm…?"

"Come here!"

Someone sauntered slowly over. Other *hevals* were standing around, dithering, smoking. The figures passed before anyone made it the few metres over to me.

"Relax," chuckled Mansur, arriving a few minutes later. It was the *kamîn* party, returning from the forward observation point in the ruined village, taking a different route back to quarters for a change.

Thanks for fucking warning me…

Typical. They'd say OK, tonight, shoot anything you see. Then later in the night someone would come climbing up over the berm to you, from the other side, out of the blue, singing gently to himself. Just some *heval*, what's the problem…?

So many times I gave the challenge to someone 10 metres away who didn't bother to say a word in reply. How many *şehids* because of idleness, forgetfulness, complacency?

And your time off *nobet* could be as fraught as your time on. Nights of straining your eyes against the fuzzy darkness, exhausting hours in ultra-alert mode, days of tormented half-sleep. As if the routine wasn't grinding enough, with the heat and the hygiene levels thrown in, the Kurdish kids themselves had to make it that bit worse.

The young fighters just didn't respect sleep. They just didn't get it. In the British army, if you'd recently come off an exhausting night duty and two teenage sprogs sat each side of your bed and started a loud conversation, or played that godawful snake-charmer music on those wretched music boxes, you'd threaten to punch them both out. Showing anger, however, was a big no-no with the *hevals*. Worst thing you could do.

One time I lost it. I was dog-tired after five hours on *nobet* and I had a day shift in just a few hours' time. A young Kurd called Merdem, who looked barely 16, despite a slightly comical old man's face with a bulbous nose and classic cauliflower ears, drove me up the wall by constantly turning the TV up and down, making a game of it and laughing at me – till I bent his arm up his back and ripped the remote from his hand. A bit rough, maybe, but sleep mattered. It wasn't a bloody kindergarten.

Perhaps all these things, the laxity, the recklessness, just indicated a wider, cultural fatalism – a sense that what would happen would happen, in time. Till then, why spoil it with anger and negativity? This was totally alien to the attitude of a conventional army, with its manic fixation on drills and discipline, and meticulously scaled punishments for infractions of all degrees.

It caused me no small concern that I was comparing everything (unfavourably) to the way the British army did things, and frequently referring to myself as a soldier. Fifteen years of anti-war politics – I'd been doing so well till this came up.

And while we were never that tight, we could always get worse.

Zinar's behaviour grew increasingly irrational. Every few days there was something else. One morning I came out and saw he'd dug out half the earth in the berm position, to make it more comfortable to sit down on. But the worst thing he did was remove the legs from his *biksî* and discard them somewhere, "so that he could use it like a rifle". He made a series of improvements on the design, involving a small canvas bag filled with sand tied below the gun with string, a carved piece of log inside a tin mug, and others – which you'd see discarded every few days as his rag 'n' bone modifications evolved. It was ludicrous: a machine gun was a crew weapon, not a personal weapon. Others had to use it, and this monkeying about was not only stupid but fucking dangerous.

His irrationality was only matched by his arrogance, as I quickly discovered when I tried to reason with him. Arguments flared up quickly and only widened the schism between us that started that day at the shower yard. Several times he called me out for a fight.

He was a loose cannon with some very disquieting features – the most immediate being That Tattoo, and his explanation for it: "It was a chick I nailed."

"When first he come here he ask me, *where are the female snipers?*" Mansur grinned, shaking his head.

I just couldn't laugh. Perhaps they viewed him as a character. Harry and I resolved to keep a close eye on him. That was all we could do.

***

An institutional apathy set in. People turned up late to *nobet*, fell asleep on the berm. Mornings to middays were a blur of lazy, sunny Sundays with barely a soul about. Daesh could have breezed in. I was thinking of fucking off before it all crumbled. Exactly where to, however, I didn't know. Say one thing for Zinar – he was the only person I never had to talk to regarding *nobet*. He got there on time and paid attention throughout, rain or shine.

I got everyone together on the berm. Bob was on duty and I wanted him to hear it as much as anyone.

"I've been watching you and you haven't looked over the top of that berm in the last 20 minutes," I said. In fairness, Levi was sitting with him, and could see over himself. But Bob had a responsibility to set an example. If a US marine couldn't uphold the standard, how could the others be expected to? Levi had been caught asleep again and even Harry had started listening to music through his earphones while on shift. We couldn't carry on like this.

"Guys, if you can't take a bit of pride in it, then look at it this way," I said. "If you can't be trusted to do your *nobet*, how can you be trusted to be taken into battle?"

At times I felt like I had my finger in the dam, watching the cracks spread. That said, for all my talk of discipline, I wasn't beyond the odd rogue moment myself. A classic dilemma: when you believe in the sanctity of order, but have no faith in the guy giving you *these particular orders.*

Jac rejoined us, one fine day. His injury was very slight; the bullet had passed through the top of his arm without touching the bone.

Some days later I woke up around 4am. Gunfire was going off all over, between us and the enemy town.

"Where's *heval* Şoreş?" I said to Mansur. I asked him four or five times.

"He is *safe, heval* Cûdî!" hissed Mansur. He'd gone out on *kamîn* with four or five others, just past the "ruined village" – a group of destroyed buildings 100 metres from the enemy.

Fuck that. I grabbed my rifle and headed off out the yard.

"*Heval* Cûdî! Come back NOW!"

I didn't even know where the *kamîn* position was; I hadn't done it yet. Mansur was still ranting at my back when I bumped into Jac's team heading back in.

"All right, mate?" he said, grinning out of the darkness. Christ, the *relief.* I'd probably only have got lost.

***

While Bob and Harry played sniper games and Zinar conducted his senile pottering on the front line, Portuguese Mario (another Kendal) whiled away the time tailoring his war-zone fancy dress: fur-lined chest webbing, a sleeveless combat shirt and some tribalesque headdress in YPG red, green and yellow. To be fair, he took a damn good photo in it all. Jac busied himself writing *420* and *SWED* (Smoke Weed Every Day) on the walls, to piss Harry off as much as anything, and I decorated the wooden stock on my rifle – scoring out a mountain scene with a setting sun and hanging, bell-like flowers in the foreground. I inlaid silver and copper wire into the grooves, fixed them down with superglue and sanded it flush, then gave the wood a wipe over with olive oil. The Kurds thought it was marvellous and started calling me a *guerrilla*.

A trip to town was a sure-fire morale boost for everyone. Stock up on confectionaries and other little treats, a priceless hour in an internet cafe if we were really lucky. Driving back, Mansur stopped the truck and called to me where I was sat on the open back, facing backwards down the road.

"Cûdî, do you see?"

I turned to face forwards. Strung high across the street was a banner, with the words *Şehid Bagok* writ large, and his photo. It felt like a punch in the nose, that distressing smell of pain. *I was laughing and joking with that guy a few weeks ago.*

We killed time however we could, but it felt like we were staving off the insanity – and doing so without the conditioning of soldiers that keeps them on the rails, or the framework to maintain it.

Levi was starting to lose it too.

He emerged from the kitchen one day following a series of bumps and crashes, and stamped towards the room with tears in his eyes, long, gangly limbs floundering and stumbling.

"He was headbutting the wall," said Jac.

Lately he'd been going whole days without eating, and looked even more slight and callow than usual, which was saying something.

I followed him into the room.

"Come on, Agir," I said, using his codename. "I know it's hard here. I don't like seeing you like this, mate." I put my hand on his shoulder.

I think my gentle words caught him off-guard, because I wasn't known for them; I was known for being a grouchy, temperamental bastard, if anything. His intense eyes, with the slight strabismus, stared into mine and the tension seemed to fade a little.

"Why don't you take a nap, mate?" I slipped him a couple of codeine and paracetamol tablets. "I'll get you a cup of tea." By the time I came back to the room with it he was fast asleep.

Poor kid. Despite first impressions, I don't think he had a mean bone in his body.

"Have I done something to piss Kendal off, do you think?" I asked him in the kitchen one time. "He hasn't said anything, but he seems really off with me today."

"Oh, no. He's probably pissed about something else," he replied. "I think the thing with him is, his emotions run very close to the surface. So he finds it hard to be nice with you and then switch to being angry at the person who's really upset him." In his calm, open eyes was an expression to overthrow weeks of abrasive machismo. "If he was upset with you, you'd know."

This Levi I found far easier to like. But I still felt he shouldn't really be there.

After Harry and I had got separated from the others to go on the Tal Nasir assault, I'd been hoping the separation was permanent. But here we all were, reunited again, one big happy fucked-up family.

Into the collective malaise an intense bitterness seeped like poison. Even Kendal, a solid character, was feeling it, as Levi had observed. The day after another of our cancelled assaults, he and Berxwadan, a tough-looking Lebanese guy with a tattooed neck, took a shotgun (doubtless found in some Daesh village on a previous operation) up to the roof and fired shot after shot at Tal Nasir, apropos of nothing, till they ran out of cartridges. Then they smashed it up and threw the pieces over the berm.

I felt an almost physical reaction. First our standards had started to slip and now we were actually attacking our own capability. I expected it from Zinar, but this was *way* out of character for Kendal. Again, I saw pure pain in his face as he brought the gun bowling over his shoulder and smashed it into the ground.

Sometimes it felt like the place would blow from its own pressure, or that we'd all become so apathetic and idle that the enemy would walk all over us. *Christ, let's have an attack soon, from either side, and give us all a bit of relief.*

"When they release us," I joked, "we'll run towards the guns with arms outstretched…"

I was at quite a low ebb when a visiting journalist asked me my thoughts on the situation. I said foreign fighters might be more of a burden than a help. It was a view I was coming to. Our cultural insensitivity (verging on outright racism), the knotty matter of tactical disparity, the language barrier and our constant complaining and unreliability made for added work and risk. There was no shortage of Kurdish fighters and maybe the YPG should just send us all home. They wanted the involvement of the world at any level, and we were a start. But maybe we did more harm than good.

People have war thrust on them, without a choice. It seemed absurd, our non-combat stress disorder. An insult, even.

An old familiar feeling was starting to come over me, one I remembered from Palestine. What was I really doing here? Could I justify it to myself?

Since the deaths of Kosta and Bagok, getting into battle had become crucial to my self-worth. Was it just my own ego in disguise?

Perhaps it was the fact that I'd been in the army but never fought, I considered. No. That bothered some guys, the Northern Ireland generation, soldiers who'd spent their careers talking about war and then seen the new set go off and do it, in Afghanistan and Iraq. But I was happy with my choices.

Was it related to my old, nagging failure to bring peace to the region of Palestine single-handedly? (To say nothing of being unable to personally Stop the War and bring global capitalism crashing to its knees.) Well, a bit, maybe.

Perhaps it went even further back, if I was going to be honest with myself. It's true to say my sense of self-worth had been fairly gored at certain stages in my life.

***

One stoned and drunken night I'd stormed out of a house party into the garden, in a daze of sudden and intolerable despair, smashed a bottle and hacked it into my wrist, severing two tendons. Blood splattered on the leaves, like black paint in the garden lights. The reason — an ex-girlfriend of mine had walked in unexpectedly, arched an ironic eyebrow towards me, and proceeded to flirt ostentatiously with one of the several guys she'd been sleeping with while we were together. She had revealed the truth when the relationship finally imploded, in cool amusement and the spirit of one-upmanship. I'd flirted with someone myself, to make her jealous: well, this would teach me.

On finding out, I'd thumped one of those guys — not because she laughingly suggested I do just that (though she did) — but for sheer idiot pride's sake. And I'd instantly regretted it. He was a friend, albeit a selfish one. Since then I'd tried to just move on, but she wasn't done. Someone had told her I was at this party, and along she had come. It turned out that various mutual acquaintances had been "in the know" for some time, and the public interest, as toxic an aspect as any, was hardly dispelled by my emotionally incontinent, self-destructive theatrics. They were all good armchair radicals, nonconformists, free spirits: saving the world with their organic yoghurt and cannabis. People who'd watch a person burn to death as happily as pull the wings off a fly, if they could accompany it with the shrill charge of misogyny.

It was the lowest point of my adult life. The following days, while half of me was making plans to finish myself off altogether, the saner half said it might be time to go and talk to someone. It was long overdue.

In the professional intimacy of the counselling suite, the doctor's calm and measured words had a strange mix of effects on me. Some were quite troubling to hear: Words such as turbulent childhood. Dysfunctional. Disturbing. Hostile environment. Unacceptable treatment. *Familiar expressions, but they'd never been made to apply to me before.*

Other words felt like a salve, without me really understanding why.

"No one would expect *you to have to deal with those things. I think it's* important *for you to realise that…"*

It was the first time I'd consciously acknowledged, with the help of an impartial and professional observer, that what went on at home when I was young was objectively – and also very seriously – wrong. That various boundaries were way overstepped in my upbringing, even by 1980s standards. That my own perceptions of events actually rang true after all.

It was tough, dredging up fragmented memories that held nothing good: only hurt, shame, anger and confusion. But after a year of weekly sessions I found myself able to understand the past in a way I never expected to, and move on from what I thought would always just be an inexplicable stone dragging me down. I mention all this (briefly) because it seems required; since people's childhood experiences obviously affect their character and the actions and decisions they take later in life. I see no need to go into detail, however.

I'd never considered therapy before: it sounded too much like surrendering my independence. And since my own past was so confusing to me, I didn't see how anyone else would be able to make sense of it, so I'd simply tried to keep it at arm's length most of the time. The coping mechanisms I'd developed had made me an emotionally inflexible and at times aggressive person, liable to walk out on a job or a relationship, or to start a fight in the street, rather than feel slighted or walked over.

At school I'd done badly as a teen, dropping from the top bands to the bottom. Teachers back then didn't care what you had to go home to; what concerned them was your attitude. Reciprocally, while they were banging on about your very future being determined by the choices you made at 15, to me the whole thing had become a burdensome irrelevance. Thrown out of home, thrown out of school. Living in a YMCA on benefits at 17, the archetypal antisocial teenager: good for nothing in my own eyes and everyone else's. Not an uncommon route into the military, I'm told. After a couple of years of short-lived, menial jobs and a few months thumbing my way round Europe, I walked into a high-street army careers office and asked to talk to someone about joining up. I had no idea what as – no concept of regiments or roles. I did the computer aptitude test, a ream of possible jobs came back and I was told to pick one on the spot. Let's see. Get a trade. How about this: driver?

The army was a last resort and a saving grace. I got a fair amount of shit in training for the "attitude" left over from my school days, but I also got given leadership roles quite frequently and discovered a physical fitness I didn't know I had. It gave me confidence and self-esteem. I found I was good at military skills and genuinely keen, and the army invests vast reserves of tender loving care in shaping someone like that. They really have seen it all.

Shortly after basic training I got persuaded to switch from driver (before I even did driver training) to pioneer, by an older instructor who was one himself. You'd get to drive every vehicle going anyway, and travel all over the *world, he said. Well, he'd had a different experience from mine, it turned out. So after a six-month peacekeeping tour of Bosnia I volunteered for commando training because it sounded adventurous.*

The military did a lot for me but I never really settled into the life. I bonded well with the other blokes out on exercise, or on PT – army stuff – but socially I was a bit of an oddball: out of place in the nightclubs, crap at pulling women, no interest in football. My idea of a good Saturday out was browsing the secondhand bookstalls in the town market. In time the structured life that I'd pulled myself up by came to feel more like a cage around me.

After the Cambrian Patrol, while our team were having our 15 minutes, I had a run-in with a sergeant who'd just returned to the unit from abroad: a physical hulk, about 15 years older than me and probably 20 kilos heavier. The reason he gave for battering me unconscious at the Christmas do was that I'd used bad language in front of his wife. The real reason, people surmised, was that he wanted to re-establish himself around here, let the new set know who he was. I'd done something commendable for the unit, and he'd given me a kicking, which in his mentality put him one higher. He was back. I woke in hospital with a broken ankle and five stitches in the face.

The sergeant was one of the old school, where you got respect for bashing kids half your size. It's not all heroes in the army. Lines get blurred between a tough regime, the work-hard-play-hard ethos, and outright bullying. There was no blurring here, though. Half the unit wanted to see him fucked for this, even those who didn't like me for my smart-arse attitude. The army was changing, and dinosaurs like him were not part of the new plan.

Unfortunately that still left the other half. He was suddenly promoted to staff sergeant while awaiting court martial. Sorted: if he got bust down a rank, there'd be no harm done.

Sick leave. I hobbled out of the shower, dried off and unpeeled the tape on the bin bag over the plaster on my leg. I stared at the walls. There was nothing on TV. The bone would knit; that wasn't the real damage.

A barrage of confused testimony at the hearing, a good civvy barrister who must have cost him a fortune, and the now-staff sergeant walked, keeping his new rank into the bargain. His lawyer actually managed to establish sufficient doubt as to who attacked whom, while he sat there doing his best impression of a choirboy throughout, mortified by the very accusation of impropriety. I'd had months of the good-old-boys trying to push me to retract my statement, of veiled threats. Now he smirked as he walked out, on his way to celebrate himself into a stupor.

My confidence suffered a seismic shock, threatened to crumble. They could smash me up like scrap and there was nothing I could do.

Despite his physique and his green beret, the guy was a stores soldier, a shiny-arse who'd done one course once and lived off it, bolstered by the other plastic commandos around him. He worked out of an office in the admin building. One fine summer morning, on my way to collect the post, I walked down the corridor and, seeing him coming, launched myself at him, battering him through a doorway and down to the ground with no more advance warning than he'd given me − 90-odd kilos of fake tough guy hunched in a ball at my feet − before people burst out of every room and I got dragged away into an office, mainlining adrenalin and laughing like a drain.

"Calm down, now!" barked Sergeant Major Miles, standing over me. "Do you want a cup of tea, Jim?"

The staff sergeant didn't smirk so much around camp with two missing teeth and a new Donald Duck accent.

Up in front of the CO, I explained my actions as a momentary loss of control. I did so out of respect. It was a big and a public enough fuck-you already.

"Private Matthews, you're a trained soldier. Trained soldiers don't experience a 'momentary loss of control', do they?"

"No, sir."

"You're a commando-trained soldier. Which means that you've been subjected to various strains and pressures to ensure that you're not the kind of person who experiences a 'momentary loss of control'. Isn't that right?"

"Yes, sir."

"And yet you still expect me to accept your version of things?"

"Yes, sir."

"I see." He paused. "Do you… feel better for it?"

"Yes, sir."

The last thing I did in the army was a token couple of weeks' jail for common assault, contrary to section something or other. When I left, I never looked back.

In my fourth and last year of service I'd taken an OU course in English and European Literature (since I had no A-levels), self-funded, which got me into university. I was already starting to think more about politics and current affairs, and to have doubts about the British army's role in them. I was probably the only commando who was also a paid-up member of Amnesty International.

Like millions of others before and after me, I came out of the army a different person from the one who went in. I travelled South America for a few months, then started uni. Study came easily, especially with my army-instilled discipline and motivation, and student life was fantastic. I got involved in activism of various sorts – early versions of the "crusades" I eventually grew disillusioned with.

The counselling in my 30s helped me immensely, but the memories would always cut deep. I've always hated those who abuse power over others, and, from that same position of power, distort reality by twisting the facts. I don't just hate it, it really drives me up the fucking wall. Perhaps at some elemental level I saw this mirrored in the treatment of oppressed cultures, in the political rhetoric of the most blatant tyrants endorsed by a biased media and an apathetic public.

So maybe, ultimately, it's All About Me. If so, I'm hardly exceptional. Go to any war zone with an international scene and you'll find plenty of grown-up, mixed-up kids – journos, aid workers, activists – still fighting their own demons, trying to make good on the past.

***

But this was me, and this particular place and time. Time to reckon up accounts again. Searching for purpose and meaning is all very well, but you should have some thought for whose yard you're doing it in.

"Do you think the YPG should send us foreigners home?" I asked Mansur on the berm one night.

"No," he said, shaking his head and laughing gently. Funny, I was banking on a *yes*, there.

"Why not?"

"Because the friends get so much… motivation, from you coming here." He always translated *heval* as *friend*, not comrade.

"We must talk," he said, "about friendship."

"OK. Sure."

"You see… *everyone* respects Zinar, a man of his age coming here, so far, to fight with us…"

It exasperated me that the Kurds didn't see what I saw, but how could they be expected to? If I couldn't get on with him, I was just making myself look bad.

The social side was crucial. *They fight with their spirits*, I'd heard it said: prizing friendship over pragmatism, apparently. It was topsy-turvy. I mean, the British army is big on *fitting in* as well, as discussed – but it's secondary to doing your job properly. But maybe that was why the Kurds put up with us at all, with all our shit – our brattiness, our troublemaking, our racism. They were looking for friends.

"And for that night – with shooting the *kalaş*. I was *so* tired. I am sorry," said Mansur.

"Yeah, I'm sorry too. It's hard here for all of us. I shouldn't get angry so quickly."

10 JUST 'CAUSE...

We sat around the porch's long table, shooting the usual shit.

Kendal was trying hard to needle me today.

"They are going to *kill* them," he grinned, leaning over the table at me.

"I expect you're right."

"And *eat* them!"

"*Yep...*"

I'd been quite fond of two ducks that appeared to have moved in, a male and female. They went waddling round together, in and out of the yards and the rooms, like they owned the place. I sat sketching them now and then. They'd been with us for weeks, living off our food scraps, when one day I'd come back from a trip out and seen a young YPJ girl holding one by the wings and the other already loaded on the back of a truck. She made a dash backwards, giggling, as I strode towards her making my feeble imprecations. The other Kurds fed me some baloney about an old man in the countryside who kept ducks as pets.

When he'd had his fun, Kendal said, "*Heval* Cûdî give me one cigarette please."

I reached into my pocket, produced my middle finger and held it up. "There you go."

People sniggered.

"It's a good cigarette. Put it in your mouth."

"Hey! Respect!"

"*You* respect. I'm twice your age."

A short while later he brought up the matter of the busted shotgun, like it was one big joke. It was a touchy subject, one I'd long decided to forget; but if he wanted it like this, fine.

"Yeah, why did you break that gun, Kendal? The YPG needs all the weapons it can get."

"It was no good."

"Not after you'd finished with it, it wasn't. Why did you do it? *Why*, Kendal?"

"It stopped to fire, *heval* Cûdî. *Khallas*."

"Probably because you and Berxwadan took it apart the day before. If a gun stops working, you don't smash it up – you give it to someone who understands that gun."

"Cûdî, *khallas. Khallas*." His smile grew hard.

"Why are you being like this today, Kendal?" I said. "It's because the operation's been put back, isn't it? It was the same the day you broke the gun. The day after we didn't attack. *Do you remember?*"

"Yes," he said quietly. The nervous mirth faded from his face. "You understand me. I love you, Cûdî."

"I love you too, Kendal."

***

Things were looking both bad and good, but not much change either way – as usual. We'd moved to the next village along, to face off a different enemy village. Now we were 800 metres from them, not 300, which meant even less action than before. But the reason given was that we were due some "relaxing" before the imminent operation.

Kendal Kobani had been less than impressed with the R&R arrangements.

"It's a dry village. Dirty, no water…" he said, kicking a hollow metal water tank. "Do you know, *heval* Baran, in the mountains, you just make a hole in the ground and it's water coming. I love the mountains. Everything is clean… Trees…

"They say we came for some relaxing. And, as *heval* Cûdî say, it was a *bull. Shit.*"

Kendal and Harry were nearly always together these days. It started with Harry asking Kendal to do a recorded interview about his life and experiences in Kobani. Since then they'd pretty much paired up. A stream of obscure little in-jokes and made-up ditties had them giggling and singing and rabbiting together incessantly. Now they were mooching around the yards, looking for water and anything else they might find of use or interest.

"At least we were getting mortared at the other place," moaned Levi, sat at the long metal porch table with me. One of my abiding memories of the last village was the two of us sitting in the mortar pit, an oblong hole in the earth six foot deep, while the bombardment rained down, singing an old trench-song that went, "We're here, because we're here, because we're here…"

A laugh was a laugh. But I'd seriously tried to give this westerners' group the slip during the move. We westerners were supposed to stay behind at the last village (the one facing Tal Nasir) when this *tabor* moved off, and join with the *tabor* arriving there as a replacement. I often thought back to my group at Shengal. The best. This one wasn't a patch, I thought now.

I'd told Kendal Kobani I wanted to go with him and the other Kurds.

"Just you?" he asked.

"Yes."

He told the boss, who got on the phone and came back with an immediate answer.

"All friends are coming with us," Kendal translated.

I'd forced myself to match their wide smiles.

***

It was getting on for three weeks since General Simko, a huge craggy bear of a man, had visited with a rousing speech thanking us for our whatevers, exhorting us all to spread the message to the western media as Harry was doing, and notifying us to replenish ammo, grenades and so forth: the operation would begin in 10–15 days, when the forces from Haseke and Serekaniye advanced.

Translating for him was a slight young German-Kurdish lad called Dilsoz.

"The world is supporting us… but the coalition is still deciding. When the operation starts we will have constant air support and we will be successful. We thank you for fighting with us, and be patient, and everyone will fight. Daesh now are very weak in Iraq and Syria and it's the YPG who have been the most victorious in pushing them out and defeating them."

10–15 days… how many weeks was it since the last time we heard that? Now it was the second time we'd gone through it, and it was looking like petering out again.

However, it was true that the planes had stepped up the bombing raids and ground was being taken. So hope held out. And that was the torment: the hope. Westerners could leave whenever they wanted; it was the hope that kept us here, the dread of cutting your lost time only to find everyone else had gone into battle just days later. The gambler's agony.

The AC130 gunship gave us another show on *nobet* last night, the constant *dum-dum* of the cannon a hollow pounding, almost sonorous, like someone downstairs banging on their ceiling to tell you to keep it down – and sparks showering up in fountains from the ground, arcing over and falling back to the earth. *Man was born to troubles…* I found it impossible to tell from the direction of tracer fire and the location of bombs and cannon-shot where the enemy and friendly forces actually were. Fire seemed to contradict itself; either the design was over my head or there was a hell of a lot of blue-on-blue going on.

Dilsoz had stayed behind when Simko took off. It looked like he'd joined the gang, eagerly chipping in with our round-the-table chatter about the upcoming offensive, speculating in two languages on where we'd go after Abdul Aziz. The corridor to Kobani, or to Shengal? Efrin or Raqqa? It was a favourite topic, as popular in the YPG as quoting Sun Tzu.

"*Battles are won in the training camp,*" pronounced Dilsoz, with a scholar's fondness for references. He'd often sit alone in deep concentration, scribbling notes on political philosophy for a book he wanted to write. Tanned and slender, there was a languorous, almost idle manner about him, contrasting with his bright-eyed intellect and eagerness to engage – in discussion or in battle. He'd never actually fought, and his keenness was effervescent, his energy infectious. He fitted in easily.

"But fighting from close, you don't enjoy," said Kendal. "When you fight from far away, OK, it's – *great fight*... But in Kobani, fighting in street, in house, when you enemy is in next building, it has been *so* bad. Two, three days you don't sleep, you don't know if it's friend or enemy coming, your mind is" – he rolled his hands, one over another – "you are tired... I hope you never have fight like that. Really, I hope."

Dilsoz grew up in Germany, and had left behind a normal European upbringing and a girlfriend three years previously to join the struggle. Before getting sent to Rojava and the YPG he had, like Kendal, spent time in the mountains. Also like Kendal, he was all about the cause; but where Kendal was a soldier first with a smart head on him and quite a persuasive voice, which might develop over time, Dilsoz was more the student revolutionary pursuing a high ideal. Kendal had been born to this, where Dilsoz had chosen it. In a straight fist-fight you wouldn't even ask.

Once I told Dilsoz the story of Zinar and the shower yard, just to hear what he'd say to Zinar's remark about German washrooms. He just gaped.

"That's *Germany!*" he gasped, after a moment. He gasped, gaped and guffawed a lot. Like Bagok, I couldn't see him getting properly mad about anything. I don't think he had fury in him.

"If we're still talking about where to actually *attack* then it's certainly not happening in the next few days," I said.

"But *heval* Şîyar (the *tabor* 2ic) says no, not cancelled."

"Well, delayed then."

Before burning rubber, Simko had joined us for a meal of barbecued chicken and ice-cream. "Must be *something* happening," Levi had said at the time. "They don't normally feed us like this *just 'cause...*"

We read signs in everything, like old women with coffee grounds.

***

Over the weeks, Levi had dropped the obnoxious badass persona more and more. You'd see him sat on a wall, happily dropping things into a drain below with one eye closed for aim and an innocent smile. One time I walked into the room to get something and heard him singing to himself, while getting dressed: "I like rolling up my socks, I like —"

Catching sight of me, he went onto reverse.

"No I don't, no I don't, no I don't…" (Hurriedly pulling his trouser cuffs down over his socks.)

That uniform with the strange hat had been given to him by his uncle (a Vietnam vet apparently) to wear here. To me, Levi seemed to have made the jump from childhood to young adulthood with such alarming suddenness he was still figuring out the controls. Whatever he was supposed to be, his best qualities for me were his sensitivity and natural funniness. This was how he represented his old man to us:

"I didn't leave part of my shin bone in some godforsaken third-world jungle to a buck-toothed gook with an AK so that you can commit three errors in a baseball game! Now shuddup and eat your broccoli!"

I was warming to the guy, and to the group in general, after so much time. But I was still concerned to keep my distance from people who were unlikely to fight. I wasn't here to socialise.

He got up from the table to go on *nobet*.

"Outta the way, pigeons!" he snarled, striding forward, M16 at the ready. A few desultory birds shuffled over a metre or so, then went back to the breadcrumbs scattered on the concrete.

The conversation drifted aimlessly around.

"It's your *calcified third eye*, dude," Bob was telling Harry. "You're not joining the dots, man." He shared a love of the weed with Jac, and had been kicked out of the marines after one year's service for pissing hot. It was the *system*, man. The Illuminati. Since his arrival with Levi, however, Bob's markedly different character had finally emerged into the daylight.

We'd done some close-quarter battle training, firstly as our own small group of westerners, and then together with the Kurds. The commander had seen us and decided the *hevals* needed some training too. Theirs was rough and ready, but "At least they had a plan," as George (one of three embedded journalists who'd recently joined us, and came to film the exercise), put it, forgiving the lack of rear cover, of all-round vision, of passage of comms – and the odd *heval* left out abandoned on the withdrawal.

The journalists, George, Mau and Mike, were all ex-army officers. I was pretty cold to them when they first arrived, telling them straight that I wanted nothing to do with their film. But after the first few days any barriers between us dissolved, particularly as George and Mike had been in two minds themselves over whether to film here or fight. It meant nothing that we carried weapons while they lugged cameras. We were one group.

I don't know if it was the presence of media that made Bob shape up, or just the reinvigorating effect of getting back into some training, but this was the time he started to come into his own, behaving like the disciplined infantryman he should have been, taking the lead on close-quarter battle drills and taking pride in it.

The team was starting to gel. It felt good. Would it ever get put to use?

The journos had been with us over a fortnight now, giving our meagre village existence of grime and thrift the feel of a reality show. We were hoping they'd provide our way into a fight. We'd grasp at any straw.

As wars go, this one was conspicuously unattended by media. In many other conflicts, the amount of press and press vehicles can be an active impediment. Here you bumped into the odd lone journo or camera team every few weeks, or months even.

"The commander is going to take you to see some fighting," Kendal told them last week. A vehicle had been booked to take them to the Serekaniye line.

"But we need to see *these* guys fight," they'd replied. *Everyone needs this fight…*

If it got us in the game, all well and good. We'd given them a show the other night, myself and a handful of other *biksî* gunners: firing into the village from every position along the berm, while another *tabor* joined in from a klick to our left and a small team went forward to put a few RPG rockets in. In was the sort of thing we did every now and then, but there'd been more of it since the cameras came. Whatever worked.

I got up and left as Mario, Jac and some of the Kurds were playing one of their favourite table games: how many flies you could flatten with a single blow of the hand. The metal table resounded annoyingly.

(*SLAM!*) "One, two, three… seven! Beat that!"

"You guys are sad. Also revolting."

***

It came through with typical abruptness. Kit on the truck, we're off to fight. Now. For real.

Months of static tension and resentment were shaken off in an instant like dust off a blanket as the war spirit cranked up. The scramble of bags, weapons, bodies and vehicles, the packing and checking and rechecking, the bouncing music and rows of dancers, the singing and ululating and excited chatter. We were energised and elated. We were off to war.

In Shengal you could die at literally any moment; you went to sleep knowing it. But the drip-drip effect of this stasis had probably been just as testing on us all. Short attacks had been ordered suddenly, without warning, and then pulled just as suddenly. Big operations had had a long lead-up, and had then just dissipated slowly; till it finally became obvious, with no official pronouncement, that they were dead in the water. It sapped your mental energy. It took an almost physical effort for the mind to repeatedly get into that state of readiness, chucking out everything unnecessary so you could focus only on what you needed to. Most people rarely if ever experience that change of states and for us it was a constant, ongoing fluctuation. I tried not to see it as debilitating; maybe it made you stronger.

Dilsoz was in raptures. "We will… go and *attack*. We will fight against Daesh. We will kill them!" he beamed, a wide smile with prominent, dazzling white buck-teeth.

"How do you feel?" asked Mau, like it wasn't glowing from every inch of his youthful, fragile features.

"Ahaa…" he gave a laugh, bright eyes flitting about in the camera's metaphorical headlights. "I'm nervous. But I feel good. I feel happy…

"I will *fight*."

11 CUTTING AROUND

The crowd parted like a sea for the Hilux, which drove into the middle of it, then round in a wide arc as though to display its live cargo to all and sundry.

A man was sitting hard up against the tailgate, bound hands dangling over the back, with a T-shirt or something similar wrapped right around his head.

People began to move in the truck's direction. This was a gathering place on the high open plains, surrounded by hills, where our numbers had swelled to the low hundreds – a day of meetings and reunions, as so often on Rojava's roads. Besides numerous YPG tabors, several families from the villages nearby had come out to greet us, bringing their kids.

"They got a Daesh prisoner," said someone.

"Kick his ass," jeered some American guy with *CHRIST IS RISEN* marked out in black electrical tape on his plate carrier.

I walked slowly towards the stationary truck, which the *hevals* were increasingly surrounding, with a sinking feeling in my stomach. I remembered Delal once admitting to me, in a rare moment, that *sometimes* the YPG treated prisoners in ways she didn't agree with.

He looked pretty young, from his physique and the glimpses of face I caught as the curious *hevals* lifted the cloth around it to peer underneath, one after another. They hurled questions at him in Kurdish and Arabic.

I saw Jac by the truck, laughing at a remark someone made, and shot him a dark look. I expected better, but at the end of the day how well did any of us really know each other? Still, I felt a jarring sense of the different instinctive responses people had to situations like this one. To me this was ugly, scary, wrong. I felt let down, alone.

They took the guy off the truck, though not roughly, and knelt him down on the grass. Berxwadan took charge of the impromptu interrogation, barking questions and barracking him.

When he cocked his rifle by the guy's head I stepped in. I didn't want to be the white guy telling everyone what to do, especially among so many strangers; but still.

"Berxwadan, *bess, khallas* (enough, stop)," I said. "He's a fucking prisoner, come on, knock it off."

Berxwadan stopped, holding his arms out. "I didn't touch him," he said.

"OK, OK," I said.

Berxwadan's brother was murdered by Daesh, I'd once been told. He (Berxwadan) was an impulsive character, a real heart-on-sleeve person at certain moments – like the time he smashed up that shotgun with Kendal in a moment of frustration. Other gestures were even more quaint: once I went to get my *biksî* and found he'd adorned it with the heads of several roses, which he'd been cutting and giving out to various people in the *tabor*. He had a real affection for us westerners, and I also knew him to be a bit of a showman, somewhat in the mould of Soran. To me, this hassling of the prisoner was more about playing to the crowd than anything else.

George turned up, camera rolling, and was sent packing pretty quickly.

Come on, I said to Berxwadan, put the guy back on the truck where you found him.

They kept him there, but gave him a cigarette, held it for him while he smoked it; others brought some water and lifted the bottle to his mouth.

An ugly scene. But no one was baying for blood.

A YPJ media girl I recognised with glasses and curly hair came and sat down next to the prisoner, grinning and posing for a photo with a broad smile. Others copied her, one after another. One of the young *hevals* gave him a playful slap, till I barked a reprimand.

Sorry mate, you'll just have to put up with it. I'd done all I felt I could. Most people were losing interest now anyway; the atmosphere was cooling.

I went and found Jac. I felt we had to talk about it. I wasn't his dad, but even so. He said yeah, it was a bit sick really. Just getting him to see that gave me some relief, made me appreciate my group more. None of them wanted to kick the guy's ass.

There was just no way to tell, right then, whether that dishevelled and subdued individual belonged to the enemy ranks or not. For me and many others, Daesh were known and thought of by their acts of infamy – just as they wanted to be. We dehumanised them, and it wasn't hard: they were the burners, mutilators and violators: terror incarnate. Daesh were bloody, obscene images on the net, they were black flags and masks. They were muzzle flashes in the night, sudden explosions out of nowhere. I found it hard to associate the enemy with human vulnerability; with a pathetic, lone figure like the one trussed up at our feet, at our mercy. We weren't up against individuals – Daesh was a mass, a phenomenon. And of course, that sort of mindset contains a whole knot of problems and perils…

***

A tank squeezed its way through the narrow streets and out into the open. It fired a shell into a small cluster of buildings, rocking back on its tracks with the recoil. A rocket came straight back from the main part of the village ahead by way of reply, bursting on the soil a few metres short of the tank. Incoming rounds started popping around our position. I switched focus back to the main village and fired controlled bursts at likely spots.

"The large grey building to our front will be known as Main Building," I said to Harry and Dilsoz. "The pylon directly ahead will be known as Large Pylon."

Serxabûn, our young commander, was on a berm 150 metres ahead, leading from the front. He disappeared through a bunker doorway at the berm's end, reappeared and sprinted back our way, shouting to us.

The call came through again: *gear up, we're off.* Just Dilsoz and me, to the berm up ahead. We dashed through ploughed earth and golden, waist-high corn as bullets cut the air all around us. Cover was scant between one village and the next. Mainly you just sprinted across bare open ground and tried not to think about it.

Dilsoz led, humping an ammo bag with 400 extra rounds for my gun. This work was tough for his slight physique. He tripped over and lay there kicking like a beetle on the ground, unable to turn over for all the metal on his back until I dragged him back up. We reached the berm and dived low as more accurate fire peppered low overhead. Straight above us, the midday sun was a coin melted smooth in a pool of dizzying white heat.

Moving again, to a berm further forward. Sweat and dirt covered me inside and out. Why did I think it was a good idea to bring a rifle *and* machine gun, plus the ammo for both? Eight full magazines in my webbing and a bagful of machine-gun belts on my back. Plus a spare barrel, plus grenades. Way too much heavy metal. Up ahead a little junior commander named Heqi raced between the corn stalks like a rat, with only a rifle, shouting at us to hurry up: *"Zu-zu-zu!"*

In a lull in the shooting on the next berm, I managed to grab half a cigarette before we were off again. Up and down, over the deep furrows, crashing through corn.

As we made it to the lone white house the *hevals* there yelled at us to get in cover, then ducked back in themselves as rounds whizzed through the yard.

I set up in a small outbuilding while the others took the main house. I tore a piece of mud brick out of the window to prop my gun onto the shelf. Dilsoz struggled to relay a confusing, conflicting barrage of directions from those in the main house. I did not envy him.

"Cûdî! Fire at big house roof!"

"Enemy right. At the bottom of the tower!"

"No, not the water tower! The electric tower." That Dilsoz was a godsend. Bloody tough job to do – I'd have had a far tougher time without him.

Half a klick out, in the enemy town, small figures and vehicles raced to and fro across our front, stopping, taking cover, firing our way.

OK, well, we're fighting, I thought, as I plugged away at them. *Took some getting here, but here we are…*

Two people appeared in front of a long building with pillars, running out of an entrance and to the right. I fired a burst and both went straight down – either into cover or shot. One got up and raced off after maybe half a minute; I never saw the other one again because I'd shifted focus elsewhere. Who knows? *Like a fly crawling across a screen, minuscule; barely consequential.* The remoteness was laced with a tinge of dread. I forced the thought onto myself: *it's a person, a human.*

The static exchange stretched for perhaps two hours, firing back and forth. Sheer concentration, intensely exacting. I'd sleep tonight.

Jets screamed in and bombs shook the town, a dull orange flash and a black cloud appearing instantly, as though stamped on the summer scene. A split second afterwards, another, followed by the double thunderclap. *Why aren't I feeling that, so close?* Two seconds later a blast of hot, dusty wind caught me full in the face, blowing me backwards. My gun clattered to the floor. Lucky I had no windows; those in the main house were shattered by the same blast.

A muffled *"Allah hu Akbar!"* rose from the new wreckage with a defiant burst of gunfire. The enemy lit tyres to smog the sky, black, poisonous gouts of burning rubber joining the gently drifting bomb-clouds of smoke and soil.

I craned to see the damage through the dissipating mist. Perhaps part of a roof was down, but it was too indistinct in the haze.

No enemy movement for five minutes, 10 minutes. No incoming fire. Quiet.

It was cool in the outbuilding. At my feet was a sackful of small fresh cucumbers and a red plastic tub full of water. I ate and drank greedily, sparking a cigarette and pulling so hard my cheeks touched inside.

The firefight seemed to have died down with the waning evening light. At dusk the commander appeared and we walked back along the track to our base village. When I told him what I'd been carrying, he burst out laughing. My back was in bits. From now on it was machine gun or rifle. Only a total bloody moron would try to take both.

CUTTING AROUND

***

Next day we entered the enemy village, group by group, just after breakfast. I gave support-fire for the first group, gun propped on a chicken-shack roof, as the *panza* raced forward in a cloud of dust.

Again, the fire directions got a little confused at times.

"One finger left of the middle telegraph pole, enemy."

I put a burst in where I thought they meant. As the *panza* emerged from the cloud and came shuttling back for us I saw with sudden dread I'd fired right near it.

A crazed scramble as it squealed to a halt, rear doors flung open. I piled in last, fighting to get my gun and ammo into the cramped, cluttered space. Last in, first out.

Bouncing over the ploughed rocky ground, stench of smoke and diesel stinging the nostrils, eyes glued to the thick, scratched glass porthole, a small circle of bright light in the dim interior. Trying to distinguish the pop and crack of gunfire from the rattle of tracks and ammo boxes. Gripping the handle above to stop my head being smashed against it. The interior of a *panza* is full of protruding metal fixtures and projections that can gouge lumps out of you if you're unlucky. Helmets are advised.

We lurched to a halt, thrown forwards.

"Right, come on! Let's go!" I shouted, as we crawled out of the rear hatch and dashed into the sun's glare, into a small yard, rounds zinging and cracking all over. *Where from?*

"Where's the enemy?" I shouted in the chaos of running and yelling.

A YPJ girl lay on the house porch, moaning and stretching out a hand – slick, bright blood on the tiles around her. *Give first aid (if they let me) or win the firefight?*

I went over but was sent packing. Machine gunner, do your own job.

We moved through the town. Slow progress, hot and tense. Checking buildings, alleys, yards, setting up and moving on. *Two human shapes glimpsed dead ahead. Friend or enemy? No one knows. Well, do we have* hevals *over there? No one knows. Just keep your eyes glued to the scenery. OK, moving again.*

Hey, heval – turn and face up that way, no one's covering the alley. Damn, I'm lying in chicken shit here.

We edged along. I covered the rear with the machine gun. Dilsoz was in front of me, tiptoeing forward, peering round corners, through windows, jerking back suddenly then relaxing again; jumping at his own shadow. An unhealthy-looking cow, tongue lolling out oddly, charged as we entered a barn and he fled like he'd seen the devil.

The tank joined us at the far edge of the village. It was all but cleared – just the school building to go. We took up positions in the small square and basically relaxed for an hour or so. I smoked one cigarette after another, tobacco fumes competing with the acrid stench of new sweat on old, steaming up from my damp clothes.

Up again, last haul. The tank fired two shells into the school. As we charged towards it I tried to caution the *hevals* about spacing, and sticking to the proven route. *Never mind…*

Village clear.

***

Dilsoz and I pulled first *nobet*, straight up on the school roof.

Inside the schoolyard's perimeter wall were colourful murals of kids and kids' things, all shot up and smeared over with black paint. In the school itself, Daesh writing and warry drawings covered the classroom blackboards.

"*Allah lul Allah*," read out Dilsoz.

"Hallelujah?"

"Yes, same thing," he said.

Up on the flat roof, the high sun was like a hairdryer held close to the skin. I cut a Daesh flag down from the pole and shoved it in my pocket. Two more were visible on the water towers of two larger towns out left. A third town, right and further away, was also Daesh.

"That's the hill," said Dilsoz. "The flat one we went up before."

"Where's Tal Nasir then?"

"Well, there's the Abdul Aziz mountains."

"But we're north of them. I thought we were supposed to be pushing north *to* them…?"

Trying to get your bearings was no easy task on this flat, bare landscape with its replicated features.

"What's the name of this village?" I asked. It'd be nice to know where we finally won a fight.

"I don't know. It's the one with a water tower, a school and a church," said Dilsoz. "And the school is yellow with two floors. It's the fucking same village wherever we go." He laughed. "I don't know which village I died in…"

Dilsoz went downstairs, out of the sun, for a rest. I could manage here by myself provided he didn't go more than one floor down. When he came back, perhaps an hour later, he told me a rumour was going around that the injured girl I'd seen was shot by friendly fire. *Biksî* fire. He didn't know any more than that. My thoughts immediately went back over the day's events. Where *exactly* was she shot? There'd been some confusion over target indications in the dust and chaos, *hevals* running all over the place. *What if it was my round, in that cloud?* I couldn't get the idea out of my head.

***

After my *nobet* I went to see the commander. No one else was going to bring it up, but I wasn't going to go round wondering for the rest of my life. I needed to go back and see if what I dreaded was possible. He stared me in the eye, his expression unreadable, and then called one of the young squad leaders to walk back with me.

We set off. "*Brindar, na boş, na boş…*" (Injury, no good…) the squad leader was saying. I had no idea if I was actually under suspicion now, or whether they were just humouring me in my anxiety.

We walked. My mouth was dry and my stomach clenched, a sharp taste of sweat on my upper lip. No one carried water bottles here; you just grabbed it where you found it. *Christ, for a sip of cold water.*

At the site we did a meticulous, forensic walk-through. "She was shot *here*," the squad leader indicated, gesturing to the corner of a building and the tiles below, where the streak of dragged, dried blood began. "You were covering from over there – ah, no, you were there *yesterday*, and *there* this morning…"

From the exact spot, there was a building blocking the view of my chicken-shack fire position. No way my bullet could have reached here from there.

We walked back again. I had no idea whether this meant anything to anyone but me. But at least now I knew. *Christ, the relief…*

***

Now there were rumoured sightings of five *panzas* in the (nearest) enemy town.

"So what's the plan?" asked Mau. "We need more people. Tanks."

What was the plan? Where was the design in all of this? Has there ever been a campaign with fewer certainties?

Everything shifted, drifted, morphed. Plans, equipment, names, facts, us. Days blurred into days, battles petered out before they'd begun, then suddenly kicked in again. Towns declared clear would be fought over for weeks afterwards, with no accounting for the contradiction. Rumours flourished. People said to be injured, killed, captured, turned up looking fine weeks later. Those who died did so in three or four different ways, depending on who told the story.

Yesterday's Chekdar was today's Soraw – you could honour a fallen *heval* by taking their name. Simiko was Genjo. Mansur was Argeş – then back to Mansur again, when it didn't catch on.

You never knew where you'd be tomorrow, and rarely the name of where you were now; friends in the next village might as well be on another continent and the wider picture of the war was a galactic dust cloud. In the progress through replicated features on a flat terrain, through unending routines and routine chaos, memories got tangled and geography confounded everyone, not just me.

When you loaded up on a truck it could be to battle or to lunch. Excess kit sent away never reappeared and you learned to do without. We rubbed and bumped along in a state of flux; you just had to stop reaching for shore, for certainties. Maybe it was a good thing.

The following morning, two of the Daesh flags had disappeared from the enemy towns.

"No, they're just hanging down against the pole," said CHRIST IS RISEN, squinting through binoculars. "You can't see 'em, but they're there."

But they weren't.

This was a worry. Those villages were earmarked for us to attack. That was *our* enemy.

Dilsoz had the news. His face was a picture of shock. "The commander is going crazy on the radio," he gasped. "Using *so* bad words! He is saying, we have been doing *nobet* for two months! And now that *other tabor* are going in our place and they are *attacking like sheep*!"

I stood and leaned over the roof wall to see the mid-ground. Eight YPG, not our group, were ambling up a track in a loose gaggle, rifles on shoulders. Stopping to meet and converse with another loose bunch in the middle of a field.

The next town had fallen without a fight.

By lunchtime there wasn't a Daesh flag in sight. A brown mood settled over the *tabor*. No Daesh? This was not looking good…

***

I'd just crawled into bed for an afternoon nap when Heqi came in and sent me out of the room. What now? The room was hurriedly cleared of all people and weapons. Heqi stood on the door looking grave.

"*Çîma* (why)?" I asked.

"Çiya." Heqi crossed his fists one over the other. *Heval Çiya's under arrest.*

"*Çîma?*"

"Rojbin." The name of the young girl who was shot yesterday. Çiya shot Rojbin?

Friendly fire. Only to be expected sometimes, I guessed. I had to feel for the guy. Consistent with YPG military democracy, the *hevals* had taken a vote in *tekmîl* and decided he must go to jail.

The room became a prison cell. Çiya was brought in and the door handles were tied from outside with a strip of cloth. One of the *hevals* was posted outside it. Inside, a 20-year-old's world was falling apart.

***

"So. Are you ready?" asked Mau.

"Yes, we are all the time ready…" laughed Dilsoz, as we prepared to set off again.

We drove in three parallel convoys to the foot of the mountains and lined out, stretching from horizon to horizon, more *tabors* and vehicles than I could count. Up there was the Daesh HQ for this region, our ultimate operational objective.

The heat-haze shimmered. Dilsoz squinted up at the ridge and the villages dotted about the mountainside below it. Occasionally the tiny glint of a car windscreen came trickling down the reddish, rocky surface like a single raindrop in the parched expanse.

"How many enemy are there now, do you think?" he said. His mouth hung slightly open, eyes widening in that typically guileless, almost credulous manner of his, as he turned away from the full glare of the sun to look at me. "I wonder – are they massacring people in those villages, right now?"

***

We made our way up the mountainside, slowly, over the following few days, encountering no resistance. That, for many people, was a problem.

"I know everybody is angry," said Mansur as we set off to clear yet another empty village, "but we have a job to do".

Finally, a couple of airstrikes put paid to the few remaining Daesh on the mountain top. Some were killed; most fled.

The area was taken, the operation over. People relaxed in various ways. A little line dance got going here and there. General Simko joined us for a barbecue. Someone found a can of yellow spray paint and in minutes half a village was graffed up with *APO* and *420*. But the celebrations rang hollow. Fighting had been very thin on the ground; a lot of people hadn't had the chance at all. Jac and Bob had acquitted themselves well in a firefight at a different village, where another young *heval*, Kocher, was shot in the leg. Mario and Mansur had run in under fire and carried the guy to safety.

A Hilux shuttled people to the top of the mountain, just for a look. I never bothered to go up there. There were enemy bodies littered around, and later Jac showed me the photos on his mobile. He'd clearly got over whatever squeamishness he'd had that night in the training academy.

After that, the *tabor* spirit became increasingly frayed at the edges. Arguments broke out. The usual chaotic polyphony when loading up for a short drive had ratcheted up to screaming, spite-filled pandemonium. Info, always scant, was deliberately withheld, our questions ignored.

Various *tabors* had converged here, at the operational end-point, bringing our group of westerners together with the others we'd met at the beginning. Only a handful had actually seen any combat. To say people felt unfulfilled would be accurate – *for them*. For those Kurds who'd missed out, the frustration and anguish went far deeper, to a level even we couldn't comprehend. Most of them had lost not only unnumbered comrades (to our three or four, perhaps) – but brothers, sisters, parents, and so on, either to Daesh or to the wider, bitter struggle for Kurdish freedom over the years. Retaking the territory was not enough.

"Even an injury would be better now," lamented Dilsoz one evening. "Over 50 friends that I know, they have fallen in the battle. And I can't... fight them back [avenge them]. It's a bad feeling."

"You're still young," I told him. "I've got a bad knee and I smoke far too many cigarettes."

***

It was a good time to go for some R & R at Qereçox, and have a rethink. I gave Dilsoz a pair of military binoculars that someone had passed on to me. Great knowing you, kid. See how long you can keep that flame of idealism alive.

When we got to Qereçox, Bob and Levi, Jac and some of the others decided to call it a day. Suddenly they were civilians again – in crumpled jeans, shirts and baseball caps that had been stuffed in bags for months – and off in a minibus.

Levi, who'd had the roughest time of all, had been in agony with a stomach bug for the past three days. Then just the night before, a dog had run off with one of his boots. We'd laughed, guiltily, at the sound of him chasing it through the hulu and yelling on the night wind.

When I gave him a goodbye hug I realised just how much I'd come to like the guy.

12 ROGUE MALE

Under the outside shelter by the cliff, I listened as an ex-Legion-naire vented his exasperation to some ten or so other westerners. I knew a couple of them; most were either from other *tabors*, or new arrivals in Rojava.

"They say, your conventional tactics have failed against Daesh, we must use guerrilla tactics... well firstly, our forces aren't even on the ground yet, secondly you're using our air support, and thirdly this is a conventional war. You're *learning* conventional tactics – just not very well, 'cause you won't fucking listen."

"Right. Guerrilla. Only with jets, tanks, Humvees and fucking heavy weapons," said another of the bunch.

"Bless their little hearts, they honestly believe this communism bullshit will work," said CHRIST IS RISEN.

"Communism. Right. Like how the kids are all in raggedy-ass shit and the generals are walking around in Jack Wolfskin. I mean the kids, they *are* retarded but at least they're *doing* something..." said another.

"Who decided these were the good guys anyway?"

"Well, there's bad and there's worse. ISIS or commies…"

"And they're saying the Christian militias are starting to fight the YPG now. So maybe go join them…"

"What's the downside to the Christian militias?"

"Well, apparently they're full of lawyers…"

"We're going to a roving *tabor*," said a Kiwi bloke I'd met once before at Tal Nasir. "*Tabori Soran.*"

"Soran? Is he a short, stout bloke with a beard? Fierce-looking?" I asked.

"Yeah, that's him."

Maybe it was time for a reunion. Was Qandil still with him? Bucky? Aras?

***

We fetched up at Tal Tamir, the cowshed.

Qandil had been wounded again – one to the arm, two to the chest, saved by the magazines in his webbing pouches – bringing the total to God knew what.

Bucky had filled out some since Shengal, and had a new walking stick.

They both greeted me like an old and valued friend, three kisses, left-right-left. From their frequent mention of Shengal while introducing me to the new faces, it looked like I had a bit of stock here based on our shared history. Well, anything that got me into battle…

There was another guy from the old days too – *heval* Bejna, the guy who'd got cold feet during that night outside at the first battle. Next day he'd been right as rain and said not a word about it.

Soran wasn't actually here. When the Kiwi had met him he was off on holiday, back to Iraq most likely, and the city he took his name from.

"We are a support group, clearing a corridor to Kobani." We sat in rows on the tarmac outside the accommodation room, while Bucky translated for a short, proud, bodybuilder type called Genjo, the commander in Soran's absence. "Please take care of your own discipline and be ready to move at short notice."

Night fell and a cheap and lurid sodium glare showered down from those battered and bent-over streetlamps that were still working.

Inside, the faces of the dead stared down from every wall, as in every YPG base across Rojava. Outside under the orange lamplight and the yellow light spilling out of the main room, blokes sat around on broken armchairs, on the tarmac and on the roof and bonnet of a Humvee, watching a small group dancing in a line by a stereo banging out a Kurdish dance track. Three or four other types of music played further off. Qandil trotted by on a white horse with a bridle fashioned from rope, turned, and headed back into the overgrown scrub. A liberated motorbike roared up and down through the dark.

This was a light-armoured *tabor* – a roving unit, following the fight, apparently; not rotating with others through months of static *nobet* and the odd whiff of action. We had three Humvees and another two in dock. Written in spot-weld on their turret plates were the names *Bagok* and *Kemal* (Kosta), as well as *Mîrza*, who'd also been killed somewhere around Tal Hamis. The names were each preceded by an *Ş.* for *Şehid*.

One evening as we lay around on cushions and rugs in the main room, smoking and listening to music, I asked Qandil to explain to me how Bagok had died. Alîn had tried, one night when we were on *nobet* together, but my Kurdish was too limited.

"We were in the *panza – not broken down*," said Qandil, through Bucky, "and we got out to fight. Bagok was right out in the open, firing at the enemy. I was behind a wall, shouting and shouting at him to get into cover. But he stayed where he was and got shot in the neck and chest; two shots."

***

It was a very different vibe here from the orthodox YPG *tabor*. For one thing, it was all-male; Soran's groups always were. ("Don't send me YPJ…" he would chuckle, head shaking. A man's man.) For another, there were more western volunteers here than in any other *tabor*: over 20 of us milling around. It looked like Soran had invited every westerner and his dog to join the unit on his way out. There was a certain air of delinquency. Men walked around with their shirts off, swore, lost tempers. The language barrier was often a blessing.

I asked a burly Yorkshireman named Baz what the meat hook dangling from his webbing was for.

"Dunno yet. Haven't decided. Last resort."

One day Harry and Kendal passed through. Things had soured further in their *tabor*; in-fighting had escalated and a young

Kurd named Rizgar had shot himself on a balcony in front of everyone after a *tekmîl* had gone against him. He'd smashed his jaw, but survived.

"I looked up and he just put the barrel under his chin and pulled the trigger. He looked a bit like Kendal — I thought it *was* him, at first," said Harry. "For a few seconds I felt like my stomach and heart were gripped in a vice. Then I looked round and Kendal was behind me."

Taken to the "injured house" near the Turkish border, Rizgar had used his injury to escape into Turkey. Another kid, Balhoz, had tried to copy him but failed — having shot himself in the leg instead, thwarting stage two of the plan.

I felt awkward seeing Kendal — something more than awkward, really. Things hadn't been going so well in the *tabor*, I explained; I didn't want to do another two or three months of *nobet*...

"Good — if you are happier here..." said Kendal, looking around.

"I just think there's more chance of fighting with these guys," I answered.

I realised I was looking down at my boots. But I didn't regret my choice, especially after what Harry had just told me. He (Harry) was on his way out, finally. Five months here had left him looking underweight and exhausted.

We languished there a few more days then assembled in the yard one morning. The vehicles had been parked in a line and we were being sorted into smaller groups.

I heard Qandil say my name and point to one of the Hummers. I was detailed to be the up-gunner (the machine gunner in the turret) in one.

Bejna was marching up and down, snapping at people and ordering them into line. A lad called Will turned up a bit late and Bejna gave him a proper shove towards one of the small groups. *Heval* spirit that was not. A mixed-race Texan of six-three, and as pliant as a rifle-cleaning rod, Will was not a person I'd shove lightly. He stumbled a single step and froze, shoulders hunching up, turning his head to Bejna with his jaw set and eyes narrowed. He gave him a long stare, then dropped it and came over to the Hummers with the slow stride of a cowboy.

Will was the machine gunner in another vehicle. Somehow we got switched, then switched again, in the mandatory shenanigans.

"Hey, man," I said. "I don't want to take anyone's place – if that's your spot, you're welcome to switch back. Or just swap the guns, whatever."

"Oh no man, that's cool," he said, placid as a mill pond.

Bejna seemed to want to pick a bone with me, too. Somehow, I don't know how, he managed to keep finding the safety off on my *biksî* and putting it right, with a dirty look to me. That *never* happened.

***

We hit the road, village to village, and took our shenanigans with us.

In a Christian village, some of the western boys broke into the church and drank the wine they found there. In another the

Kurds sprayed *Apo* and *YPG* all over the walls, straight after a *tekmîl* in which we'd all agreed to respect the place and leave things as we found them.

With Bucky and Keith – a thin, greying American in a loose position of leadership among the westerners – I explored a wrecked and abandoned town, shop after gutted shop along a deserted main road. We walked maybe two miles, attiring ourselves in blazers, "cunt-caps" (Keith's term) and other random bits of costume we found, and giving impromptu dance and street-theatre performances to passing YPG vehicles, and to the rest of the boys when we returned to base. Bucky found a new walking stick.

A village or so later, I sat behind the headmaster's desk in an abandoned school building identical to all the others. Will was lounging on an armchair, like a man who didn't know quite where to put all of his legs.

"Will," I said, rapping on the desk. "You've let the school down, you've let your parents down, but *most of all, Will*, you've let yourself down."

Familiarity fell across his face as he stared straight ahead at the wall, hunched, and replied, "How many times you gonna give me this speech, Mr Davison?"

Drake was an adjective I'd heard used to describe Will. Dry as a salt cracker.

In that same village we helped an old man, one of the few remaining inhabitants after the enemy had overrun and devastated the place, to move some furniture from his house onto a truck to be taken away for safekeeping. Looters were coming in from other areas, clearing out the abandoned houses with dubious papers of authority, taking advantage of the chaos. Some months before, the old man told us, Daesh had abducted some 280 women and girls from around this area.

"What – *Christians*?" asked someone.

"Well, they're probably Muslim now," replied Keith. Islamified through sexual violation, according to Daesh credo.

***

The larger part of the *tabor* headed off for Girespie, in the stretch of territory between the Kobani and Cizire cantons: part of the effort to link them. Our Hummer, with a smaller squad, set off for the Abdul Aziz mountains, where I'd fought my previous battle.

I gave the handle a turn, rotating the gun turret left, then right; gave the turret's tiny square windows a wipe, to no effect. Bulletproof glass so smashed up the dirt had seeped into the tiny glass fragments. Crammed into the Hummer below me were four westerners and two Kurds. Bejna was the leader of our squad.

***

"Woman in red dress, garden, left. Woman in blue dress, front. There's a lot of fucking civilians here, guys," I said. "Just –"

"– stand fast," finished Keith.

He parked up, jogged from our Hummer to the group of vehicles behind. Villagers were appearing in gardens and doorways: barefoot children and women in bright-coloured dresses, brilliant against the monotone surroundings of brown earthen dwellings and dry, brown-earth terrain, and the drab fatigues of the YPG troops striding from yard to yard, house to house through the village.

An old woman with tribal tattoos on her face came up to our Hummer and started railing at us in Arabic. A YPJ woman, also speaking Arabic, tried to placate her.

"Looks like the Sea Hag from Popeye," said Keith, climbing back into the driver's seat.

This village was pretty much cleared, he said. The next one almost certainly had enemy – and we were going in first.

It looked as though we were here to give Hummer support to a *salderî* (infantry) unit. Also along with us were a *panza*, an armoured bulldozer, a motorcycle scout and several Hiluxes, some with Dushkas mounted, others laden with *hevals*, inside and out. We drove in convoy for a while, then most of the troops and vehicles broke off and dispersed throughout the wider area, presumably to other locations.

Our enemy village loomed up in front of us; as we approached, I glued my eyes to it. Of the convoy there was now just the *panza* and one Hilux in sight. They parked up together on the road, about a klick away from the village. We rolled off the road into the scrub, around its left-hand side, and pulled up.

The *panza* fired its Dushka into the village's main cluster of buildings. Immediately, an old man appeared on the road, raising his arms and crying out as he strode towards the *panza*. The Hilux came tearing down to meet him. He stood there remonstrating with the driver and gesturing behind him, to where a group of civilians – mainly women and children – stood huddled together. Slowly they started moving towards him. A village elder looking after his people.

Come on, hurry up; get out of the way… I thought, and was immediately disgusted with myself. What did their homes, their lives matter to our war games? They walked away up the road in a group, leaving their village to our enemy, and us.

We rolled on forward. The spattering of enemy fire crackled somewhere to our left, well outside the village.

"Anyone see the enemy?" I shouted, down through the hatch. "Muzzle flashes?"

Worth asking. But if I couldn't see anything with my head out the turret, the others had Bob Hope from down in there. Their small square side windows weren't much better than mine: crazed with repeated battering from countless battles. *Maybe that berm up ahead, or that grey shack…* I scanned the scrolling terrain as we rolled on.

A cluster of figures appeared suddenly, dead ahead, as we rose up sharply over the undulating ground. I brought the gun into the aim, closing one eye. It took a second to register that they were standing up, motionless and pressed together. Combatants would move, spread out, get down. Drawing closer, I saw they were mostly wearing dresses. *Christ. Nearly raked fire across the lot of them…*

An itchy trigger, a momentary slip of judgement, could mean irreparable tragedy, monstrous crime. At times the *lack* of fear was the scariest thing – how remote and detached I could feel in the cold and necessary concentration of the moment. *What did I nearly do?*

The group made off the same way as the others, moving sadly into the barren beyond.

Incoming fire continued to wing around us, closer now, as the unseen enemy got our range. We had driven so far out by now it was just us and the enemy, wherever they were. Suddenly everyone was clamouring to direct me at once. Baz reckoned he'd seen the glint of a scope; the others, some movement.

"Stop saying, 'Over there'!" I yelled, exasperated.

"Patch of grey earth between the pylons!" shouted Keith.

"That's better!" I swung the gun round and rattled off a burst.

The gun jammed, almost immediately. It was clean as a whistle and a new one, but I'd never had a chance to test it.

"*Fuck!*"

As I fought to clear it the Hummer lurched violently forward, accelerating, slewing from side to side in a tight S-bend, throwing me left then right against the hard metal of the turret. Earth burst upwards in a V-shape 20 feet to our front, then again somewhere behind us.

"*RPG!*"

Keith jerked the wheel round again, braked, then floored it once more. We screeled around spaghetti style, speeding up as two more rockets exploded in the near ground. Great bit of evasive driving, *well done Keith…*

Baz passed me his RPK (a bigger Kalashnikov, basically, with bipod legs) and I gunned with that as we raced back out of range.

Now the fire was coming from the main village. We crawled forward and went static at a range of perhaps 700–800 metres. Someone fetched me the spare *biksî* from the boot; the guys opened the heavy armoured doors like wings and stood out behind them, peering over for better visibility.

We settled into a stand-off, picking targets as the dry Syrian headwind sang and scraped off the rough edges of the turret's welded, up-armoured plates, and the occasional round spanged off the Hummer's bodywork. A *chirrup!* as a low round came through the gap above the gun and split the air by my ear. As so often, it seemed like nothing at the time.

An up-armoured bulldozer pulled up just behind us and started heaping the soil into a berm. A Hilux appeared and eight *salderî* piled onto the berm, then jumped back in the Hilux after maybe ten minutes, and roared away.

Things played out much the same way as my previous fight: aircraft screamed over, dipping low and soaring at a sharp angle, and two monstrous trees of earth and smoke grew up in an instant – silent at first, then the double report and rush of hot air and dirt. The guys gave a loud cheer; a faint "*Allah hu Akbar*" came back from the village.

"Must've killed someone," said Keith.

Our vehicle was suffering. A tyre had been shot out, but kept going on its solid inner core. The wing mirror had also been shot off. According to Keith, we'd been hit ten times in total;

eight by enemy rounds and twice by Bandu, the other Kurd in our group, who'd taken the other *biksî*, cleared it, and then gone running around doing his own unilateral thing all this time. At one point he'd even taken cover under our Hummer. Keith had nearly killed him.

Absurd though it was, we had to leave the fight and make our slow and painful way onto the main road, where we flagged down a YPG low-loader and rode to a local garage.

Three hours later we returned to the battle site. The *salderî* had moved up and were lined along the enemy village's outer wall, about 25 of them now, some firing randomly into the village. A guy in a green bandana was holding his rifle up over a high wall, firing at the sky. At the last moment our newly repaired Hummer refused to start – an electrical fault, now.

Keith fought like hell with it, but to no joy, not even with three boisterous Kurds muscling in and taking over, randomly pushing, flicking and turning things, scratching their heads and arguing.

We piled into a waiting *panza* with a bunch of the *salderî* and raced around the left flank, debussing amid the smoking rubble of the airstrike and dashing for cover as rounds popped past us to our right – most, if not all, from our own side.

They worked through the village in no order at all, firing into windows, throwing grenades and kicking in doors. Bejna and I handrailed the town's left edge till we reached the far end, then worked into the buildings inside. Green bandana caught up behind us and, as rounds from our own *hevals* back at the perimeter wall cracked through and past us, started firing back in their direction.

Where the hell were the enemy? I was sure the *panza* took fire on the way in.

"What about over there?" I said to Bejna, pointing to a berm some way out. *No*, he said, *no problem*, and moved further into the village.

I decided to go check it out anyway. Halfway there, the dead ground beyond it grew visible. Immediately I saw five figures, armed, maybe 150–200 metres away, sauntering away in a line; leisurely, unhurried. They wore a mix of different military dress; a couple seemed to have their faces covered with balaclavas or something similar. They'd delayed us for a day and were falling back unscathed, leaving the YPG kids to run harum-scarum through the town.

They moved so nonchalantly that I could barely believe they were the same people we'd just been swapping fire with. Unsure, I shouted to them and fired a round over their heads. They broke into a run. If five enemy made it to the next village and got reinforced they'd probably regroup with others and stage a return attack. I started to chase them, then stopped and turned.

"*Penj durzmin* (five enemy)!" I shouted to Bejna, who was already sprinting out of the village behind me.

"Yes! Come on!" he yelled.

The *salderî hevals* watched us from their newly taken positions behind the village perimeter wall. The five enemy broke track and cut across the scrub towards a cluster of houses on my half-right, moving left-right across my front now. As I gained on them, the hindmost two, closest to me, went down into the long grass. The others kept running.

Fire zipped past me as I sprinted forwards, zigzagging left and right through the shining gold and dull-brown terrain towards an enemy I couldn't see. Twilight was coming on and I thought, *is this where I die, then?* I felt like I was on a souped-up airport travellator – carried relentlessly along, unable to stop or reverse.

A rocket flew over my right shoulder and crashed somewhere behind me. I took cover, prone at first, then, finding it impossible to see through the grass, up on one knee. The first three enemy were well ahead now, off to my right, fleeing without stopping or returning fire, with Bejna and Bandu behind them.

My two were using the dead ground well, popping up and down, running in short bursts and disappearing again, firing my way. I fired back on single shot from the knee at the rearmost figure, the closest to me at maybe 80 metres. My first fall of shot I didn't see. He took cover again as the other guy ran a short stretch.

My second shot raised a cloud some way past the guy. My third took him down. His screams reached my ears, stirring a faint, remote but tangible feeling of guilt and dread. The second guy started to run back to him, then the first yelled something and he turned back and carried on. Did the second guy abandon the first as he cried for help? Or did the fallen man tell him, *"No, keep going"*…?

My rifle wasn't firing now. I racked it, changed mag, shoved the first down the neck of my shirt (quicker than fiddling with webbing pouches), went through the drills. Round stuck in the barrel. Maybe I got dirt in it during the up-down.

A small, orange explosion blossomed up ahead, followed by a cloud of dirty smoke. The second of my two had blown himself up with a grenade.

"Cûdî! Come on!" screamed Bejna.

He and Bandu were well ahead of me now. My fight had slowed me down and I'd done twice as much distance on the pursuit curve while they'd headed straight right. Turning right I ran on, sprinting like hell, with no weapon to use. The *panza* came racing past us from behind, chugging out a cloud of white diesel smoke and battering away with its Dushka at the cluster of buildings that the remaining enemy had probably reached by now. The smoke was full of muzzle flash and tracer.

No weapon. I had to get into that cloud.

I reached it and found Bejna and Bandu blatting away from the knee at the houses. Gilo, a young American from our Hummer squad, appeared behind me, throwing himself down into prone.

"This fucker's jammed!" I said. "I've got no fucking weapon."

Gilo got his bayonet out and had a quick go at loosening the jammed round. "That guy's dead." He nodded towards the smoking pile of rags that had been my enemy number two. "Take his."

When I got to the burnt and butchered heap, in a shallow dip in dead ground, Bandu had beaten me to it. "Stay back," he warned, standing over the body. "*Mayn!*" And proceeded to strip it of loot.

Mayn (pronounced *mine*) was a general word for IEDs of various kinds. It seemed equally likely, however, that Bandu had meant 'mine' in the possessive sense. As in, *all this is mine...*

Reluctantly he threw me the weapon. The metal casing was red hot from the blast of the grenade, and the wooden stock had been blown off. I found it lying in the grass, jammed it back on and gave the weapon a test fire; two shots. It worked fine.

Just then the *panza* came chugging back towards us, scudding over the choppy terrain like a fast boat. We threw ourselves in the rear hatch and raced away. Inside, Bandu was admiring a watch he'd taken from the dead man.

When we got out it was dark. A huge moon hung low in the sky, the colour of old, rusty oil. We walked the rest of the way. I stopped to drink from a water tank, putting my mouth to a jet of sun-warmed water spouting from a new bullet hole. Bandu washed blood off his new watch.

"You just walked over a dead body there, Cûdî," said one of the others.

I kept walking as they stopped for photos.

Back at the village we met 20 or so Kurds, moving out the way we'd just come, passing us as a larger organised group.

"Good, Cûdî!" grinned one, to me.

Bejna was jubilant to the point of apoplexy, chanting slogans and cheering: only our *tabor* came out to chase the enemy, we were the best... I tuned him out.

Well, said the voice in my head. *Now you've shot someone. Another human being. Till now you could always say you never seriously hurt anyone. Now you can never say that again. So. How do you feel?*

"Ask me later," I told it.

You couldn't just let the enemy leave – that mistake had cost too many of us – and this wasn't an outdoor sport, even if it sometimes seemed like it. But I felt far from celebrating.

Thank God the guy was shooting at me.

***

The next morning we got into the Hummer, now working again, and drove on to another village already cleared and held by *hevals*. We got out for several hours of hanging around. Bandu, who somewhere along the line had decided he was in charge of us, fell to ordering people to clean weapons and do *nobet*. He contributed nothing himself.

It was, as usual, baking hot. Returning from a scout around for some bottled water, I was met by Baz.

"They've just shot a fucking *gundî* (villager)," he said, looking off into the distance. "Stupid cunts."

"Where?"

"He's over there, crawling on the ground. He were riding away and they shot him off his bike."

I scanned, couldn't see anyone.

"We were shouting don't shoot, he's a fucking villager. Bejna were like, '*Some-theeng! Some-theeng!* Shoot, shoot!'…"

"I can't see him. He's over there, is he?"

"Yeah, he's crawled into the grass."

"Right. Get me the fucking med pack."

"I don't know, mate, that area's not been cleared yet."

"Get me the med pack."

I went to Bejna. "We just shot a *gundî*?" I pointed in the direction Baz had shown me.

"Yes."

"I'm going to go and treat him."

"No no *no*…"

"Yes, I am."

"No, no problem Cûdî. Hummer coming. Ambulance. Wait."

"The guy could be bleeding to death while you wait."

We were fighting in Arab villages in this area, and the attitude was worrying. Baz brought me the med pack from the boot of the Hummer. I opened it, flicked through the contents, zipped it up. Bejna started shouting.

"Fuck him,' I said. "I'm going out there. Are you with me, guys?"

"Yes!" shouted Keith. The others agreed, if less fervently. No one relished the idea of strolling out into uncleared ground, but it was the right thing to do. I slung my rifle over my back and set off, carrying the med pack in my hands, the others following. The yelling behind me increased, Bejna screaming blue murder for me to get back and Bandu making up a chorus.

One of them fired a volley of rounds over my head as I walked on.

Baz turned and raised his weapon at the two of them as I stopped and yelled, "You better fucking cut that out NOW!"

Suddenly they were all yelling, threatening, shoving.

"Fucking sort it out, all of you," I said, stamping off. I looked back after 10 metres or so. Only Botan, a young American, was following me. The others were dealing with those two loose cannons.

I told Botan to stay 10 metres back from me. I had only the med pack in my hands. "I'm not holding my weapon because I don't want to scare them," I said. "You need to have eyes all round, 360, OK?"

"Gotcha." Botan had inherited the *CHRIST IS RISEN* body armour from Mr Kick-His-Ass, who'd gone home, but so far he seemed pretty OK.

We walked forward, not knowing if we'd get shot by Daesh in the front or by the YPG in the back. No one was visible on the empty plain ahead – just a couple of small, silent houses. I opened the med pack and took out some large, square white pads, holding them out and up as I walked.

Four Arab women, different generations of the same family, emerged from the nearest house, wailing, keening, arms raised. A short way off, a fallen motorbike lay on the ground.

"*Brindar*?" (Injured?) I shouted.

"*Aiwa!*" (Yes!) they cried.

"*Kudere*?" (Where?)

They pointed, talking through tears and sobs.

A man's voice, pained and angered, joined from the left. The guy, maybe my age, was lying on his front at the edge of some long grass the other side of a track.

Botan dropped to one knee and covered me as I went over.

He'd been shot in the backside; an awkward place to dress a wound, but the bleeding was ebbing. I taped one of the pads down over the small bullet hole, took the *keffi* from my head and tied it right round his waist. That would have to do till they got him to hospital.

As I helped him to his feet his face was a mixture of shock and ignominy. The oldest woman, a tiny grandmother with facial tattoos and tears streaming from both eyes, was asking me *why, why?* She wrung her hands, waved her arms, her heavily lined face contorted in anguish. Tears in my own eyes, I gestured back in the direction of the *hevals*, shrugged, raised my hands: *I'm sorry, I'm sorry…*

I held my hands out towards her and she took them in hers; all four hands stained with blood. Huddled together, the group walked painfully back to the house, the women supporting the man on all sides. At least he was able to walk.

On the way back I held my weapon properly in two hands, turning and checking.

It was Bandu who'd fired over my head, I found out when I got back. If the others hadn't got in the way I'd have killed him with my bare hands.

"Fuck your mother!" he spat as I lunged towards him, running behind two Kurds from another *tabor* and grabbing his rifle. *Sooner or later, matey…*

"Who shot the guy?" I asked.

Chekdar, a bull-necked, ex-Royal Green Jacket with cropped grey stubble and a colourful criminal past, raised his hand.

"Why did you fire?"

"Because I was told to," he said quietly, looking down. His remorse was genuine but not unalloyed – with it was an iron conviction that he'd followed orders as a soldier must.

"Guys, you've got to use your judgement a bit more out here. It's not a professional army. Chekdar, you're lucky you don't have the death of a civilian on your conscience today, mate. I don't know if that would bother you. Everyone's different."

Chekdar nodded quietly. "Yeah, it would. I was relieved when you said the wound wasn't too deep."

He hadn't asked, though. And that wasn't exactly what I'd said.

"Yeah, I know where you're coming from, Cûdî," said Baz. "But if you're told to shoot, you shoot. *We* don't know who the fuck's enemy, who's friendly, out here. It's down to the Kurds."

Well, this wasn't Harry, Levi and Jac I was with now. Nor Dilsoz and Kendal, nor Kosta, nor Delal.

Up at Qereçox, and in the lefty press, Rojava was building the polyethnic dream, the egalitarian utopia. But down here, far from the intelligentsia, the academics and spokespersons and air-conditioned offices and press conferences, it could seem a tenuous prospect.

Eventually another Hummer drove towards the house of the wounded man, picked him up and took him off – to hospital, we were told. We told Bejna we were going to go talk to the family. He voiced his permission to our backs.

The women, and a very old man, gave us tea in a cool, bare room. The sun through the window glinted dully off a smooth poured-concrete floor. In one corner was a cabinet stacked with dishes and glasses. Botan brought out a packet of orange drink crystals and mixed them with water brought by the old woman, handing some to the older of two boys, maybe five years old. He was on medication for some kind of mental disability, they said. The other kid was a toddler. I pulled out a multicolour biro and tore some paper from my notebook, scribbling on it on the bare concrete floor. I handed it to the kid, who had a go with it, then started to cry. We sat awkwardly on cushions, focusing on our tea.

I talked to them, haltingly, in beginner Kurdish and beginner Arabic.

"When will the YPG leave?" asked the old woman.

"After Daesh leave, YPG leave," I said, hoping it was true. We hadn't the numbers to reinforce and hold every village, even if we wanted to. There were hundreds like this.

"Keith, can you do me an exchange, US money for British?" I said, discreetly going through my neck-wallet. I stood up and placed a $100 note on a high shelf under a glass. The old man started to object but I cut him off rudely – it hadn't happened. When we left I picked up the motorbike and wheeled it to the house, grateful that they'd asked me to. "Thank God you are here," said the old woman. I've rarely felt lower.

Back at the Hummer, Bejna had come to a decision.

Kit on, he told us. We're going forward. Now. My webbing and rifle were by a wall where I'd left them. "Get it on," he said to me, picking it up.

"I've fucking told you, I'm done fighting with you people."

He insisted, I refused. It ran and ran.

Keith tried to reason. "Cûdî *will not fight*," he said to Bejna.

"Cûdî, come on mate," said Baz. "The younger lads need you."

I thought about it. Baz kept on and on at me. *Who'll take over on that machine gun if I give it up, and what'll happen next?*

"Right, OK then. Give it here. But after this operation, I'm done."

Bejna and Keith boarded the Hummer with a crew of just Kurdish fighters, bar Keith driving. They were off to get it repaired, said Bejna. They'd be back for us. As it pulled away, Bandu went sprinting after it, waving and shouting.

"He's *begging* to be let on that Hummer," laughed Baz, as it stopped. "He don't want to be left here wi' you, mate."

Bandu jumped onto the boot of the Hummer and off it sped.

I found an outside water tank, washed and drank from it. The water was close to scalding.

Baz was examining a new hunting knife, taken from the hand of a dead Daesh guy who was little more than a hand himself at the time. "Look," he said, holding up a photo of a severed, blackened arm on the ground. "Quite a bicep."

Maybe two hours later Keith returned – without Bejna, Bandu or the Hummer. The Hummer was at the garage and they were on their way to hospital.

In an attempt to make good on the morning's disaster, they'd raced off to another enemy village, with no plan, leaving us behind. Straight into enemy fire. Bandu was shot in the arm and Bejna had taken more than one to the body.

"Hate to say it, but, poetic justice," said Keith.

***

After five days stranded in the hulu, we got the Hummer repaired and made our way back to Tal Tamir, where things disintegrated further. An American threatened to pull the pin on a grenade when they wouldn't get him his bag out of storage. Kurds and westerners drew rifles on each other. It was bullshit.

"Cûdî, do you mind being my number two?" said Keith. "Just till normality is resumed?"

"Resumed?" I cackled.

But not many days later, the whole group of us renegade foreigners got driven out to a transit point near Tal Abyad and, over the following days, dispersed to different units. It wasn't working.

I was more than ready to kick the dirt off my boots and head home. So much for fighting the good fight. Mixed in with the swirl of negative emotions came that old familiar disappointment, one that smacked of inevitability. The altruistic crusade bumps up against reality and comes off worse once again.

Well, at least I could say I'd fought a bit by now. And as it turned out, fighting wasn't everything. Who knew?

I grabbed the first Hilux heading for Qereçox.

"Thanks for coming out with me that day," I said to Botan, before we parted. "Make sure you stay like that. Not everyone here's got a moral compass."

"Sure, man. I know."

"What was going through your mind at the time? Just out of interest."

"Aah – that you were fucking nuts?"

13 THE MOUNTAINS

Qereçox, up high. Windy Hill, as the westerners were starting to call it. The ground beyond the cliff edge was like a patchwork quilt, browns and yellows.

I made a report about the villager shooting. *Heval* Kamura, one of the commanders at Qereçox, assured me it would be taken seriously, and he meant it. He was generous, sympathetic and moral to a fault, and had been treated as a soft touch on occasion by unscrupulous westerners in the early days, who'd claimed money from the YPG for fictitious expenses. I suspected, however, that (notwithstanding Kamura's own integrity) the sealed, handwritten pages containing my report would just gather dust.

Will had come back here too, with Baz and a couple of the Americans. They'd had it with the shenanigans and were off to Iraq to try the Peshmerga.

Will was one of the best people there, in my estimation. I think that was why we struck up a friendship quickly. Those of us with military experience tended to divide people up into military and non-military types, but he made you think twice about that because although he was the latter he had something of the natural soldier about him: reliable and diligent on duty, proficient with his skills, quiet and sensible. Pity we hadn't been side by side in battle. I hoped he'd find the Pesh more to his liking.

***

Nothing happened too quickly at Qereçox. I was lounging around under the outside shelter, chatting to a Kurd called Roberto. If you found someone with great English you tended to make the most of it.

Yes, he said, there were many mistakes made. They were not professional soldiers, in the end. They grew up with weapons from the cradle, more or less, but they lacked proper training: medical training, tactical training.

"Well, there are people here who could provide that," I said, "but they won't *accept* our training. They make us do it *their* way all the time."

"Yes, because no one helped us before," he said.

This was the first time so many people from around the world had taken such an interest. The Kurdish people have been passed over throughout history, left to suffer in obscurity under the regimes of Iran, Turkey, Syria and Iraq, denied the wherewithal to build anything better for themselves: education, skills, resources, rights. Even forbidden to speak their own language. Through that lens, their insularity and pride were understandable, retrograde or otherwise. That young fighter who treats you like you know nothing, who laughs in your face when you try to talk pragmatism to him might not, in the end, know why he does it. It's an attitude inherited, a reflex of cultural defence and survival. That political superiority, that almost religious resistance to technical progress, may be veneers over something that runs much deeper than the here and now.

In the Arab towns we were taking, Kurds had been treated as second-class citizens for jobs, education, healthcare, a driving licence and untold other essentials, and that sort of a balance is never righted smoothly. In one sense the Daesh phenomenon was a gift.

We volunteers were the first generation of hopefully many more; bridges were being built right now, in spite of everything. It was uncharted. With the decline of the Daesh threat and of its promise of adventure and violent thrills, fewer volunteers would come, but hopefully more suitable ones.

It was always amazing what coming back to Qereçox did for your perspective; here, up high, the air was clear and you could almost see the curve of the world from horizon to horizon. So many people made up their minds to leave Rojava and then reversed their decision after a few days here, turned round and headed back in. It wasn't just because you found people like Kamura and Roberto, who understood a bit better what it was like for us – though that certainly helped. It wasn't even the most comfortable of places, though you could have a shower, and they might let those with phones have an hour of internet a day, and give you a run to the shop in town now and then. I didn't know what it was. Perhaps it was just getting out of the villages, where you could feel like you'd been buried. You remembered your sympathies and high ideals at Qereçox (if you had them). You remembered why you'd come.

A girl I vaguely recognised came down from the HQ and media office on the other hill.

"Do you know me?" she asked. "I made the video with you over there..." She pointed to the cliff where we made our statement. "With you, the Australian, and *şehid* Delal."

Delal?

There are some people you just never consider that it can happen to. It doesn't cross your mind. Delal was such an integral part of my picture. I couldn't imagine her lying still and empty-eyed in the dust somewhere.

But there it was, on a mobile phone with a scratched screen, a *şehid* photo. Star in the top left, head and shoulders, green background. The hint of a smile at the corners of her mouth. A trace of that spark in her eye, perhaps.

I turned away.

Killed in Siluk, trying to take a village.

Shot twice in the stomach.

Died the following day.

No, the same day, the media girl corrected.

Adjust. Get used to it. The war without Delal in it, out there somewhere. We had so much further to go. There were things I wanted to say. The timing was all wrong.

The news had taken a month to reach me, like light from a dead star.

I stared a long time at the rocks, where I'd made the video with her, Jac and Ronnie nearly half a year before. Where she gave me my name. Everything I'd done here since, and everything I had to say about it, was suddenly worthless.

And just as I was on the brink of leaving, once again, that old sense of desertion rose up in me.

Kamura said I could go to Shengal.

***

The kid was 11, and obviously westernised, with his well-fitting, ironed jeans, clean T-shirt and fluent, Antipodean English. Well bred, polite, and without the hard, angry eyes of the ragged kids of the refugee camps who went up against tanks and jeeps with fistfuls of stones. He'd grown up partly in Australia, and had only recently moved back to Palestine to be with other family. His father was still in Australia. Why hadn't he joined them?

"He is afraid," smiled the boy. His dad was a wanted man here.

He looked at home, sat on the sofa watching TV in the humble concrete surroundings with their bare trappings, though he was obviously used to better.

A look of recognition crossed his face as an English-speaking politician came on screen and said something about the Middle East situation. I asked him who it was.

"John Howard," he said. The Australian prime minister.

"So what do you want to be when you're older?" I asked.

He turned to me and smiled a full smile, with his large bright eyes and perfect teeth.

"A martyr," he said.

***

Shengal with its arched corridors, its crooked steps and rat-runs through mouseholes bashed through wall after wall; its obstacles, ramps, sniper screens, and short stretches where you sprinted, doubled over, from the view of the city.

What was I actually trying to return *to*? Was I looking for Kosta, Bagok, Cûdî Vietnam? Even Delal herself, in the most illogical way? Or just hoping that something of that group spirit, which I'd cared so little for, may have lingered in the yards and corridors, like dust in the air?

I only knew I'd been happiest there.

***

Tirej was a guerrilla. Not some YPG kid *calling* himself a guerrilla – joined up for a free pair of trainers and all the cigarettes he could smoke – but the real deal. He was only 23, but had paid his dues in the mountains. Not these, the Shengal mountains, nor the Abdul Aziz mountains, but *The Mountains.*

The Qandil mountains on the Iran-Iraq border are part of the Zagros mountain range controlled by Kurdish guerrilla forces. The terrain is harsh, extremely tough to reach, and hence routinely bombarded by Turkish and Iranian air power.

Among Kurdish fighters, the mention of The Mountains evoked powerful emotions, almost a sense of the mystical. They were the heartland of Kurdish resistance, of cultural survival and more: a geographical symbol of the sacred ideal.

We were on night *nobet*, in a small yard down the bottom end. We sat on two chairs facing one another, talking low, right by the rubble pile that had buried Bagok and Cûdî Vietnam the previous winter. Tirej had been there; he'd helped drag them out.

"I came and I saw feet and hands under the stones. And I think, they are *şehid* for sure. Then one hand moves, like this…"

I got up and went to look through our spy-hole, crawling through a cramped and cluttered space under some stairs to an opening in the wall. I looked out onto the track where the suicide vehicle had pulled up and detonated. Beyond, the scrubland sloped down to the city.

There was a strange, serene hush when it was like this. The moon and stars in the clear summer night sky, the crumbling arches, the stillness. I thought it must be a happy, peaceful place in normal times. By day this courtyard was shaded with a cool gloom. By night the whole place waited.

"We worry about him," said Tirej, as a tall, slightly gawky kid walked through the yard. A nice guy but clumsy, and none too bright. His deadpan stare and the set of his jaw had something of a Frankenstein look, and you could hear his heavy, clopping feet from a mile away.

"He's young," I said.

"Yes, he is young, but he is *new*: two, three months. Lot, lot of *hevals* be *şehid* in this time. Turkey TV make anti-propaganda – you know what it is? – it say, all die in maybe two years. True, but more, most in *this* time."

"When did you join?"

"At 17 years."

"Six years ago?"

"Yes. I lost all my friends from then. They kill my command-er, tie him to *panza* and drive through village."

"Do you ever see your family?"

"No, never. One time they came, but I didn't want to see them. Later I meet someone in city – and he tell me, my brother have child, my sister married, my uncle die…"

I said I always found it astonishing, the complete lack of fear shown by so many people. I'd never seen anything like it anywhere else.

"Yes, when first you come in the mountains, you are maybe afraid to die. But in our *ideology* we learn about what is life, what is death, and there is nothing to be fear. When we do attack every-body say, I want to be in first group. Sometimes even a person say, I will shoot myself if you do not let me in first group.

"If *bomba* comes to you, you lie on it. Sometimes our commander throw to us… fake *bomba*, and everyone –" He mimed a scrum of bodies, all pushing and fighting to be the one to throw themselves on the grenade.

"And Daesh *not* like this. Sometimes we find a dead Daesh, he has made his leg like this –" Tirej bent his leg double and mimed tying something around ankle and thigh, together – "to not run away. If someone of us do this we do not say he is *şehid*. This is *shame*."

I was no stranger to the torture of missing a battle, the agony of being spared. People threatened, even tried, to walk into battle against orders, refused to have injuries treated so as not to miss a precious chance to fight. Plenty of people in the YPG could be cavalier about death. But that paled in the shadow of The Mountains. This sounded almost like a drive *towards* it. A few stops further down the track that begins with making the choice to fight.

What Tirej was relating seemed pretty close to the apogee of the martyr faith. You see a tattered *şehid* poster on a pockmarked wall, and it can never mean the same thing to you as to them. You see tragic loss, youth cut down before ever even getting a handle on life. What a waste. They see a soul that's crossed over, come into its own.

And maybe that was part of it. Naturally these kids had less world experience, more intense emotions, were more susceptible to brainwashing. But that term itself needs scrutinising. If they *were* cannon fodder, exploited by older leaders, then how else should a culture in crisis react to the threat of impending genocide?

Unfathomably fearless freedom fighters, laying down their lives for future generations – or brainwashed young acolytes who'd had their self-preservation methodically drummed out of them? You can't have one side of a coin.

At any rate, this conversation cleared up any bafflement over the YPG's apparent fatalism and resistance to tactical orthodoxy, however well proven. *That's how our enemy fights*, they'd answer, if you tried to convince them. They looked to the mountain guerrilla, not the western soldier. The latter was anathema, and it ran deeper than pragmatics or politics. They'd dance their own way and no one else's, even if it killed them.

They had no helmets, no body armour, no heavily defended compound to fall back to. No helos on call, to come out and strafe the area flat when they ran into trouble. And no rigorous conditioning to fall back on. Where a soldier has programming under the skin (of which the scaled punishments mentioned earlier form an integral part), second nature overwriting his base instincts, a guerrilla has *ideology* for the same purpose. And through that lens, pure pragmatism may well diminish in importance if it comes at the expense of *heval* spirit. Not a few professional infantrymen from orthodox armies had come out here and gone home again, shaking their heads and thanking their lucky stars they survived to relate their unfathomable encounter.

All of which had me wondering why the YPG accepted US air power. Doubtless they'd prefer to win without, but we'd never have swept so decisively across the area and pushed Daesh back had they refused it. In this regard the YPG high command favoured pragmatism over their anti-capitalist/imperialist principles and their strongly fatalist and romantic outlook. One wondered why that same utilitarianism wasn't applied further down, by giving the *hevals* a better level of training and equipment, at least in first aid, if not security and tactics. *Happy to take a bullet, but not to learn first aid,* was how I'd started to describe it.

In a previous conversation, I'd talked Tirej through the British infantry's basic ambush procedure. Unusually for a Kurdish fighter he'd been enthralled, and had related it to the commander, excitedly, at the first opportunity – using a pencil and paper to show rendezvous points, cut-off groups, rear protection and so on. He'd absorbed every detail in one telling. But as he spoke the commander grimaced, shook his head slowly and leaned away from him. He said a few simple words, with an unmistakable note of sadness, and that seemed to close the subject.

"Is he not impressed?" I smiled, to Tirej.

"He *is*. But he says, this needs discipline."

"But they have good discipline in the mountains, surely?" I said.

"No," said Tirej. "It's a problem."

The thought occurred to me later: who needs discipline when your troops are queuing up to throw themselves on the grenade?

I could see both sides. More than see. The dichotomy struck a chord deep down. On one side the idealism of the guerrilla, on the other the soldier's pragmatism and discipline. Both called for self-sacrifice in very different ways.

Everywhere I'd been out here, people spoke of the mountains with a sense of reverence. I remembered Kendal's words: "Do you know, *heval* Baran, in the mountains, you just make a hole in the ground and it's water coming. I love the mountains. Everything is clean... Trees..."

I asked, "What will they do with my friend Delal's body? Take it to the mountains?"

"If family wants, we send to them. If not, we take to the mountains."

I preferred to think of her there.

THE MOUNTAINS

"Cûdî, why don't you come to the mountains? You like to walk, to shoot. You are soldier. You will like very much the mountains. It is better there."

I thought about it. But I'm no disciple.

***

I knew Shengal wouldn't be the same, and it wasn't. The right-hand corridor had been cleared and blocked off, made into a room with carpets tacked to the wall. It looked nice. The *nobet* house was finally sorted out, cleaned up; new partitions formed of rows and rows of sandbags, neatly stacked; the right-hand blast-hole was sealed up, professional. The yard was swept bare, the accommodation at the top was no longer reached by ramp but through a hole to the left, then up some steps.

The place *I* knew existed only in my mind, and in the mind of a very few others.

I wrote Kosta, Bagok and Mîrza's names on the walls. They'd fade in time, like everything, like the echoes of their voices I could hear now among those walls. But in the Shengal in my mind it was a freezing cold night. Soran was singing to the enemy up on the berm and Bucky was under the stairs in the *nobet* house, firing at nothing. Cûdî Vietnam was hunkered below an upstairs window, saying, *Watch your six*. Bagok was telling him a joke, and laughter echoed through the rooms and corridors. In the secret sniper spot, Kosta snapped on the safety of his M16, turned to me and said, *Did you just call me a cunt?*

I was the only westerner there now; the fact that I'd fought in Shengal all through February meant nothing. Fair enough. Tirej and I walked, talked, paid visits to other *hevals*. Did some target practice in the ruins of the suburbs. But whenever something happened, I was kept at the rear.

If I'd said yes to Tirej, I'd have had a role there for sure. That seemed to be the choice facing me in Shengal. Join The Mountains, or be part of the furniture. No one put it to me like that, because I didn't figure even that much in their day. I was welcome to stay, eat, chat over *çay* till kingdom come. Or I could go all in.

"What you gonna pay me?" I'd joked, when Tirej suggested it a second time, at a barbecue laid by some Peshmerga friends in the warren of tunnels up on the high ground.

"Well, we have no money, but I can offer you the love of the friends…"

"OK, *heval*." I clapped him firmly on the shoulder. "*Serkeftin* (best of luck)!" And I stalked off, as if towards the sunset. I turned and we both laughed. Looking back, it's a bittersweet joke.

I made my decision, and after that there was no point hanging around. I said my goodbyes to the family and left for Qereçox.

Speeding through the low, brooding mountains at night, past the lights from camp fires and bare-bulb shacks where refugees squatted on the earth, wondering how much more of this misery they'd have to endure, I knew I was nothing here: just a speck blowing through, not even forgotten because not even noticed.

***

I'd been out here six months now and my batteries were low. I'd come here to fight and I'd fought, for what it was worth. A six-month tour was respectable enough, I told myself. I needed to get away and take stock and I couldn't do it here, to-ing and fro-ing from Qereçox and the front line like a yo-yo.

Heavy with misgivings, I bit the bullet and told Kamura I wished to leave Rojava and the YPG, for now at least.

"OK, Cûdî…" he smiled.

I voiced a few wan sentiments about maybe coming back at some future point. He nodded, without saying anything.

"*Can* I come back?" I asked, unsure after the trouble with Bejna and the fuss I'd made.

"Yes."

Good to know. Even if I never intended to.

***

They smuggled me over the border in a Peshmerga uniform three sizes too small. Back to Sulaymaniyah and the safehouse where my suitcase was waiting. My own clothes, own laptop, phone, watch… such rediscovered treasures.

I flew to France, and holed up with the parents of an old friend in a tiny Breton village. It had everything I needed. Bars, shops, countryside to walk in. I'd reintroduce myself to city life tentatively, look up some friends in Paris, while I thought about my route back to the UK. Jac had been hassled by the British police and made to give over Facebook and email passwords. It'd be nice to avoid *that*, if possible.

I paid daily homage to a hotel bar, normally empty, the only place in the village with wifi apart from the local library. Set up nicely, with my laptop plugged in, a cold glass of French lager by my elbow and no plans for the day... Ironic, that a quiet village with unnumbered empty days stretching out before me was suddenly a prospect to relish.

Among the raft of emails in my inbox were several from the teachers' recruitment agency that had sent me to Saudi – quite predictably, asking where the hell I was. Needless to say, my bridges there were well and truly burnt, but still I felt I ought to email them with an apology – at some point.

I thought to reflect on the past six months at a distance. Put things in order in my mind. On Facebook I wrote,

> Starting to collate my notes from the last 6 months. Slow going reading my own scribble and it seems every other person I'm writing about has since been taken away from us. In my head they're walking and talking, arguing, watching for enemy and doing daily stuff, being everyday people. Just one of us, not icons on a wall like they are now.

Not long after – and completely unconnected to my post – a photo popped up on the feed. A *şehid* photo, yellow background (for a man), star in the top left corner. Çiya: the guy who'd accidently shot Rojbin on the operation to clear the Abdul Aziz mountains. Since then he'd returned to the front and been killed.

It was the first of a series of bombshells that came barrelling into my fragile oasis of European tranquillity and blew it to pieces.

Beritan and Tekoshin, two young YPJ women from the Tal Nasir group, were also dead. *Christ! What happened?* Tekoshin was a mischievous, hilarious girl, responsible for spraying half the 420s that Jac got credit for. She'd once tried to walk off with my kneepad and gone into a right strop when I demanded it back. I say girl because I'd put her at 19, tops. Now she was still, cold, her battle and her journey over.

The next day there was more news.

Kendal Kobani, dead. Just like that.

The next day it was Dilsoz. No… not *him*. Not him, please, Christ, no. Shouldn't have favourites, but please, not him…

There were seven deaths in total, from the Tal Nasir group.

Devrim, a rough-necked young scally who'd replaced Dilsoz as my assistant. Just the sort of tearaway, as Mau saw him, who'd be out twoccing cars if he hadn't found the YPG. After a bolshy start with me he'd been conscientious to a fault; every bit as eager as Dilsoz and physically better suited to humping those ammo bags around.

A lad called Havram, who no one had really got to know; he'd give you a shy smile in greeting and back away to busy himself with something. Who'd have known he was *Hazan Taybet*: undercover Special Forces?

That group (the Tal Nasir group) were getting rotated out of the action, back to *nobet* in some anonymous village somewhere.

That was what all the strife had been about. That was why I'd left. To chase the fight…

Well, fighting isn't everything.

Though the news had come piecemeal, in ones and twos, they had all died on the same night, bar Çiya. He'd not spent long in jail, as the *hevals* had collectively judged that he only deserved so much of the blame.

All I could get was, they'd fought and taken a village near Raqqa and been left to hold it by themselves. Daesh had counter-attacked in the night and overrun them.

My mind went back to those stir-crazy days at Tal Nasir. Days without end, on the brink of imploding through inaction. Then the bitterness at the end of the road at the Abdul Aziz mountains. Then, what they had most yearned for had arrived in the night, unannounced, and taken seven of them off. No considerate notice, no time to prepare, to say your goodbyes and get your affairs in order. Gone.

It didn't go in. Even Kosta and Bagok hadn't gone in. But at the same time it was becoming dreadfully familiar, this kind of news. It carried a tinge of inevitability, as though the jury was out on those you hadn't heard of for a while, until you heard of them again.

The network pages filled with tributes. I grabbed photos off them, anxious to regain a fragment of what was now lost.

"*I don't know what village I died in,*" Dilsoz had said, when we fought together in the shadow of the Abdul Aziz mountains.

I asked, but no one else seemed to either.

He had a future! So did Kendal. They all did.

I looked at the note Kendal wrote, the night we waited up for a cancelled attack:

Cûdî is ferind from Beritanya and he helping us whis faithing agist Daes

Later I drew a cartoon of a YPJ warrior for him, which he carried around in his pocket. I gave him no end of grief for smashing up that shotgun.

He didn't have Dilsoz's advantages, but still, he might have gone far, I thought, in spite of that. He had that focused intelligence and inner drive. Maybe that was why he had such a bond with Harry.

A day or two before, Harry had actually said to me, in a Facebook chat, that he was worried about him.

I'd replied, "I keep thinking about the young fighters I know, going over them in my head, thinking shit, I hope he/she doesn't die next. And then they do."

Maybe he'd find his resting place in the mountains too. *You just make a hole in the ground… Everything is clean… Trees…*

Dilsoz had had a European upbringing and saw things more from the outside, which I'd tentatively encouraged. Frankly I'd hoped he'd think through his options eventually, and consider getting out. When time stops like that it's totally arbitrary. I was old and I'd wasted plenty of mine. It was unfair.

And where was I? Out of it. Again. I felt sick with guilt.

I don't know what drew me into the village's ancient stone church. I'm not religious in the least; not even secretly, in times of misery or fear. I was the only person in there, surrounded by gloom and stained glass. Thin candles stood beside a coin box near the altar. I paid my penny, lit one and staggered out, drenched in tears, hoping no one saw me.

I couldn't rest. I couldn't allow myself to. Just grieving for my friends in the normal way felt like an easy get-out. There was only one place I could justifiably *be*, right now, and it wasn't France. A less than rational decision, maybe. But it was go back or go nuts.

I moped and deliberated for a few days, got drunk for a few more, then started pricing up flights to Sulaymaniyah. It wouldn't bring them back, but I just didn't know what else to do.

In a normal army, you all go out on tour and come back together. The people I knew were still fighting out there. It got under the skin. I couldn't just switch off and say OK, see you later. I'd do it someday, but not yet.

***

Getting in and out is always touch-and-go. Some people get arrested, detained for months; others just get refused entry and turned around. Going through customs at Sulaymaniyah, my mouth was dry. *What if the gate was closed to me forever?* When I got through, I was walking on air.

Less than a month after leaving Rojava – for good, most likely – I was back at Qereçox.

"Cûdî... Why you go, and – *come back*?" said *heval* Kamura. With his face darkened by the high sun dazzling behind him, I could only just make out his kindly, quizzical expression. He had a patch over one eye and was due an operation on it soon.

"Because seven of my friends were killed," I answered, gritting my teeth against tears and a painful lump in my throat. Seven, and then some...

The answer was as neat, pat and simple as the one I gave Delal at the river that time. *Why do you come here?* And as gapingly incomplete.

So what? My return wouldn't bring them back.

So – *why?*

There was a sense of obligation, certainly. The shame of desertion, which put an unbearable spin on an already devastating loss. The high and noble wish to *honour their memory*. To "finish what I'd started", however such a notion could be cashed out in real terms and real actions.

Fine. But there was a deeper draw.

The misgivings I had, caused by the experiences of my last operation, hadn't gone away. They were constantly at my shoulder. Yet still, I *needed to be here.*

OK, deep breath: *the wish to revenge myself on the enemy, and the wish to kill.* That took some admitting, but eventually it was too stark not to see. I hadn't felt it before, when Kosta and Bagok were killed. Yes, I'd been devastated, but they'd signed up and accepted the risks. I didn't feel they'd been *murdered*. Once I'd even argued to Delal that killing wasn't a goal in itself. At the time I'd felt the point needed making. Now, that just smacked of so much empty prating. Now I got it.

The risks of injury, trauma and death are factored in, if you've got any sense. But these roads can take you where you don't expect to go. Tracks get tangled. Your thread leading back may snap somewhere along the way, and you may push on blindly till you finally find the monster in the maze, and by then it might be you. Never saw that one coming. Live and learn.

And even *that* wasn't the core of it.

Because despite this newer, darker compulsion, paradoxically, my desperation to fight for fighting's sake had abated. I mean, I still *wanted* to. But now I knew more about the fighting here, missing out would never be such a torment again. I could live with it. I'd even told Kamura I didn't care where he sent me; I was happy enough just to be back here. I felt closer to my lost friends already.

Which was closer to... *what*?

An irresistible pull, which remains nameless for so long, for so many.

I may have declined my invitation to the inner room last time I was in Shengal. But I wasn't immune, given the right pressures.

The Kurds, and others, celebrate the martyr. For uninitiates and outsiders there is no such varnishing. The dead are just the other side of a short wall, beckoning, *come join us*. But of course Delal and Kosta and Dilsoz would want you to live. It's the part of yourself that seeks oblivion; maybe there's a seed of that in your coming here in the first place.

"Seven of my friends were killed," I repeated.

Kamura looked in my eyes and nodded. He understood perfectly, without elaboration. How could he not?

***

I collected my weapons there and on my way to the front, pitched up at one of several typically ugly concrete shacks scattered around the stretches of anonymous, bleak and barren fields; craggy, poor soil full of litter and the furrows of heavy vehicles. Lines were being redrawn, lots of ground had been taken and five or six *tabors'* worth of assorted war vehicles roved about the area day and night, churning up the ground.

I bumped into little Merdem, from the Tal Nasir group. I'd never paid much attention to him before: just a kid, a bit of a pest, too young to be there. He and several others had stayed at Tal Nasir when the majority of us pulled out for Abdul Aziz. Delal's unit had replaced us there and he'd joined them.

In his face now was a sadness that mirrored mine, for all our various differences. We stacked a few broken blocks on the concrete porch and sat down together.

"She was killed at Siluk, right?" I asked him, in my broken Kurdish.

"No, not Siluk," he corrected me; it was a town called Mabrukka.

That night, she'd gone with a small group to check out a house and had surprised some sleeping Daesh. They'd killed them and taken the house, and then more Daesh, based nearby, had counterattacked in the night, surrounding them completely. Rounding the corner of a building, she was brought down by a shot in the leg, then hit again on the ground.

As the overcast sky darkened through evening, we were joined by other, half-familiar faces. People I'd half-known in my short time hopping from one *tabor* to another, trying to chase the fight. After customary warm greetings and a few more words about our departed friends, we just sat around, saying not much, while Merdem's last few words about Delal rang afresh every so often in my ears. *She said you and Jac were good.* I could almost wish he hadn't told me.

I found I was happy to be with people who understood. I'd returned here for that as much as anything, I suppose. For the first time I felt I got why the Kurds were often so content to just *be* in one another's company, sharing the silence. Sometimes it was enough.

14 AL-HAWL

The following two and a half months were a major lull for the YPG everywhere. I spent them more or less static at the cowshed at Tal Tamir, while the YPG prepared for a major offensive. Jac was in Iraq, in the Peshmerga with Baz and Will.

It was Tal Nasir syndrome again: *we go in 10–15 days…* and the days stretched on.

There was another reminder from the Tal Nasir days too: Mansur was here, kicking around in limbo like me. The *tabor* had been disbanded and dispersed, for the sake of everyone's morale following the tragedy.

They'd gone way out of Cizire canton towards Raqqa, the de facto capital of Daesh in Syria. They'd taken a village and had been left to hold it themselves, undermanned, unsupported. As with Delal's group, Daesh had counterattacked in the night, from three sides at once.

"Devrim came running to me, crying, saying, 'I am shot in the hand.' I said, 'Go around, behind this building.'" Mansur spoke in a monotone as he pointed at what he was seeing in his mind's eye. "Then more Daesh came from that side and… they killed him."

Mansur was shot in the stomach. It was believed that Kendal, stuck out on a limb with the machine gun, injured, and seeing he was surrounded, had pulled the pin on a grenade and gone up with it, taking some of the enemy with him. Mansur didn't know how the others had died in that night of bloody chaos.

We sat outside, on old half-demolished armchairs on the debris-covered concrete, smoking and whiling away time in the evening twilight. We'd had many bitter moments between us at Tal Nasir, but post-mortems for that were unnecessary. That was one thing to the Kurds' credit – they didn't go in for grudges. Yes, they drove you up the wall and yes, it would be your fault by default. But all they wanted was for the bad vibes to go away and everyone to be friends again.

"I think the tea is ready," said Mansur, getting up.

We passed whole days and nights like this: chatting, wandering round the compound. Endless movies of Shaban, Turkey's legendary comic actor, on the battered old TV. "Reminiscing" about the Tal Nasir days. Not really the word, but you had to see the glass as half full.

The characters we knew. Levi and his moods, and movie recitals. Zinar and his inexplicable antics. I couldn't help but bring up *that biksî gun* of his.

"Yeah, the *biksî* was *terrible*," laughed Mansur.

"But why was it only me saying so?" I asked. "Why didn't you agree with me?" Half-amused, I felt that old exasperation rise up even now. He'd always stayed well out of my and Zinar's arguments. But I knew the answer already. He'd tried to explain, in those fraught days, what mattered most to the *hevals*.

A pause. We each lit another cigarette. Into the sultry summer air, thick with the smell of the wild vegetation overtaking the place, seeped the night's inky blackness. The compound's street-lamps flickered on, humming audibly. Sticking to the shadows, the stray white horse came to examine a pile of half-decayed tomatoes thrown out of the kitchen block.

"I want to die... like a *soldier*," Mansur sighed, suddenly. He gave a shrug, raising his hands and letting them fall again. His days of front-line service were over, for the time being at least.

I said, "Look, Mansur. We haven't always agreed on everything, you and me. But you're an intelligent adult. You're not some village kid, all *Apo–Apo–Apo–*" I waved a hand in mock fervour. "You can help the cause in different ways. There's no reason to stay in a party that's going to get you killed."

See sense, mate. You've fought a few battles, got your trophy wound and a few good stories. Now quit while you're ahead.

***

Tal Tamir. How I grew to know – and loathe – every inch of that place. Wandering the vast concrete sheds, the patches of overgrown scrub, day after day. The insane heat, the different species of biting insects that would torment you in shifts, one species handing over to another throughout the day and night. In your face, in your clothes, in your bedding. That poor horse, driven mad through loneliness and abuse, who'd appear by night like a ghost in the flickering lights, momentarily still, before skittering off into the darkness at your slightest movement.

Conscience had compelled me to return here. It was all I could do. Friends had tried to talk me out of it but it was a feeling deeper than I could explain. But I wasn't immune to second thoughts in these long, hot, empty days.

I mooched around. I climbed on the roofs. Dug a curious object out of the ground with the toe of a boot and examined it, before throwing it into the scrub. Put the odd window through. It reminded me of my childhood.

Like most kids in the 80s, we lived our lives outdoors, and the truly bright moments that stand out from my childhood are because of that. As long as I wasn't grounded I was generally happy, as I remember. Lost hours spent wandering along disused railway tracks, following a stream into the Park Hall hills with our shoes hung round our necks, breaking into the derelict, boarded-up buildings that made up half the city. Smashing the windows. Climbing in the quarry that was out of bounds after the police showed local schools a video of a boy being rescued from the quicksand there.

While half of Stoke-on-Trent was derelict, the other half was being built. Construction sites, scrapyards and wood yards, devoid of any security, made other, fantastic playgrounds.

One Saturday, me and Dave Williams spent a whole afternoon lobbing bricks, rocks and jagged chunks of cast-iron drainpipe at a cracked wall on a scrap of waste ground, till the whole side of the building came down and Dave had to dive for his life. Another time we found an assortment of capsules in an old doctor's surgery and filled them with ball-bearings to turn them into magic jumping beans. Taking them to school was a mistake; it prompted my first visit from the police.

For all its deprivation, the so-called urban decay had a charm, a touch of the exotic. I have a vivid snapshot in my mind's eye of a Victorian terraced street, red-brick houses a thousand hues and shades of baked local clay, with nettles and dock leaves, thistles and dandelions shooting out between the crumbling bricks and broken paving slabs, translucent leaves lit up by the sun, steaming in the damp summer heat after the rain. The leaves in the trees lining the road glow with same luminous greens and yellows. Two little Pakistani girls in bright satin dresses of crimson, green and gold, wait to cross the road, chattering and holding hands.

The disused factories were ancient ruins of irresistible mystery, just crying out to be explored. We dug up chunks of opalescent, translucent glaze from around the pottery factories and speculated on their likely worth.

It was the time when I was happiest, and felt I most belonged – because I wanted to, I suppose. But we moved every few years, so I became an outsider everywhere. Years later I revisited the place and got lost; buildings had been torn down, roads altered, spaces built on. The routes I knew, through back alleys, abandoned yards and scraps of wasteground, existed nowhere except in my memory, fixed there the way they'd been. Such mental snapshots would mean little to anyone truly local, who lived through the area's continual transformation, precisely because the town was perpetually both a work in progress and an abandoned lot.

Like Shengal, maybe: another place of the mind.

***

For several weeks I latched onto the sabotage unit stationed over the back of the base. At least they were doing some rough-and-ready fighting drills, in and around the empty blocks and sheds. A couple of times we went to pull IEDs out of the ground in the Abdul Aziz mountains, after the *tabors* stationed there repelled a renewed attack. Picked over the bomb-craters and the rubble of homes, strewn with the odd enemy corpse here and there. One was laid out on the ridge of a crater, a hand over his breast, the other thrown out wide; head tilted back. He resembled some kind of figure from a religious tableau.

"Look Cûdî – Daesh!" said Demhat, one of the youngest Kurds in sabotage, walking over to the body and spitting on it.

Other than that it was days and days on end of nothing but *nobet*. I hung around most of the time with Joe Akerman, a British guy who'd crossed from Soran's *tabor* to sabotage some weeks earlier, and had been injured by an IED that killed a quiet, self-effacing young Australian called Reece while I was navel-gazing in Shengal. Every now and then Joe chucked me little bits of cash for the internet cafe in town and for credit on the phone someone had given me. He kept me going. The bugs drove him so far up the wall that he started walking round like a

Polar explorer, clad from head to toe in scarf, gloves and coat in the crippling heat, hood up and goggles on, grousing and cursing. Once he spent half a day attempting to construct a fly swat from a strip of plastic and a piece of perforated cardboard. I kept him going, in turn, by laughing at his misery.

I'd have done better staying in France and recuperating a bit more. But you can never know, and anyway, I couldn't have done it.

***

In late October, just as the horrible heat was losing its edge, the YPG rolled out on the next offensive, to clear the area right up to the Iraqi border and take the strategic city of al-Hawl.

I was back with Soran's *tabor*. I had been feeling at a bit of a loose end, not really gelling with the sabotage lads, when I bumped into him passing through Tal Tamir.

After fond greetings, he asked what I was doing. *Not much…*

"Do you want to come with me…?"

I was hesitant after the debacle last time I was in his *tabor* – but of course, he hadn't been around then. When he was, it could be the best of groups.

Of the familiar faces, besides Soran himself, there were only Aras and Aso, the tall lad who could never take anything seriously and always seemed to be getting the sharp end of some command-er's tongue. Soran's maverick approach suited him, I guessed. I liked Aso: an inveterate bullshitter, unreliable, but he could be the life and soul. Now, he kept us entertained for hours as we idled away our time in another tumbledown room, bongo-drumming away on the underside of a cooking pot and singing freestyle verses, dancing and joking. A mind (not the sharpest one, granted) that didn't understand why we couldn't just laugh and dance and sing the whole time and forget all the rest.

Bucky was still floating around out there, probably making a report at an HQ somewhere (one of his favourite pastimes). Qandil was out: gone clear. As Keith told it when I last saw him, he'd flipped out on a mission near the Turkish border. They'd taken incoming fire, and Qandil was convinced it was an inside job: that Genjo was setting them up to be killed by Turkey. Ranting and yelling, he started hurling accusations and spreading suspicion throughout the *tabor*. Then he and a couple of others deserted a few nights later.

I wasn't sorry; hopefully it meant he'd live. Qandil, who'd been in three armies and wounded more times than anyone had kept count of. Presumably he'd had enough.

Aras, on his way to becoming a legend, was still around, still irrepressible with his long, heroic songs. This was taking its toll on him, too. Unlike Bucky he actually needed a walking stick, and looked constantly tired.

Apart from those two, my *hevals* were a new set.

It was easy to like the Iraqi Kurds that Soran favoured; there was less of the Apo chat with them – they had their own lives, girlfriends back home, phones and so on. The Syrian or Turkish Kurds in more regular *tabors* could be a bit one-dimensional at times, with their one-track partybabble.

We pottered around a few villages before hitting the warpath proper. I managed to snatch a few days at Qereçox. Mansur was there now, in a new position in the YPG media section. He looked as happy as I'd ever seen him.

At Qereçox was Alîn, too – also, now, working in the media section.

We hugged – a long, tight embrace, our bodies moulding into one another's in a way that was borderline illegal in the YPG. Paradoxically, the intelligentsia at the HQ bases seemed more relaxed about that kind of thing than the lower commanders in the villages. I'd come to the HQ and media block with three other guys to collect a Hilux to take us to Derik town for internet and shopping. When it arrived, I told the boys to go on without me; I was going to hang out here instead.

We went into an empty office, just the two of us. I sat on one sofa, she on the other, facing me, feet up, legs crossed, knees bouncing slightly as she talked, animated and excited. My Kurdish had improved to the point where we could actually have a basic, broken conversation.

"I heard you had left, Cûdî. I was so sad…"

"Ah. *Sorry*. I left, but then I came back."

So much catching up.

"What about the older guy, the *biksî* gunner, who gave me the pen?"

"Oh, yes. Hugir. He's in Kobani now."

Absent friends, alive and dead. The old days. Bagok. Back then, she'd tried to explain to me the sequence of events, but my language wasn't adequate. Maybe I could understand her account a bit better now.

"We were in the *panza*, still, after the rocket hit us…" she recounted.

"So if Bagok hadn't got out of the *panza* that night to cover you…"

"We would all have become *şehids*…"

What happened to that little girl in the *tabor*? I asked her. Very young – "*Kem şişko?*" (A little bit fat?) I said, suddenly thinking of the girl in Delal's group who'd come over to chaperone us that day. I hadn't thought of her for a while, not until now.

Her name was Sosin, which I'd changed to Susan; she was irrepressibly happy no matter what was going on and how miserable everyone else got. She was proud of speaking both Kurdish and Arabic, and once squealed in excitement when I asked her a question in basic Arabic. One afternoon, I'd lugged some sandbags up to the roof for her and her schoolgirl mates. "*Heval Cûdî boş e*," (Cûdî is good,) she'd said to one of her friends; it was so cute, the way they'd vigorously agreed on the judgement. If you were down, she'd try in her child's way to fix it. Once, when I went into a glowering sulk over a missing knife, she fished out a knife of her own and gave it to me with a smile. It was a useless little keyring trinket, something that I would keep forever.

Yes, Alîn nodded. Sosin was *şehid ketin*: martyred.

It was a pure, tragic accident, less than a month after I left that group. Her rifle had caught on the ring-pull of a grenade in her webbing, apparently, and pulled out the pin. It had exploded and killed her instantly.

I thought back to one cold, wet afternoon near Tal Hamis. Susan had just come up to the flat roof to take over from me on *nobet* when the lunchtime rain built to a drilling, drumming crescendo. She'd have stood there the whole shift, unmoving and uncomplaining, as her maroon woolly coat soaked it up like a sponge. She protested as I took off my Gore-Tex jacket, till I made her understand that I was going straight inside. I helped her on with it, fastening it up like I was dressing a child for school, but didn't bother getting the detachable hood from the jacket pocket for her because I'd have been drenched myself by the time I'd attached it. Her headscarf and thick hair would have to do. For some reason that troubled me every time I remembered it, my not going that last step. I could see her now, hands in pockets, rifle on one shoulder, smiling through the grisly weather as I went back down the steps like she'd just won a prize. She was 16 years old.

What on earth was a kid that age doing in such a place, walking around with grenades to begin with? But I'd addressed that kind of judgement already.

"Do you see?" said Alîn, pointing to a framed picture on a shelf. Delal. I touched the frame with my hand.

Alîn showed me on a laptop a bunch of photos of herself in the mountains with her tribe, long lines of fighters in traditional dress marching through the lush greenery, by waterfalls, lakes, caves, campfires. So happy, so at home. I had to sit on the sofa next to her to see the screen. Our legs brushed together. I allowed my hand to pass lightly through her hair. She smiled shyly and leaned in towards me a fraction. As those huge dark eyes stared into mine, my chest was pounding away like a runaway gun. I stroked her cheek. Then we cut the electric current between us by mutual action, as somebody outside walked past the office's glass doors.

The boys arrived back. A few hours had passed in an instant.

I said goodbye to her on the outside step, warmly and simply. Every time you say goodbye to someone it just might be the last time.

***

Fires burned in the tarmac grounds of some large, anonymous industrial compound on the Haseke city outskirts, converted from who knew what original purpose to an operational staging post. The festivities were well underway as we arrived by night: the familiar, rousing tunes blared out of five or six truck stereos at once, rows of dancers kicking up their heels in the light of the flames and the harsh glare of vehicle headlights, and the odd daring soul leaping right over the fire. Other groups sat in circles on the ground feasting from the takeaway trays of barbecued chicken and kebabs, cans of soda and other rare treats circulating in abundance – more food (and better) than anyone had seen or would see for weeks. This operation had been a long time coming.

I waded through the milling crowd, greeting the friendly faces that floated up out of it every so often, chatting, joking, smoking. Meetings and reunions.

Jac was back. Sick of the Pesh, where they'd had comfortable conditions but done fuck all besides playing pranks on each other and posting up the results on Facebook, he'd returned and joined the newly formed /223 group: an all-western unit, finally, created by Peter after months of petitioning and campaigning among the YPG command. Bagok, the first international *şehid*, was killed on 23 February: 2/23, as Americans write it. While making a stencil for them, on request, so they could spray it on their base wall, I'd pointed out that the forward slash should go between the numbers; but they'd said no, keep it like that. It's more mysterious and looks badass. So /223 it was.

I went to give Jac a hug but he stiffed me. Not in front of Peter. *Fine…*

I introduced them to Dan and Damien, two American *hevals* new to Soran's crew. Damien was a short, stocky Puerto-Rican/American, compact and intense, with colourful native tattoos on his forearms. He claimed to have learned his weapons skills in LA street gangs as a youth. I'd taken him through some machine-gun practice and found him a decent shot.

Dan seemed the opposite of Damien in appearance and other ways. A tall blond Georgian, a bit of a jock, good-looking, with Cherokee blood and hatchet cheekbones. He seemed to like to see himself as a southern gentleman, so we treated him as a backwater hick at every opportunity. Annoyingly, he seemed equally proud of that. Other contradictions – we all had them – included a penchant for history books and a casual racism and homophobia whose depth I found impossible to gauge.

Once he said: "I don' approve of *aaah*, slavery or nutt'n. But for a lot of folks down south it wasn't as bad as things like Hollywood and so on make it out to be, I mean no one's really looked into the real extent of *aah*..."

"Well why would anyone *bother*, man?" snapped another of the Americans, cutting him dead. "It's a fucked-up practice that was abolished...!"

I liked Dan's easy nature and pleasant, unselfish manner, even as I felt uncomfortable with some of the things he'd come out with. Out here I made common cause with all kinds of people. The anarchists back home would forgive me that; but for liking their company, never.

"So, you back with Suicide Soran then, Cûdî?" Peter grinned.

We laughed; you had to, but it wasn't all jokes. Peter harboured deep reservations about Soran's style of command. Last time I'd seen him, at the mountain camp on my way out, I'd asked him straight, "What do you think of Soran?"

"Well. A lot of people have been killed under his leadership. He didn't reinforce Bagok when the panza broke down. At 500 metres away you can see what's going on."

"Kosta really looked up to you, you know," I said.

"I know..." he sighed. "We had a deal. He was going to work on his Kurmanji for a couple of months and then come to my unit, and I was gonna take him under my wing. Nothing you plan in Rojava ever works out. Must be something in the water."

***

Around the perimeter of the grounds were one-room, low-roofed brick chalets, bare inside but for a thick carpet of soft dust. Using some leafy branches, we brushed one out as best we could and laid our blankets on the floor.

We spent most of the following day watching others go out ahead of us, waiting our turn. The grounds emptied; we were among the last. When we got down to the low tens we set up some cans on barrels and had a shooting match across the bare space. Soran and I built a small fire in the evening and got some tea on the go. The grounds were empty now.

He was trying to tell me about his previous occupation, back in Iraq, before the YPG.

"*Seeya*. You know, like police, but for information. Same like America, *See-ya*."

"*Seeya*…? Oh! CIA?"

"Yes. I do this. We come when there is many people making problem, take away people."

"Really? Wow."

A few weeks earlier, while on a flying visit to Tal Tamir, Peter had invited me to join his new outfit. I was mulling it over, stalled on the six-month commitment he wanted. As the al-Hawl operation played out, our two units worked closely side by side anyway, clearing village after village with our battered and faulty Hummers.

Another night, another fire in some random village, nibbling pumpkin seeds and drinking *çay* with some *hevals* from other *tabors*. Aso was absorbed in the art of flipping a cigarette upwards towards his mouth, trying to catch it between his lips: a bafflingly difficult move which gives so little back by way of effect, but one that some people seem bent on mastering. He sat there now, cigarette bouncing off his face time after time. Finally his tenacity paid off and he grinned with pride at his supposed audience. God love you Aso. Don't ever change.

Soran's radio sparked up and the mood switched as suddenly as the expression on his face.

"OK," he said to me. "Am going." (*I'm going* meant, *let's go.*)

We rumbled over hard, unforgiving furrows like a stony sea in the pitch dark, all lights expunged. I climbed high into the gun turret to see out over the top, rather than through the battered glass and the small slit round the gun. Straining my eyes for any sign of movement, I turned the turret handle forwards and back, moving turret and gun left and right slightly, as though to limber up. The gears slipped occasionally on the left turn. The night was so dark that the division between ground and sky and the outlines of trees and buildings were all but blotted out. Up ahead and left, a light flashed suddenly, illuminating a treeline at the edge of the field, then cut out again. Directions crackled from Soran's radio, and we turned off on a new angle towards the light as it flashed once more.

We followed a series of such signals to a village, where some of the /223 guys were ranged along one edge, silent and still, in fighting positions behind walls and buildings. It was they who'd called us out.

A casualty was carried out past the tense fighters, still with a job to finish. The deck of the Hummer was cleared and a thick quilt put down. I climbed up right into the turret to make room, perching on the narrow, curved bit of ledge around the hatch, my back to the raised lid. He made neither sound nor movement as they laid him on the quilt. From where I was I could see grazed skin on his back where his shirt had rucked up; otherwise he looked OK, I thought.

We retraced our journey, accompanied by a Hilux with a few of the /223 boys. At least now I knew what we were doing: a straightforward medevac.

A Heyva Sor (Kurdish Red Crescent) ambulance drove out to meet us at a place deemed safe to use lights. I stayed in the turret while they transferred the casualty over and the crew went to work. A group gathered at the back. Though concerned, I didn't want to join them; it seemed unseemly. Anyway, the guy looked OK.

"What's going on in there?" I asked to Damien, down on the ground with the others. Face pale in the harsh glare of the vehicle lights, his impassive expression was unreadable, till he turned to me with resignation in his eyes and voice.

"Well, he's pretty much done. They're just trying to bring him back now…"

The guy's battle partner, an Israeli of about 22, looked on, frozen, as the medics fought for his friend's life. I climbed down just as they covered him up with a thin yellow blanket and started to pack their equipment down. Damien muttered a few words of consolation and put his arm round the shoulder of the young Israeli, who lowered his head and slouched away.

***

Next morning, I woke on the flat concrete roof and stowed my bag on top of the thick blanket. I threw on my webbing and rifle and walked through the mist and dust and early light to see the /223 guys and pay my respects.

A Canadian guy called John Gallagher. Codenamed Gobar, new in-country. *Şehid* Gobar, now. I'd met him just once. The assault was a joint effort, the /223 and a Kurdish *tabor* together. Firhat, one of the Kurds, told me that Gobar was killed by a suicide bomber, but the /223 said he was shot, and I was more inclined to believe them. Everyone was agreed that he'd found himself at close quarters with an enemy in the dark and some words passed between them before John was killed. Plenty of people would have shot first and asked questions afterwards.

We hung out on the steps of the house they'd appropriated for their accommodation, chatting, cleaning weapons, as the sun climbed higher. Someone tossed me a can of Taqqa, the local energy drink, from a crate they'd brought along. A rare treat. People pottered in and out of doors, where their gear and quarters were (unsurprisingly) impeccably squared away, attending to various bits of daily admin.

"Guys, please make sure that the person waking you up for *nobet* knows where you're sleeping," said Nichivan, their Canadian 2ic. "It's a ball-ache when you have to search around for someone in the dark, waking everybody up."

"Yeah, and try not to sleep with your face covered up as well," added Jac.

People murmured their agreement.

Most of the /223 were of course ex-military – infantry, marines, airborne, and so on, from all over the world. Jac wasn't, but he'd seen a bit of combat by now and was holding his own with them by the looks of it.

Another returnee from the Peshmerga had just turned up, replacing Gobar almost as though it had been planned. Will had also got sick of kicking his heels in the Pesh and was back in town. He slotted straight into the /223.

My most abiding memory of him was from Tal Tamir, the last time I'd been in *tabori* Soran, *sans* Soran himself. In the last days of that particular incarnation of the unit, even the junior commanders were hardly ever around. Three young Kurds had formed a little clique in their absence and assumed an authority no one had given them: trying to push us around; skiving off duties while insisting we did ours; freely going to shop in town while trying to incarcerate us on camp, and so on.

There was a motorbike in one of the sheds. Of course, only they were allowed to ride it.

Late one afternoon they came tumbling out of the accommodation block at the sound of its engine, and started waving their arms and shouting at what they saw. Down a stretch of track, Will was facing them off like a cowboy with a long shadow, legs bowed around the bike, the sun behind him, flicking revs like he was going for his six guns. He released the brake and roared towards and through them, shouting, "America, YO!" as they scattered. Two of the other Yanks donned flags like superman capes and danced up and down, and the rest of us fell about laughing as Will burned up and down the track and the little dictators yelled and grabbed at him again and again. An absurd way for grown men to act, of course, but you had to be there.

It was great to see Will again. I was still turning over Peter's invitation, but there was no hurry. I liked my relationship with the /223: a sort of friend of the family.

A day or so later, two of our Hummers pulled up at an isolated row of houses surrounded by ploughed fields, maybe a klick from the nearest village where sporadic small-arms fire could be heard, just peppering lightly. Leaving the machine gun in its mount in the turret, I dashed upstairs to the flat roof overlooking the village.

Lined out along the near side of a long, low building on this side of the village were half the /223 and some Kurds. The fire we could hear was coming from the far side.

"They're pinned down over there," said Nichivan. An ex-infantry marksman, he had a rangefinder on a tripod set up on the roof's surrounding wall, and was making calculations for windage with a notebook and pencil. There were 20-odd Kurdish fighters and a few commanders up here too, talking on radio to the Kurds down in the village with the /223.

I offered to spot for Nichivan, a second pair of eyes. He passed me a pair of binoculars.

Scanning… logging reference points. *Small church, demolished house with white pillars still standing… and…*

…the ragged outline of a sniper's ghillie suit, rifle barrel clearly visible, like some murderous scarecrow from a horror film.

"There's a sniper on the roof!" I shouted.

The figure brought the weapon up into the aim.

Nich got into a firing position with his *karnas* and squeezed off a couple of shots as I relayed the indication into his radio.

"We know he's there but we can't do anything!" came the reply, from Sher, a Croatian guy.

Seeing what Nichivan was doing, one of the young Kurds picked up somebody else's sniper rifle and started copying him, firing randomly at the village. *Monkey see, monkey do.* Nich politely told him to cut it out before he killed one of our friends.

A fountain of earth whooshed upwards suddenly, about 100 metres out, in the middle of the field, followed by the loud report.

"*Fusa!*" shouted several people at once – a rocket, fired from a tripod-mounted launcher, bigger than a shoulder-launched RPG. The sort that killed Kosta.

The next explosion was closer, and they weren't coming from the village. Over the radio Sher told us they could see a mobile rocket team out there, driving around in the dead ground.

We had a few minutes' quiet then, maybe 10; and then the next rocket hit home – smack on top of a neighbouring house in this row, four or five down from ours.

Down the steps we ran, towards the sudden cloud of dirty fog, the stench of weapon chemicals and building materials stinging the nostrils. We dragged a guy out of the smog, blood pouring from his nose and from holes gouged in his arm and cheek. Will, Nich and a couple of the other /223 guys were at my shoulder, producing bandages and tourniquets. "Put something round his face," I said. Will came forward with a roll of gauze and wrapped it round and round the head under his nose.

We walked him to the Hummer and packed him in gently. Two Kurds jumped straight in with him, so I told them to keep his head stable and not let him sleep on the way back, and went to slam the door shut.

"Cûdî, Cûdî!" said Soran, at the wheel, beckoning me inside, "Come on!"

I squeezed back in, sitting on nothing in the overcrowded space, facing the casualty and holding his head gently.

"*Na raze* (don't sleep), *heval*," I said, patting him on the arm whenever he looked like nodding off.

We raced away. Every now and then I had to yell at Soran for smashing over the bumps in the ground.

"*Hedi hedi* (slowly slowly)!" I said, to the inevitable yelling, grabbing scrummage of Kurds that greeted us back in the village where the Heyva Sor ambulances were stationed.

As I swung open the door the injured man shrugged us all off indignantly and made his own way to the ambulances.

I washed off the blood covering my arms and hands with bottled water. One of the Kurds came to hold it for me, pouring it onto my hands bit by bit.

"*Spas* (thanks), *heval*," I smiled. My trousers were slick and wet with blood as well.

I clambered over the Hummer bonnet and jumped into the turret from above – quicker than opening those heavy doors and closing them again. As I got settled, one of the medics threw me a sterilising hand gel. *Spas, heval.*

Two guys from some foreign military, here on specific business of who knew what nature, were stood together behind a low wall, stiffly in their clean new YPG uniforms, worn to blend in. They watched me, impassive and expressionless, as we roared off again, back towards the gunfire still audible at this distance. I gave them a wave, and after a second one raised a tentative hand.

Back at the position I forced open the rickety wired-up tailgate of the Hummer and fished my spare pair of combat pants from my bag, peeling off the bloodsoaked ones: a frantic scramble out of one pair and into the other before being seen by the YPJ milling around all over the place.

Back up to the roof. Nich was on the radio to the /223. A YPJ commander was hovering at his shoulder, looking agitated.

"Hey *ahh*… I'm getting that there's some confusion between yourselves and the Kurds down there… *Uh*, your way of working; so if you could work *with* the locals…"

In the fields below, the *monkey-see* kid was having a go on an unattended Dushka gun, rounds bursting up in the grass miles from anywhere. No one seemed agitated about that.

Nich lowered his binoculars and ran over to the YPJ leader.

"There's a truck!" he pointed. "Heading straight for the village – it's a suicide truck!" He thrust his binoculars at her. Before many more seconds we could all see it: welded steel plates all over, rumbling along heavily; clad like an armadillo and rammed to the gills with barrel bombs. A VBIED (vehicle-borne improvised explosive device).

As I grabbed the radio to warn Sher, the truck changed course.

"It's heading this way!" I shouted, as several Kurdish voices filled the air.

The roof cleared in seconds as the Kurds poured down the steps like water and scattered into the fields behind. First time I'd ever seen a group of Kurdish fighters run like that from *anything*. Fucking powerful psychology, those trucks.

Left on the roof with me were just Nich and Will.

We fired shot after desperate shot at the truck with our rifles as it came hurtling forwards, growing rapidly in size and detail – barely a chink in its armour. Ghost of a chance, but you have to try. I raced to the wall, stuck my foot on it and rested my elbow on my knee to support the rifle, trying to lead my shots.

"Hold your fire! *Hevals!*" I yelled to the other two, as the VBIED raced past one of our Dushka trucks and the small team of *hevals* fleeing from it. It rattled on and we resumed fire, following along to the roof's right-hand edge as the truck veered slightly, the track still leading it towards our row of houses, but further to our right. We screamed warnings in case any *hevals* were still over there. As it drew close it went out of sight, obscured by our roof's edge. I jumped up onto the wall, leaning my back on a washing-line pole, trying to get an aim, get a few last shots in.

"Watch for that sniper, Cûdî!" shouted Will. I jumped down again just as the truck exploded, deafening, not far from where the *fusa* had hit. *Hope to Christ people kept away from that area since.* The roof trembled and debris filled the air, raining dirt and fragments down around us; the wave of foul pollution followed along in seconds.

We dashed down the steps again. No one hurt, apparently. *Incredible.* Soran returned and everyone, Kurd and westerner, abandoned the buildings and drove or walked out into the fields.

"Good man, Will," I said. "Thought we were properly fucked for a moment there."

"Oh, *maaan*," he sighed, shoulders sagging.

We laughed with relief, catching our breath.

The Hummer parked up with a couple of other vehicles. The ground was higher here, giving a view onto the enemy terrain. The late afternoon stretched on and all was quiet for hours. I sat in the front passenger seat; Dan and Damien, and a Canadian called Dilgeş, were in the others. Twilight came on slowly.

The Hummer doors were wide open on account of the heat, but the edge had gone; nights were getting chillier. The rainy days wouldn't be far off. My Gore-Tex jacket was full of small holes by now, and my posh leather gloves were burnt and cracked from one of our fires. My fancy sleeping bag had long disappeared too – placed in storage when we were told to streamline our kit for one of the numerous scrapped operations at Tal Nasir; and never seen again. Since then I'd just scavenged for blankets whenever we came to a new place, like everyone else.

"Well. Looks like another night sleeping in the fucking Hummer, unless we're gonna move villages now," said someone.

"Which I doubt."

"Well, we can cuddle up."

"Fun times in Rojava," said Dan.

"Yeah, for you it will be. Because you're a *gayer*!"

Like with Jordan in Shengal, it had become routine for us to remind Dan several times a day of his essential gayness, since he'd expressed his somewhat conservative views on the matter.

"Leave off him. Some of my best friends are homophobes."

"I may be homophobic, but yew ain't supposed to be, Dilgeş. *Bad* Canadian."

"What's that gay festival they have every year in Georgia?"

"Ain't no such thing."

"Yeah there is. It's huge. Everyone goes. Southern Decadence, that's it."

"Never heard of it."

"Sure you have." Dilgeş described the flamboyant LGBT festival in some detail for Dan's benefit.

"*Heh heh*," he laughed, finally. "Well, good for them…"

Dan played up to the redneck role as much as we'd typecast him in it. There was some truth to it, but it was stretched on both sides for comedy value. He was too chilled and smart to get actually riled about anything like that.

Sometimes it fell back on me, this bantering; I'd cast him as the honky hick and he'd respond by peppering his speech with words like *nigger* and *jiggaboo*. I'd be the one who lost out, because I had the handicap of actually giving a shit. When the fighting was done here, or he'd had enough of it, Dan was interested in getting into some kind of voluntary work with the refugees in Kobani – "Helpin' folks." It was his Christian beliefs as much as anything that motivated that desire. Well, almost anything, bar the girl he was pining for in Kobani town.

"Şerzad reckons that Zoran kid's gay. Tried to stop him leaving the *tabor* because he had a crush on him."

"What, Şerzad tried to stop that Zoran kid leaving the *tabor* because he's gay?"

"No. That Zoran kid tried to stop Şerzad leaving. Because Şerzad wanted to cross to our *tabor* because he wasn't fighting, and Zoran kept telling him the commander said it wasn't possible. And then in the end Zoran said to him, *I wanna put my penis in your butt-hole.* And Şerzad just went nuts, told the commander, told everyone. Not because he was gay particularly, but because he'd blocked him for weeks instead of just passing on the request. And now it's this big thing in the *tabor*. The other Kurds giggling and saying, *Zoran gayer, haha.*"

"Zoran's from Fallujah."

"Jesus. Imagine growing up gay in a place like that."

"Yeah. *Shit.*"

"I mean – what the fuck would you *do*?"

"Well. Leave."

"Yeah, easier said than done, though…"

"Right."

"My teacher at college actually *was* gay. She was a lesbian. But I woulda still slept with her, though."

"Oh, that's very progressive of you, Dan…"

"Dilgeş, any chance of some music...?"

Dilgeş had some battery on his phone; enough for maybe half an hour of sounds. Even though I promised not to, and I really meant it when I said it, I still found myself ruining the Sia track when it came on by singing, "I'm gonna swing/from a panda's ears..." over the chorus. I couldn't help it any more.

The slow, slow afternoon passed, like many such afternoons.

"Fun times in Rojava," said Dan.

At dusk we pulled back to our base village, leaving half the /223 *tabor* still lined out along that wall. Young Jac was down there with them and I wasn't easy with it at all, less so as night drew on. But there was nothing for me to do. He was with capable people, as was proven when Tony, their British team leader, decided enough was enough and marched them out of there after several more hours of hanging in limbo with no ammo resupply, no reinforcements and no info. I was happy, but it wouldn't bode well for their group in the eyes of the Kurds.

***

Another misty morning, another village. I moved inside in the wee hours, down from the concrete roof with my blanket as the morning chill set in. At dawn I rose stiffly, cracking my neck and back. Before the sun cooked off the moisture in the air and baked the ground, I gathered up my monkeys and parrots and dragged my aching bones on the hunt for some sweet, life-giving tea. *Try that fire over there, by the parked Dushkas.*

"*Roj baş.*" (Good morning.)

"*Roj baş.*"

"*Çay heye?*" (Is there tea?) I said, giving them my most winning smile.

"*Ere, heye,*" (Yes, there is,) said one of several YPJ women, indicating with her foot the big blackened kettle and small silver one with steaming spouts, nestling in the ash at the edge of the fire.

Sugar too. Happy days. No glasses though. I cut the top off a discarded plastic bottle and poured slowly as it warped and softened.

As I savoured the holy nectar and sparked up the first and best cigarette of the day, someone appeared with an armful of warm, fresh flatbread wrapped in thin polythene bags, a light steam just visible on the inside. She dumped them on the ground as others laid out dishes of white salty cheese, olives, chopped tomatoes and cucumber. There were also tubs of jam and tahini. They sat down, beckoning to me.

"*Heval Cûdî, xwarin, xwarin.*" (Come and eat.)

Good timing, heval Cûdî, I congratulated myself. Breakfast with the delightful ladies from Heavy Weapons.

Soran came and joined next, in fine form today.

"*Ala rasi, ala rasi! Ala aini, ala aini!*" (On my head, on my eyes!) he said. It was an Arabic greeting he seemed particularly fond of just lately.

The Heyva Sor crew, who slept on their ambulances, came along to join us; we shuffled out into a wider circle to make room. Having finished eating, I went to get some more bread and refill some of the bowls with olives and cheese for the others.

Then, as an added bonus to an already lovely morning, who should happen by but Alîn, camera in hand. Greetings between the two of us were warm, if not as charged as the previous time at Qereçox (we weren't in the company for it).

"Cûdî, are you ready for *fighting*?" growled Soran, between mouthfuls of bread and tea, with a cut-throat grin through his beard. I assured him I was.

"Very good!" He thrust a raised thumb at me.

"*Heval* Soran, *Inglesi zanî*?" (Do you know English?) asked Alîn, impressed.

"*Kem*," (A little,) he answered her, with a gentleman's modesty, cocking his head to one side. "You know, Cûdî, I was 12 years in England. Coven*tree*, Birming*ham*…"

"Yeah, I know. What did you do there again? What work?"

"*Mushrooms*."

"Hm. Why don't you speak English then?" I grinned.

He cackled. "Because I… *very busy*, in this time."

"Just joking," I said.

"Hey Alîn – put the camera down and get a *silat* (weapon)," I said. "Come fight with us. You're a warrior."

Her smile could have lit and warmed the whole village on the grimmest of mornings. Today it was the perfect send-off.

Today we were up. Going forward.

***

Two *hevals* lay on the ground with bullet wounds where we pulled up behind a small group of houses on the open, undulating grassy plain. Gritting his teeth against the pain, one guy raised up his shirt to show a sort of half-tunnel bored out of the muscle above his hip. I whipped my *keffi* off my head and pressed it gently to his side, taking his hand and placing it on top. *Keep it there.* The other already had a tourniquet high on his thigh, above a dark patch of blood. A kilometre away, the enemy village where they'd been shot sat still and silent as the air around us; not a soul in sight, part of the scenery once more. *Don't bother me and I won't bother you*, it seemed to say. We hauled the casualties into a Hilux and dispatched them to the ambulance point. At the last second, a tall, nervous American with a black bandana leapt onto the back of the moving Hilux.

"Hey, that's *my* tourniquet! I need it back!" New guy, panic all over his face.

"Here!" I fished a recently-acquired tourniquet out of my top pocket and threw it to him. *This is why I never have any stuff.*

He stalked after me, gabbling away, as I made for my Hummer.

"These guys are fucking crazy!" he spluttered, arms awry, in battle-shock from the brief skirmish. "They drove *straight* into the line of fire when there was *no* fucking reason to, and that other guy started shooting up at *nothing*, and…"

I jumped into the turret, put my shoulder to the machine gun, quick turn forward-back on the handle to rotate it either way – gears still slipping on the left turn, they told me they'd fixed that – and we set off. *Yep. That's what it's like here, mate. And the next one will be like that too.* Make your peace with it, or leave.

With Soran at the wheel we raced over the lumpy terrain, bouncing and shaking. The enemy village disappeared from view as we plunged through dead ground, then hoved up over us as we crested a rise with a jolt. Damien, the up-gunner on the other Hummer, gave me a thumbs-up from his turret as we headed around one side, they the other. As I returned the gesture, gunfire burst out from somewhere and winged around us. I clenched my teeth and the machine gun's pistol grip, cramming my shoulder into the butt and bracing my stance, focusing utterly on the view through the small gap in the shield plate around my weapon sights. Focus was going to be tricky here, and crucial.

"Cûdî! You see *this house!*" pointed Soran, as we lurched to a halt. I half-bent, half-squatted, craning my head round the gun and down through the roof-hatch to look out through his small bullet-crazed, bulletproof windscreen at a two-storey house with walls of real stone. *Nice choice.* My view up top was severely narrowed. The vehicle's turret had small windows either side, but they'd taken more of a battering than even the windscreen – their glass reduced to crumbs and powder, only held in place by their coating of ripped plastic film.

"Daesh in this house! Shoot here!"

I sent a few short bursts through the windows and door, before the view whipped away as we veered and swerved out of the answering fire.

The Hummer floor had no turntable deck, so whenever I rotated the turret I had to walk my feet round with it. *So this small area of deck is all mine, right? Kept scrupulously clear so I can operate…* Dream on. Two Kurdish fighters each were sat in the rear seats to either side of me, four guys in a space meant for two, crammed against my legs. Every other spare inch was filled with an unsecured, random shitpile of ammo and other gear. I felt a distant, familiar invitation to panic: not from the bullets or the driving or the even physical constriction, but from all the above with guys who *just don't get it*. Cry as you might, they won't understand. They've never known any other way. You just have to master the fear of that chaos before it masters you. Squash it down and get on.

Yelling and clamouring, they fell this way and that as we sped along, angling their rifles clumsily out of the tiny windows in the cramped dimensions and firing, filling the space with deafening reports and flying, livid-hot brass. They pitched and fell against me with the force of a rugby tackle, buckling my legs under me and then trapping them; there was the crashing rattle of loose ammo shaking out of open boxes as I squirmed free of the human sandwich, kicked out and shouted at them in the heat of it and we raced on round and about, firing and evading.

"Now this house, Cûdî!"

As we wheeled and scrawled around I wrenched the turret handle forward and back to keep up with Soran's incessant volley of fire directions. The gears were slipping more and more on the left turn, and the only thing for it in our constant weaving was to wind faster and faster, knowingly increasing the damage just to get anywhere at all: diminishing returns and ever-decreasing circles.

My hand was a blur on the handle as my gun sights inched grudgingly around. By the time I was lined up on target the scene — trees, mud huts, a well — flew away again as we sped off. A rising surge of anger boiled up within me as I fought to keep us on track and get rounds on target. *I TOLD Soran this needed fixing! Now look!* ("OK Cûdî, OK, we fix, we fix…") Now he was going mental down there and I was too fucking slow. The danger wasn't bothering me nearly as much as the sheer fucking unfairness of it. *It's not my fault…*

Then the left-turn on the turret went altogether; the gears slipping smooth, biting on nothing. I was verging on both tears of frustration and peals of laughter at the madcap idiocy of it all, as our two Hummers raced past each other and on through the town in this crazy, drive-by-shooting ballet.

This was one of *tabori Soran*'s signature battle tactics, if tactic is even the right word; it was what got us our reputation as kamikaze-cowboys. Barrelling on into an enemy location and racing round and through the gauntlet of fire, over and over, all guns blazing, to soften it up for the infantry.

"Now here, Cûdî! Daesh here! Shoot here!"

My left-hand side. I turned right, the only way I could turn, taking the long way round the barn through 270 degrees.

"Shoot!!!"

By the time I'd got round we were burning off again, enemy fire bursting all round us. The view was a madly scrolling screen and I was getting spin-dizzy. This workout would be tough enough in a functioning turret; like this I'd be better just waiting still for the target to flit across my sights again. And I could barely stand up for 20 unbroken seconds at a time.

This will never, never do.

Dragging my feet out of the tangled, squirming mass of bodies below me, I climbed right up through the hatch hole, perching my arse on the narrow ledge of roof inside the turret, leaning my back against the raised hatch-lid behind me and jamming my feet against the shield plate, bracing with my legs. Leaving the *biksî* in the mount, I somehow wrestled my folded AK from where I kept it stowed behind the hatch lid and propped it on the top edge of the rough-cut, rusted steel plates welded to the turret to raise its height.

The turret gently started to drift of its own accord, and I edged around to compensate. One of the enemy houses was about to pass in front of my view. I braced and strained more, raising my head and shoulders right up out of the turret to see down the rifle sights. Gunfire resounded from somewhere but I *just hadn't got time* to worry about that; I was falling behind with things as it was. I loosed off a shot. Hardly marskmanlike, but we were finally getting rounds down in the right direction. I fired off another.

Better switch to bursts, I decided, firing one more on single-shot – just as the vehicle nosed into a ditch and bounced up out of it, throwing me back-forward against hard metal in the same violent instant, leaving me dazed and winded. In the rusted vertical surface a metre from my nose gleamed a silvery weal, brand new: a dent half a centimetre deep in the steel, with rippled edges like a frozen splash in mercury. *I just fired a round inside the turret.* It took a second to compute: if that 7.62 had bounced straight back I'd have been sitting here now with half a head. *A miracle,* I thought, as the scenery rushed by.

The boys were yelling up at me, "What's going on, Cûdî…?"

"*Pirsgirêk* (problem)!" I said, pointing to the handle and slapping the turret's sides. One of them relayed it to Soran.

"OK Cûdî, OK."

I experienced a small sense of relief at the thought that they *got it.* We thundered on.

As we came round for another pass, it occurred to me that I could use the bigger gun the same way as the rifle (i.e. just as badly and dangerously) and its weight might actually be an asset. Releasing the catch, I awkwardly freed it from the mount, bringing it in through the shield plate into my lap. The Hummer tipped sideways and I nearly fell straight down through the hole on top of the others, gun and all. The ammo belt snaked out of the makeshift metal box welded to the mount and hung down from the gun, swinging about and whipping me on the knuckles as I propped the gun on the turret's top edge: muzzle *well* forward this time.

Here we go again, enemy house in view, and I fired a good, long, satisfying broadside as we swept on past. Under these conditions one round in 20 *might* make it through the window, so 20 it must be. Besides, I was playing catch-up here; I was a few bullets in hand.

My leg jerked in sudden, intense pain – hot round casings, rolling and collecting on the ledge, burning my arse. The turret-drift had lessened considerably now as they'd become jammed between its underside and the roof. *Good days.* I'd get a cushion up in here next chance. I found I could right the turret now and again with my foot on the handle, too, as long as it was a right turn that was needed. This wasn't so bad.

A familiar *whoosh* and a slight, sonorous *dink!* – clear and distinct in the melee of background noise. Two neat round holes drilled straight through the parallel metal sides of the gun mount, where the grip slots in. The catch lever was bent out like a broken finger. A round just passed straight through the turret, in and out again, where the backward-angled shield plate left a tapering gap between it and the turret housing; a big chink in the armour. Right where my fucking hands were, less than a minute ago.

I might just die in the next few minutes, I thought, sitting back with my head down, just below the edge. If that round had entered on a minutely different angle it would have been pinball in here, with me in the middle. The miracles were stacking up. I was suddenly aware, as if for the first time, what a tiny space it was inside this rusted box. The boys down below were cursing and firing, yelling and falling. We were getting swung around like a fairground waltzer and I heard myself burst out laughing because suddenly it was all too much. It felt good, so I laughed louder, louder, letting it out. Below, a Kurd named Herdem turned and looked up at me, wide-eyed and drawn, as though I was some kind of nutter.

The gun's extra weight *did* help steady it, comfortingly, against our constant jumping around, but every time I got it set up one way the vehicle turned again, making me wrong, and I had to throw it up and over the other side. Though nicely balanced, it was way more cumbersome than the rifle with that ammo belt trailing down, and I was getting smashed around inside the metal turret like ice in a shaker.

Herdem stood up through the hatch, between my braced legs, to try and give me support by shooting out with his rifle, but it was even more unworkable with two up here so he ducked back in again.

The drive-by whirligig lasted maybe 20 minutes, after which the two Hummers circled the perimeter, blasting away in an orderly fashion at the two established enemy locations.

"Yes! Good, Cûdî!" shouted Soran, after I put in another sustained volley. As we settled and slowed down I could feel for the first time how bruised and battered I was.

We braked suddenly and the door flew open. Herdem dashed towards the enemy house, through an orchard of small trees.

"Cûdî, cover him!" shouted Soran, but I couldn't see him from up here for those trees, so I climbed out and down with the gun. No sooner were my feet on the ground than Herdem came racing back, fire ringing out behind him.

We drove around for another pass, and then pulled back 200 metres or so, parking up behind a house. We debussed and Damien's Hummer joined us.

"I didn't actually *see* a single fucking enemy," I said, wiping sweat from my face and neck. "Did you?"

For the first time I noticed my hand was bleeding, from the rough-cut edge of a turret plate most likely. I'd just streaked blood across my own face.

"Yeah, I saw one guy go down and I made sure he was dead. Another guy tried to run and they ran right over him."

"Fuck…"

"Man, Cûdî, you were standing right up out of the fucking turret, man…"

"Yeah, the rotate mechanism's screwed. Only way I could actually aim out."

Feeling myself starting to cool down, I walked over to where Herdem and the others were squatting in the shade. I gripped them by the shoulders. "Well done!"

Their smiles and hugs said there was no need for translations, nor for the profuse apologies I made for kicking and yelling at them in the heat of it all. I showed them the shot-up gun-mount. A round came in through the window below as well, they told me.

The *salderî* were gearing up now, preparing to go in on foot. I grabbed the *biksî* and joined them, manoeuvring forward from cover to cover. Shots burst out but I was pretty sure they were all ours.

As we took our positions around the enemy house and put in some tentative fire, Pişko the mad dwarf ran right out in front of everyone, waving his arms and issuing impromptu battle orders. *Just what the fucking hell is he doing…?* Damien went up the outside steps to check out the roof, and as he came back down Pişko lobbed a grenade into the solid concrete porch they led to, where it could hurt no one except Damien himself. Pişko just wanted to hear the bang. We screamed like madmen and Damien dived, avoiding the blast by a whisker.

Before anyone could do anything he threw another, right into the middle of nowhere this time. *Looks like that was his last one, thank fuck.*

Finally the remaining enemy were isolated in one house. After hitting it with a barrage of rockets and bullets we pulled back and the sabotage team moved in, planted a charge, rolled out their command wire and blew the building to crumbs. Smoke and dust rushed outwards and made us cloud-blind for several minutes. No one in there was getting out alive. I didn't dwell on it as we drifted away, passing troops coming in to secure the now-taken ground.

***

We headed off for a rest, back to base. Another village notched up. Good day's work.

"*Tu şîyar*," said Herdem, as we stretched out.

"What does that mean?" I asked Jac.

"You're a lion." Jac's Kurmanji was eclipsing mine. A bit embarrassing for a language teacher, but I could no longer deny it. Little fucker was whipping me.

"So you did a fucking drive-by?" Jac laughed. "Sick, mate. *Well* gangsta!"

Well, maybe. It was hardly army, whatever it was.

"We, aah, had a *tekmîl* just now," said Will to me. He meant his unit, the /223.

"Oh. OK. Useful?"

"Ye-*aaah*, it was. We talked about the battle, you know, with Gobar and stuff, and about the other day with that VBIED."

"Righto."

"And *aaah*, I did a point of critique, on *myself*, because when you shouted to cease fire 'cause the *hevals* were in front I fired one more shot after that…"

I hadn't even mentioned it; it was only now, thinking back over it, I remembered there had been one more shot after I'd shouted, so I'd said it twice.

"Man," I said, "don't worry about *that*. It was one of those situations."

That he stayed up there at all was what counted. But he'd wanted me to know anyway. No one made you do self-critique; it was a voluntary thing, by definition. Will had obviously been doing some hard thinking. His error, if it could be called that, said little if anything about him, considering the context in which it was made. But his act of conscience spoke volumes.

Later, when I thought back to the Hummer battle, I realised I'd been at least as afraid of blame and criticism, floundering away in that rogue turret, as of the physical danger around me. It mattered, what others thought of you.

I never really figured Will out, which may be a funny thing to say for a place where you never figured out anyone that well; but it bothered me that I couldn't get a better handle on the guy – on who he was, what he thought of me and what I really thought of him.

Bill or Will, it seemed he hadn't totally settled on one or the other yet. I was Jim or James around a similar age. Maybe for some people, working out who they were was all part of this. Will was sombre and tight-lipped, stony, drake. Laconic smarts and a withering stare, not a heart-on-sleeve man at all. But he could brood to beat the band, you could almost *hear* the guy thinking. At that age you preoccupy yourself with all kinds of things that never really get worked out.

So many things are open in Rojava, in so many ways. You don't know where you or the person next to you will be next week, if you'll still be in-country or even still alive. When you haven't seen someone for a while it's like Schrödinger's cat till you see them again. You don't have time to know people well, so you go with your instincts on those around you: what they're really like, whether you can rely on them, why they're here, and so on. You share these brief, illuminated moments of laughter, camaraderie, mutual support in mortal danger, reciprocal gratitude afterwards. A word or two of comfort or encouragement in the really shitty times. Moments of connection – through the shifting mists and fog-shadows that make up most of the past and present.

***

I was sitting in the turret reading a book about the Norman invasion, borrowed from Dan. Typically anomalous; besides being a good old boy he was something of an amateur historian, and several exchanges had taught me to come at him armed with the facts and not just a bunch of liberal sentiment.

The YPG mechanics had set up shop in this village. The place was a chaos of snaking cables, flying sparks, grinding and welding and hammering. After I showed Soran the bullet holes in the gun mount, he brought us there to have the turret up-armoured some more. A guy took a couple of measurements and cut two rough triangles from a thick sheet of steel, then welded them to the sides of the shield plate, reducing the gaps. With the resources available, the boys had a go at reinstating the mount catch and the rotate mechanism too. They battled away and jerry-rigged some small improvement, but realistically I'd have to carry on omitting both features, riding high on a cushion with the gun out.

Dilgeş, Damien and a few of the Kurds were here too, milling around, sunbathing, scratching their nuts. Waiting for stuff to happen.

"Shengal's finished. It's done. Liberated, whatever," said Dan.

"Really?" I sat up.

"I just heard from the sab guys, half of them are over there now. Almost no fighting. Daesh just packed up and cleared on out."

"Shit." I'd like to have seen that, but I had my chance...

Joe Akerman was out there with the sabotage guys, clearing mines on the enemy's doorstep and fighting them when it came to it. He was injured twice by IEDs, seriously, but so far he had no thought of calling it a day.

"Wonder if there'll be any more fighting for us on this op," said Dan.

"Nich reckons we're done," answered Damien.

"Nich," Dan snorted. "He talks the big game, likes to give the impression he knows what's going on. I don't think he knows."

"If there is any more I want that fucking dwarf nowhere near me," said Damien.

"I wonder if he *does* qualify as a dwarf. Or midget, whatever," said Dilgeş.

"I heard his family sent him here to kinda man him up 'cause he's such a screw-up at home," said Dan.

"Right. So send him to a front line. Lucky us. Did you fucking *see* the guy?" I said.

Pişko was just under five feet tall. He had a slightly feral look about him: wide face, a heavy brow-ridge and a tuft of beard like a circus ringmaster. There was a mad, sometimes malevolent gleam in those eyes that seemed to see the world, and this war, as one big fucking fairground.

The first time he'd really come to my attention was when I'd allowed him up in my turret on a road journey, when he'd just joined us. From my seat in the back I looked up to check, and found he'd taken the safety off the gun and was squinting keenly down the sights at Dan and Damien, riding on the open back of the truck in front. I'd gone nuts on him. He'd laughed his disarming laugh and cocked his adorable little head. And that was how it went on.

No one had a good word to say about Pişko.

"I told Soran, but he just acts the cute little kid and gets off."

"Yeah, or hides behind his brother's legs." Agiri, Soran's number two, was Pişko's elder brother. He was solid enough, ex-Iraqi army apparently. But you were pissing in the wind criticising his little bub.

"In a real army they'd treat him just like anyone else," I said. "Starting with several years in jail. You know he borrowed my rifle and when I got it back the Picatinny rail was missing? No front stock, just the bare barrel. I asked him where it was and he said, '*Bomba*.' I'm like, *yeah right*. A grenade unscrewed the fucking Allen bolts and sold it to one of your mates."

"Did you see the baby shoe?" laughed Dan. "They found a baby shoe and fixed it to the straps on his *ract* (webbing). He was going crazy, fighting with it, trying to get it off."

"Should have shot him. He's gonna get someone killed." I forget which one of us said that.

***

Later in the day we blagged a Hilux and Aso drove us 10 or so miles to a couple of tiny shops out in the hulu. There was nothing to really buy but crisps, soft drinks, coffee and different cigarettes, but in our present mode of existence such a prospect had us fizzing over with excitement.

Aso was feeling the need for speed. Well, they all drove like maniacs to be fair. The truck screamed down the dirt track, jumping in and out of ditches, veering over the track's raised edge and nearly flipping now and then.

"*Stran heye*?" (Got any music?) said Aso, hopefully, turning right round in the driver's seat and forgetting the road. He plugged in the USB stick I passed him and soon I was having second thoughts as he took both hands off the wheel and started air drumming to Tom Petty, eyes tight shut, head waving as though in sync with the vehicle's slewing movements.

He was even more charged up than usual because he reckoned he'd scored with one of the YPJ the other night.

"He's a fucking lad, isn't he?" laughed Jac.

Back at the fire, we had a little party with the energy drinks, chocolate, sachets of 3-in-1 coffee and other goodies. Soran was singing a long, heroic song full of improv verses which included us all. I threw up a sign when he dedicated a verse to me, nodding and clapping along. *Pretty sure he's saying nice things.* Ararat, an Irish guy who'd just joined the team, shrugged, scowled and refused to join in because Soran had left him out of a battle. Well, he wasn't going to get in like that.

"*Ala rasi, ala rasi! Ala aini! Ala aini!*" I growled, as the song ended. Aso and the younger Sorani boys fell about pissing themselves with laughter, egging me on for an encore. Now that Soran was trotting out the expression every five minutes, I'd started impersonating him; stretching the roguery and giving it a senile tic, more paretic than piratical. A hit with the kids.

My Kurmanji was elementary at best, and Soran's boys spoke more Sorani anyway. But the bond develops quickly, however few words you have between you, when you've bawled blue murder at each other under gunfire and danced hand in hand around the campfire, shared your last cigarettes, halved a cup of tea on a cold night on *nobet* – everything bad and good. We weren't lean, green fighting machines, or steely-eyed dealers of death. We were *hevals*.

Time between battles dragged and sped by, alternately, on that operation. Party spirits at the Haseke base, meetings and reunions, music and great food. Old friends and new ones. English Humphrey with his bristling colonial moustache. The smiling "Somali" whose humour would make a sailor blush. Aso and the cute little YPJ girl, singing a rally of traditional songs by the fire, blatantly flirting. "One in Kurmanji, then one in Sorani," she was saying, running the show. *Look at Aso, just eating out of her hand...*

Meeting and greeting the small, newly-arrived Arab militias, come to join the fight alongside the YPG. Watching them at their morning prayers while we ate breakfast, smoked and drank tea. Practising my bad Arabic with them. Practising with the Arab village kids as well, getting them to help me clean my weapon. Chucking packets of cigarettes from my turret to the villagers walking round smoking their heads off, now those neurotic religious fuckheads weren't there to punish them for it. *Smoke up, Gran, you've earned it.* Soran in his element, round the fire, around us, singing, holding court. After the blows and the frustrations, the hardship and boredom and tragedy, it was an operation to remind you what you came here for.

We didn't work miracles but we did take ground. It was what it was; a good fight with some bad sides. It needed doing regardless, and pessimism was bad company.

And good company was what it was all about, really. Shared moments, the human connection. One of us might not be here around the next fire. How much gold I stepped over in my search for worth and meaning. *Fighting isn't everything.*

The operation concluded in al-Hawl city, where the familiar YPG convoy, Wacky Races style, met another one coming from the Iraqi side.

Townsfolk streamed out of their houses, surrounding our vehicles; some waving flour sacks tied to sticks – makeshift white flags, others scattering rice over the motley troops and vehicles and serving tea on trays. You can't always be sure, but they seemed pretty happy to see us – Kurds *and* Arabs.

Pişko rode on the Hummer bumper, waving and shouting left and right, playing the mascot. Soran was leapfrogging every vehicle to get to the front, provoking horn-blasts and angry shouts all down the line.

Suddenly we veered off the road and pulled up. He'd spotted something.

"Cûdî!" he called up to me, getting out. "Hummer…!"

He pointed, beaming. I nodded; I'd clocked it already. An abandoned Daesh Hummer, desert colours, not green like ours; half-in, half-out of an open garage.

Soran was in raptures. *A kid at Christmas…*

"Be careful," I shouted. He raised his thumb and walked towards it.

He went softly at first, looking all over, through windows, underneath; then just went for it, flinging a door open. I was hunkered right down in my turret. Our convoy crawled on past, forgotten now, as Soran got on the radio to one of his many contacts to organise a pickup. I accepted a glass of tea from a smiling kid with a trayful of them, and settled back on my turret-cushion, watching the boy disappear with the thinning crowd as twilight came on.

As with the start of the op, we were among the last to leave on the get-out. The Heyva Sor had taken off, *tabors* were heading out their separate ways. *See you on the next one...* Those villagers who had left were trickling back in, reclaiming their houses, putting things back in order. I always imagined the arguments that must ensue over the blankets and cooking pots that made their way from house to house.

We huddled indoors from a foul rain. It was just Soran, me, Aso and a few other Kurds: seven of us. The rest had all gone on ahead. We had a tiny mudbrick room and the dim flame of a sputtering stove-ring, connected by rubber hose to a gas bottle on the dirt floor, which we'd all crouched round. Late November now, nights getting colder.

We were singing to raise the bricks off the thin tin roof; the rain shattering down onto it hadn't a chance. When it was my turn I gave them Camptown Lady. Think what you like: they loved it, clapping along and drumming their feet as I sang the one verse I knew again and again. *Sing anything, just be in. Laugh. Share. Connect. We are still here today, with fire and song and... maybe some tea. If we can find sugar round here.*

We were inside, and the dark and cold and loneliness were outside. Tomorrow was outside; outside was the next operation, and more *şehids*.

Great, here was the tea. Immediately someone spat theirs into a corner, cursing. Some idiot had put salt in the sugar. Oh well. Spark up another cigarette. Who dies of cancer in Rojava?

***

We made our way back to Tal Tamir, and several of the Kurds split, back to Iraq. That's how it went with Soran's boys – a high turnover. Goodbye guys. Good knowing you. Not time to know you well, as it so often goes. But some bright moments and you're all still alive into the bargain. Thanks for the memories. *Hevals* for life, even if we never meet again.

I turned to the others – Dan, Dilgeş, Herdem, Aso, dear old Aras. Still among us, ready for the next op. Nichivan reckoned it would piggyback straight onto this one, with little if any gap in between. We'd be rolling out before we'd had the chance to unpack.

"Pff. He don't know..." said Dan.

Soran took off for Iraq as well, having ensconced us in a lone mansion on the main road between Tal Tamir and Serekaniye, well outside the main base. Gone to his city to recruit fresh blood.

Some days later, we took our first real casualty.

I dashed outside to see what the commotion was. One of us – Aso – lying on the ground. Blobs of blood puddling on the tiles by his head. *What the fuck?* I hadn't heard any shots.

Around him were fragments of ornamental cast concrete and bits of smashed woodwork. No time for a mystery. I waved the guys away from their fumbling around him and fished out a quick-clot bandage I'd scored from someone recently. The cut in his head was deep and vicious. I wrapped the bandage round and round, drawing some false relief just from not having to see the wound as I covered it up. *Oh, fuck, Aso… What happened?*

As sheer blind luck would have it, right at that moment a smart, newish minibus pulled onto the forecourt with Peter at the wheel and a few of the /223. Just a social call. *Thank Christ.*

Into the van and off to Serekaniye hospital for Aso. He sat hunched over in the back. I had one hand on his shoulder and the other just resting lightly on his forehead to stop it hitting the seat in front. *Don't sleep,* I kept telling him.

"*Nave te çiya, heval?*" (What's your name?) I said.

"Aso."

Good. *He knows to use his codename, can't be completely cabbaged,* I told myself – knowing I was grasping at straws.

"Have you got any music?" I said to Peter. "This guy loves rock 'n' roll." I turned back to Aso. "*Stran. Boş.* (Music, good.) Yeah?" I said, groping for things to say, as we sped along to a mix of 70s classics. He grunted incoherently.

By the time they wheeled him away on the gurney, he'd turned ghostly pale and completely unresponsive. I felt the blood drain from my own face, as if in imitation.

Right, what the fuck happened? I rounded on Herdem, who'd come with us to the hospital.

The guys were throwing things off the balcony, and Aso jumped off the roof, Herdem said – or rather, mimed.

What, head first? I said, searching his eyes.

Herdem shrugged and said more, which I couldn't understand. Was that a guilty look? *Did someone throw something down on
his head?* I said, miming as well.

No!

With Peter's better language skills we got to the bottom of it.
A bunch of them were throwing things off the balcony to smash
on the ground below, *for a laugh.* (Why else?) Launching a piece
of heavy furniture over, Aso had leaned against the ornamental
ceramic balcony, which gave way. Down had come furniture,
balcony and Aso, head first.

Christ. The only guy who could *şehid* himself in peacetime
with no bloody weapon.

"Sorry, Herdem," I said. I shouldn't have doubted that guy:
he was as stand-up as any of us. I felt a rising anger. "He never
fucking thinks!" I shouted, then translated it so Herdem wouldn't
think I was angry at him.

"*Fikir nina*," (Thinks nothing,) agreed Herdem.

"Fun times in Rojava," said Dan, as we slunk back to base.

15 AFTERSHOCK

We had a dual role today. As well as providing perimeter security, we were here to pay our respects, at an open-air public service in run-down public gardens that had seen better days, like the rest of the town. A funeral wake on a large scale, as grand as they could make it. Giant Öcalan portraits were up in place, along with more than 30 faces of the dead, printed large on canvas banners, looking down on the rows of mourners seated for eulogies as the cavalcade drifted past: hearses made from vans, jeeps and minibuses, open-hatched, where grandmothers rode with coffins draped in flags of red, yellow and green. They sat straight, facing out back, rifles propped on their laps, pointing skyward in defiance as much as commemoration. A poor, proud procession, drifting on and on, through tomorrow and the next day and the next. *And I would rather be anywhere else, but here today…*

Later, back among the bare white walls of the mansion we'd squatted in like pirates in a palace, a shrill incessant wind howled away, finding its way through to the raw nerve like a dentist's drill. It wasn't the carnage that had floored me, but the impossibility. Floundering in the blood and chaos, accomplishing nothing most likely.

Three car bombs had exploded simultaneously in Tal Tamir, in the heart of town. We heard the blasts from our house, 10 miles away.

Out of bed, weapons, gear, get going.

Armed to the teeth we'd raced down there, off-roading round the checkpoints and tailbacks, and found the town a gutted wreck: utter chaos. Buildings down, streetlights out, no electrics, no medics, no plan. *Where are the Heyva Sor?*

Two craters, like those made by airstrikes. I felt like a chump walking up and down the milling crowd with a machine gun. What was I going to shoot now? *Give it over, get in with the rescue effort – such as it is.* The scene unfolded before me: yelling men pulling in different directions, hauling rubble and furniture off bodies buried under heaps under sagging hanging floors. Working by torches and phone lights.

Following the light to a group in a smashed building, over piled angular concrete – tripping, naked pair of female legs poking up, moving slightly. Look around: what's on her is just too big for hands to move. Further back two guys wrestling another out between leaning pillars, ducking spikes of rebar. One treads on the exposed foot, which shrinks away, gradually and slowly.

Grab the injured guy through the gap, step back over the rubble, out onto the street. Let's get him to the Heyva Sor. The Heyva Sor's gone. Hospital targeted. That's why no medics. Had root canal work there last week, now it's fucking rubble. *Herdem, mate. Get him in the truck and off to Serekaniye.* Hope that's where he goes, I don't ask.

Rush back to those legs, what can I DO? Now they're fighting someone else out the same way, woman grey with dust stretchered on a quilt passed through the gap to me. Over those legs again; sorry madam, you're going to have to be very obliging and stay there and die if you haven't already; can't get you out and you're in a through-route. I'd be quick about it if I were you.

Help who you can. Don't waste time on who you can't.

Staggering down the road through the crowd with the woman on the quilt, blinded by the lights of a bulldozer ploughing through the debris, bucket down, towards us. Scream STOP but he doesn't, clotheslines the lot of us with dragged telegraph wires from downed poles.

Patient dropped on the ground, everyone forgets her, yelling and bollocking the bulldozer driver; get her back up and let's fucking GO! Slapping and grabbing them, *come on, lift, move…* Desperately flagging down any vehicle, please, *fucking stop*. She's dead weight, crammed through a van's sliding doors, can't get in properly myself to set her straight, OK she's on her side, which is more or less right, hey you – *you!* Sit here, stop her rolling off onto the floor again for fuck's sake. Doors slam, vehicle drives off God knows where.

Back in again, next building down, industrial freezer upturned on a guy sat against the demolished heap inside, all dust and caked blood. Yelling shoving fighting, roll it this way, lift it, push, pull, OK it's off him, get in there, radial, carotid pulse, nothing. *You doctor? Afraid not, mate*. Behind him a glistening jagged bloody chunk, presumably human unless this was a butcher's shop. He's dead. *He's dead*. We can't fucking know that, get him out. Forget what vehicle we put him on. Squelchy white paint all over me from somewhere. DIY shop maybe. Why couldn't you die in a fucking lorry repair shop or a carpenter's you inconsiderate bastard?

Down on one knee after carrying the third person. Such a rush, such a strain, cramped spaces, sweat-soaked in thermals and other warm gear, weapon and ammo added to the weight of bodies and my fitness sabotaged by a year of smoking my head off and sleeping in the dirt and eating crap. Get up, rest later.

Hm, some cute girls walking around tonight – What?! – *Get moving*.

Another body, another building. Lift these slabs, drag him out, onto this metal door pull his pants up for God's sake everyone around the door lift let's go to the traffic island no pulse hey stop your car help this man.

Can't I'm going somewhere else.

Start giving CPR. OK, OK, says someone, car coming. Pickup truck pulls in tailgate dropped, slide the metal door with the guy on it onto the back, jump on with him. Racing and bumping along, trying to keep him from sliding off, to stay on myself, to keep his chest going all at the same time – never know, get him to the medics, wherever they are. THEY will say if he's dead or not. Have to keep trying till then. Off the vehicle, what *is* this place? Carry him through an entrance into a yard – with dead bodies stretched out and wailing women. Fuck I thought we were going to a hospital, give the guy a chance. Sorry mate that's your lot got to give up now no one's coming.

Where am I now? Are you driving back to Tal Tamir? No? What about you? Hey! Are you –? No, sorry mate. Fuck, which way is it? Walking through the dark, strange streets, strange stares, armed white guy covered in white paint, blood and dirt. Don't know who's friendly, who isn't. Totally disorientated. Nothing's familiar in the small smashed darkened town. Follow lights to a crowd – fuck, this is a different bombsite. Vehicle marked AMBULANCIA, shredded. One of the suicide vehicles or just caught in the blast?

Daesh did this to punish the town for being so friendly; can't think of another reason. Arabs and Kurds have bought it equally. Death count? Fuck knows, won't know for days.

Walking round and round everywhere looks fucked, whole town gutted in seconds. OK, here's Herdem, Agirî and Hassan, finally. OK looks like we're going. People could probably be saved if we were organised, had medical supplies, somewhere to take the wounded, if I had a team with me on the same page, just one other westerner with me to back me up, speak my language, help me slap and bully these people into order.

Middle Eastern buildings create voids when they fall because they're big concrete slabs that lean at angles on collapsing; western bricks just crumble and crush tight. Buried people may have a chance here if there's a proper rescue effort, if the machines are used carefully and methodically instead of just barging and gouging and clawing away, if the diggers realise they may suffocate people by shaking dust down into the voids, if there's cutting equipment, if there's any – where are the FUCKING MEDICS? Dunno if we saved anyone's life here, should have checked that woman's airway, done this, done that. Should have folded my rifle down, wouldn't have caught on the wires, on everything, slipped off my shoulder, I could have got into that van, sorted it, didn't think. Such a rush to get people out.

Medics appearing in ones and twos as we're going, when the crowd is thinning out, away from the digging and bulldozing. Smart, composed, taken aback, white gloves.

Where are the wounded?

Fuck knows now, mate...

On the truck going back, trying to hide the fact that I'm in shock. Leg won't stop shaking. Freezing fucking cold. Wish it was my other leg, then Hassan, sitting next to me, wouldn't know. He looks at me and tells the driver to close the window.

Want to stop at the base where the /223 are. Get a shower, talk to them, hot tea; but I need to get back to our guys, back to our small exposed undermanned house on the main arterial road and put them in the picture, security brief, it can happen here boys, stupid fucking place to be anyway, be on that gate at all times, the family next door know how many we are, what weapons we have and when we're here or out. Stand-to positions are: you on the roof with the machine gun; you assist him, etc; Dilgeş in charge when I'm not here. We've all been slack.

Images of the night won't go away. Amphetamine jump-cuts, lurid, overexposed. I don't know how many wounded fighters I've patched up and packed off to hospital this year, but these were civilians. It's different.

***

I don't know if we saved *anyone's* life that night. I'd frantically tried to get people onto vehicles and off to Serekaniye hospital, but it was miles away and the traffic was frozen, all checkpoints suddenly on belated high-alert.

The town's alert state had downgraded organically over the preceding months, as Daesh were pushed further away across the region. Now it had paid the price. Perhaps basic terrorism like this was the shape of things to come, as Daesh's pretensions to statehood withered.

Our own security situation on the main road was hardly more in order, even after the bombs. We'd lost some of our best people since the al-Hawl op. They'd gone home to Iraq and whatever they had going on there; till the next time, maybe… I wished them well, but we were a poorer group for it. One day I put Pişko on *nobet* on the front gate, and when I went to check on him twenty minutes later I found he'd flagged down a vehicle and gone into town for the afternoon, leaving his post abandoned.

Before, we'd been a solid enough group to absorb the impact of a character like him; but now others started to play up in Soran's absence too. My team of westerners and four or five good Kurds held things together, each person doing far more than his share.

And if that wasn't enough, Soran's fresh blood, when he finally returned, brought fresh concerns.

Hamza was back. Not seen since Shengal. Rehabilitated after a long spell in YPG jail, by his own account – which clashed with other people's. According to him, he punched a general. The more popular view, not propagated by me, was that *Hamza's Daesh*. Maybe it was just because he was an Arab. But if so, his own behaviour hardly did him any favours. Never thought I'd see him again; but then, Rojava was all about reunions.

As if having him and Pişko wasn't enough, we had a newcomer called Kesra who just seemed like trouble from the off. He could have been an extra from a Middle Eastern version of Happy Days, with his greasy quiff, pocket comb and fake biker jacket over his combats. Into everything in the first five minutes, pushy as hell. I'd been put in charge of a Dushka gun on one of our renovated Hummers, and as soon as he saw me working on it, stripping and cleaning, he was all over it, grabbing bits and yammering away at me. He was obviously clueless, and finally I just grabbed him and shoved him away. I'd long learned not to do things like that here, but I'd had a shorter fuse since the night of the bombs at Tal Tamir and one more know-it-all clown in the unit was all I needed. He stumbled a few steps, then smirked and said something he knew I wouldn't understand.

When we pulled out on the next operation (it turned out Nichivan wasn't too far wrong about a quick turnaround) to clear the villages south of Kobani and retake the Tishrine Dam, my top priority, as leader of the western group in our *tabor*, was that *no one here dies stupidly*.

"Everyone in this squad has a battle partner. So please stick together and if they try and split you up, refuse. Even if it's Soran, I don't care. If you dismount in battle, get straight into cover, stay in verbal and visual contact with your partner. Cover each other. Even if everyone else is bumbling through, you move properly. You have to be a bit more of an adult in this unit, because they just don't look after you the way other *tabors* do. If they tell you to do something that you think's unsafe, don't do it. We can only rely on ourselves here. When I know more I'll pass it on. For now, let's keep weapons with us at all times, and *racts* (webbing) on, please. It's an operation, let's treat it like one."

We drove on. Days of low cloud, green hills, wet roads and smashed towns, all soot and debris. I perched high in the turret, sometimes swaddled in blankets in the freezing fog, rain and occasional snow, sitting on one hand then the other to keep the feeling in them. I nearly always sat up in the turret now, on a cushion. Occasionally we got a repair and I could stand down, get in cover, rotate the thing properly, but it never lasted. "Garage" here meant some guy with leathern skin and a pair of pliers.

We gave Hummer support to a *salderî tabor*, clearing village after village. In one, we had a textbook shootout from a concrete stairwell. Like so many others, decided by aircraft. I nearly got scalped at one point by low-flying RPG, and Dan came close to meeting his maker after I pulled him out of cover and sent him back on the Hummer with a casualty. As the Hummer returned with Dan in the gun turret, a suicide truck came roaring up its arse and blew up, close enough to scar the Hummer but no more. The truck wasn't up-armoured with steel like they usually were; just some battered old wagon, red with multicoloured swirly paintwork in that Middle Eastern style. I never fired, because I only realised what it was when it accelerated hard at the Hummer; two seconds later it was just a loud cloud. I'd been worried that Dan would be pissed off with me for sending him off the battlefield, up till then.

"I saw you carrying that little girl on your shoulder," he smiled, in the village that night. "It looked... *poetic*, man." He'd got some shots off at the VBIED before it went up, so he was happy enough. Another good war story, and he'd kept all his fingers and toes into the bargain.

An Iranian YPJ woman, young and darkly beautiful, sighed inconsolably, heartbroken at missing the battle. When would her time come? Soon enough, *heval*. Be careful what you wish for.

In the now-taken village the next day I met Kocher, the *salderî* Kurd who'd directed the firefight, and gave him a hug. *Good job yesterday.* The last time I'd seen him had been at Abdul Aziz, just before he'd gone to fight alongside Jac and Bob and had been shot in the leg.

The *hevals* went to pick over the Daesh corpses littered around the deep lunar craters that replaced three of the four enemy buildings. Dan took the boots off a corpse and put them on. I got his old ones.

We rolled on.

***

Dilgeş quit two weeks in. Took off after Pişko nearly got him killed with his battlefield high jinks. I wasn't there, because his Hummer went to one location and mine to another. The next time we met he was on his way out and nothing could change his mind – not that I would have tried. I totally got it.

Now there was no one I could confidently hand over to, even if I wanted to leave. Dan was good but didn't have Dilgeş's military background, and however different things were out here, that still mattered.

Of course nobody could stop me leaving any time I chose to. But living with myself afterwards would have been harder, especially if something happened to one of these boys after I'd gone. So I was locked in now, until the operation wound up or I could convince my team to quit and go to a more organised *tabor*. And as things unravelled more and more over the following days, that's what I dedicated myself to doing.

Several villages later, a barrage of confused, multidirectional fire by night. One dead Daesh, Chinese, was stretched out on the ground the next day, staring skyward, a chunk of his head ripped out. One casualty on our side, bullet through the thigh; hundred to one it was friendly fire. A YPJ fighter poked at the corpse with the toe of her boot. Mikro, a Norwegian combat medic (who treated our casualty the previous night and possibly saved his life) grabbed its wrist and hauled, causing blood to dribble out the back of its lolling head as it sat half-up. He wrestled a set of high-quality tan-coloured webbing off the body, drenched all over in fresh, bright blood, and put it on.

The dead seemed like movie props. Rubbery. Like that severed hand I saw from a berm on the al-Hawl op, tossed away in the clear-up after a village was taken. Or the enemy corpse with a lid of skull removed somehow, the interior hollowed out by chickens still pecking at the edges, next to another body, incinerated like a clutch of tarred sticks, fused to a charred motorbike skeleton. Where was that? Somewhere around Tal Hamis – or maybe Tal Barak, before Tal Nasir. Or the countless other corpses in various states of repair. Funny how movies seemed real, I thought, but when you saw the real thing it looked artificial. I wondered what to feel about that.

We rolled on.

***

Kesra was still at the wheel, despite having totalled at least one, maybe two, of our fragile, ailing Hummers with his reckless driving – another mystery of Soran's troop management. Dan reckoned he promised them things like this as part of his recruitment drive.

Kesra treated vehicle care and weapons care (and care in general) like it was something for the old folks. Skin thicker than a tank's armour against any kind of reproof. *Come back Aso, all is forgiven.*

Soran's groups, and his operations, could be the best or the worst. A lot seemed to depend on how much he was around. Whether he realised it or cared was anyone's guess. His mind was always elsewhere these days, as was he – not singing round the fire, laughing like Henry VIII and leading from the front like on the last op. We saw him every few days. And when the cat was away, the mice were inclined to play. Just like before.

Detach, concentrate, keep your team safe. Don't leave them hanging mid-op.

As we entered one village, Kesra nearly garrotted me in the turret for the umpteenth time by driving under low wires, ignoring my warnings. Villagers glared and shouted at me, arms raised, as the wire snagged and snapped and clean washing slapped down into the dirt. I shrugged guiltily and bawled myself hoarse at Kesra, whose knuckleheaded features waxed baffled and faintly amused, as they had yesterday when I yelled at him for firing off the Dushka on a whim in a civilian area. Those bullets would go through three or more of these mud walls before stopping.

At this stage shouting had become a habit, a reflex. Otherwise, inside, I felt quite comfortably numb. The lethal idiocy was a constant, a fact of life to be worked around like the weather and the mortar bombs landing on top of us every few days.

We pulled up at another lone, exposed house in the perishing, bullying wind, unloaded the weapons and other gear, and the boys went scouring the abandoned dwellings nearby for blankets, firewood, a diesel burner and other essentials.

"Daesh coming here yesterday night," Soran said. "Throw *bomba*, one my friend kill-*ed*."

We needed a sentry on the roof and one patrolling the grounds. He took off again in the Hilux. These cold and lonely promontories he found for us, then left us to.

I started scoping stand-to positions and sorting out the sentry list. As soon as I showed it to people, they wanted to fuck the schedule around again. Amazing the way those guys could argue till dawn over who was on when. At least our squad were taking it seriously, thank God. Dan suggested we stand to an hour before *roj baş* (reveille). I was diffident about selling that to them, frankly, so it was more than a relief. Self-preservation just kicked in after Tal Tamir, for some of us at least, thank fuck.

The al-Hawl op was more fun in general. We rarely saw the /223 group on this one either. Jac was no longer with them anyway. He'd dropped the ball once or twice — not in any major way, but they were serious guys, the /223, and ran a very tight ship. They didn't expect him to equal their military standards, but they did want to see that he *got* it. They'd come down on him, but also given him his chance to redeem himself, which he just hadn't taken despite my own attempt to explain things to him. In fairness, he'd come a long way from the callow kid I'd met in Sulaymaniyah. But he'd never had the rigorous conditioning of a real army and it showed. He was missing this op. He wasn't missing much.

A Kurd we sometimes referred to as The Dude, who'd got us all out of bed a few days ago by firing at a tree in the dark (he was stoned on hashish and the tree was "moving") came to me one evening in stark cold fear. Pişko was on *sûbay*, he said. There were enemy all around and we'd all catch it in the night. He drew his hand across his throat, wide-eyed.

"Don't worry. I've got it," I assured him. No way I'd trust that little headcase to keep the guard rota going either; I wouldn't have trusted him with a burnt match. I stayed up the whole night, yet again, a blanket draped over my shoulders, drifting around the perimeter like a shapeless ghost. Hassan, supposed to be on *nobet*, sat hunkered down against a wall out of the wind with his face buried in his jacket collar against the cold. I just couldn't be bothered to tell him. It was an accomplishment just getting him out of bed; half of them wanted to do their *nobet* from under a blanket.

Pişko got up in the night anyway and immediately decided to light a fire on the outside porch, in a metal wood burner we'd scrapped.

"Pişko. Look around," I waved an arm at the night. "Why do you think there are no other fires?"

It was one thing after another.

My team did stand-to like proper soldiers every morning, taking up positions at first light and remaining alert; and whenever an extra duty needed filling, a bunch of hands always went up. I felt proud of them as I shuffled off to bed.

In the warmth of the Hilux, Pişko and Hamza were disputing the ownership of a Columbia lock-knife. Pound to a penny one of them robbed a body for it. OK, Hamza robbed a body for it, but he lost it and Pişko found it. *Give me 3,000 Syrian pounds and you can have it back*, snarled Pişko. Grasping, conniving little bastard. They settled on 1,000.

Hamza, Kesra and Pişko had the fatalism, the *laissez-faire* outlook of the Tal Nasir guys, but none of their devotion. There was no aspiration to martyrdom – tinged with the ineffable draw of death itself – for those three. I understood that draw and respected it, misgivings notwithstanding. After a year of this I had a foot in both camps. But these three musketeers wanted a Samsung Galaxy, cash, a better weapon. They were cowboys and worse. One mad, one bad, all dangerous to know. Just before this operation the Irish kid, no longer serving, rang Dan up and warned him to get the hell out of Soran's *tabor*.

In another village the enemy brought the fight to us, but they picked an unfortunate time – just as we were on our way out to do a night attack of our own. Daesh thought to surprise us but they found a joint force of maybe three *tabors*: 60 or so *hevals* ready and waiting. The first shots rang out as we were sat in the Hummer, waiting for the off. *From where?* Obvious first thought: *is that some of our lot getting overexcited and starting early?* We sent the hapless aggressors packing with a spirited response. Soran fired from the rooftop sandbag position. The air was filled with shouts, cheers and the occasional "*Biji serok Apo!*" (Long live leader Apo!) A good time had by all. At one point I even gave them a bit of a song: "Happy birthday to you! Happy birthday to you...!"

At times I wondered if I was losing it. I was due a spot of *leave now*.

Next morning another Hummer *tabor* rolled in and we watched them clear the outlying buildings all around, as the welcome clink of glasses signalled a couple of *hevals* making the tea rounds along the berm. Shahin, the boy who taught me the dance steps a year ago at Zara village, was one of the Hummer drivers. With rough stubble on his face and responsibility on his shoulders, his year of combat had turned him from a laughing boy into a grizzled vet.

The count of enemy dead circulated from mouth to mouth.

"*Tene yek*," sighed a guy I'd been chatting to. Only one…

Together with the sabotage *tabor* we went for a long drive, up and down the roads, on the lookout for mines and IEDS planted around the area.

As the search wound up, Pişko went out on the ground, looking for things to scavenge. He searched through some workers' huts, then made for a couple of dead Daesh bodies, stiff as tailor's dummies, limbs askew. He scrabbled through pockets and pouches, hauled on webbing straps and rolled one over. Shiny bullets fell to the ground and he scampered around collecting them like a malevolent clown snatching up coins. Then he stepped back, fired a couple of shots from his rifle into the body. Bored, he returned to the Hummer.

We headed back to our base, in convoy now with three Hummers from other *tabors*. I signalled to the gunner behind me to turn his gun and pass the message down, till all guns were facing 360.

Groping for sleep that night, I saw Pişko in my mind's eye again, riding on the Hummer's front bumper like some totemic hood ornament, signalling all that was wrong with us. Those grinning, goatish features, that scruffy tuffet of beard.

The infantry *tabor* started using us less and less after I argued with their commander. They'd tried to split up battle partners in my team, and I'd dug my heels in. *No way.* There'd been instances of people getting left out alone on previous operations and it wasn't going to happen here. *They go out in pairs, or not at all.* The blokes knew I was reducing their chances of battle, but they also knew my only authority was by their consent, at the end of the day. Nothing would happen to them for going against me.

One morning after the stand-to I gathered them in to talk about the thing I'd been turning over in my mind all night – for days, actually.

We collected on the cold, windy roof to include Karker, a young German lad on *nobet*, new to the group, in the Serious Talks. I'd nearly thrown Hamza off this same roof a few days before, for taking random potshots at passing villagers with my machine gun. Even so, my heart was hardly in it even then. I just felt it was something I should do…

"Boys, this unit goes through good times and bad times. When the Hummers are in good shape and we've got plenty of decent people, we're the tip of the spear. Other times, the guys are 100 degrees south of useless, the Hummers are fucked and the *tabor's* on its arse.

"And what about this: besides the danger to ourselves, do you want to be implicated in the murder of a civilian? What happens when this lot shoot up a car and you spend the rest of your life wondering if it was *your* bullet that went through some kid's head, because you supported them in the moment and opened fire?" It had nearly happened the other night.

"Soran won't resent you for leaving him – I did it before. He puts his needs first and so should you."

"Well. If there's no fighting…" said Dan.

I'd learnt that fighting isn't everything. But you have to find your own way to that. Finally we were all agreed. They'd leave for another *tabor*, and I'd just leave.

We went to give Soran the news. We were out.

"That was like kicking a puppy," said Ararat, afterwards.

***

Next morning at breakfast Soran was singing loudly, full of forced merriment and bonhomie. I felt a twinge of guilt. This time, when his *tabor* broke up, it was largely my doing. And while I had what might be called a love for him, I had no second thoughts about this course of action.

The boys took off in a truck for Kobani city to get reassigned. The *tabor* was too small to continue now, so the rest of us headed back to the cowshed at Tal Tamir and most of the Kurds decided to bail as well. Soran was down to Hamza, Kesra, Pişko and Herdem, who was also planning his exit, apparently. I hoped so.

Leaving them at Tal Tamir, Soran and I travelled to Qereçox.

Qereçox, where you could almost see the curve of the world from horizon to horizon. Where you remembered why you'd come, and turned round and headed back in. But this last op had drained me to the dregs; it was time to get out for a while before I started to make mistakes of my own. The signs were there: taking a bit longer to get out of bed for my guard shift, putting off cleaning my weapon till later… signs of my edge getting blunted. And ignoring them could be costly, possibly even lethal.

I was, as ever, *pretty much* decided; with the usual doubts and misgivings in place. Out here, little was certain and almost nothing was final. And back home, an argument with a boss, a conversation with a *heval* on Facebook, and you find yourself pricing up flights… but, for the time being, I was set. I'd got through a year of this unscathed – physically at least.

Goodbye, Soran. I gave him a hug before we parted.

"You good friend," he said.

Maybe he'd build it back up again, from the charred remnants. Maybe I went back to him because he had the heart of embers, the genuine unrefined magma that drew people towards him. But when he left you out in the cold, it was fucking cold.

Young Jac was still out there, in a sniper *tabor*, I heard. He'd missed this op. But he didn't need me any more – if he ever had.

16 DECOMPRESSION

Portsmouth International Ferry Port
February 2016

The confined, sterile interview suite is a world away from the open plains of Syria and the countless squalid, tumbledown rooms I've spent the past year in.

Arrest wasn't entirely unexpected, but still I'd held out hope that the ferry crossing from France would be a safer bet than flying into Heathrow. The badly hidden expression on the passport controller's face said it all, much too late.

"*Oh…* Could you wait over there for a moment please… sir…?"

Shuttled from point to point, stood up, sat down, stripped, searched, questioned. Passport, laptop, phone, clothes, every stitch and item I came over with, whisked away. Handwritten journals, personal files, private thoughts fingered and thumbed. I'm in prison plimsolls, joggers and jumper. My body isn't mine any more, and neither is my mind. The hooks are in deep; I'm suspended midway between guilt and innocence. No longer a full and private person. The jury's out.

Head still clearing the three pints of Guinness on deck, the sea spray and the rhythm of the boat, my focus zooms from floor to table in the glaring light as the questions come tumbling through the air. They are vague at first, a meandering fishing expedition, until I'm formally arrested under the Terrorism Act and more experienced officers take over.

Was it your sole purpose to fight ISIS? Or was your mindset more closely aligned with the aims and goals of the Kurdish forces?

The interview suite is boiling but my muscles contract with cold. Sitting in the broken turret, in the winter mist. Contemplating my wrecked boots with their layered stains of dirt, blood, paint, diesel, and the moments that caused them. Trying to separate them out, get the order right.

Were you given battle plans or strategic plans for the engagements?

What intelligence was there for identifying your enemy?

Barrelling through the enemy town, bullets entering the vehicle above and below. The guys yelling and clamouring like it's a galley-slaves mutiny down there.

What were your fellow fighters like? Professional?

Was there anything particular you saw that you didn't agree with – anything done or said that wouldn't have been allowed in the British army?

Pişko waving his arms like a mad conductor in the line of fire, throwing grenades around like firecrackers at a street dance.

What do you feel you achieved by going there?

DECOMPRESSION

Pulling the dead and dying from the wreckage of the town. Teenage warriors dancing in rows by night, fire-shadows on the wall. Disappearing one by one, the others dancing on.

You were in Syria twice. Why did you leave in June 2015?

Why did you go back again?

Friends lost. A photo on a scratched phone. That spark in her eyes.

How did you feel about it?

How did that make you feel?

17 REMEMBRANCE

All I want for Christmas is my dead friends back, wrote Levi on his Facebook page in December 2015. In the new year he went back. For more and more westerners who've been there once, Rojava is a revolving door. Why? It gets under your skin. People go there for one reason, and go back for another. Harry, Bob and many others also returned at different times.

Levi was killed at Man Bij, searching a booby-trapped house. It was no great surprise to learn from the press that he'd never been a marine after all. But he *was* a fighter in the YPG. And a good man and a friend. A *heval*.

Will was also killed at Man Bij. I can still see him on that motorbike at Tal Tamir, standing in the middle of the track, revving the engine.

That's how it goes: friends you once sat with to remember the dead have gone to join them. The veil that separates us is thin.

They were all far too young to die. And Aras, dear old Aras, was too old; meaning, they should have found him something else to do, away from the front. I don't know which hurts more. Last I saw him he was driving the logistics truck and again very happy. Singing, smiling, making up goodie bags for our *tabor*, his favourite drop-off on his circuit. He was captured by Daesh out on a supply run and beheaded, I'm told.

***

In the static position facing Tal Nasir, those long, tormented summer months, we all had to pass the time somehow. Portuguese Kendal (Mario) had his tailoring, Bob and Harry their sniper games and Jac his dumbass vandalism. Seeing me sketching a cartoon for Kendal Kobani, young Diyar – a chubby, tough-looking machine gunner with one of the nicest, gentlest dispositions you could imagine, asked me if I'd draw him. I said why not, gesturing to him to sit down.

As I started roughing the outlines, up came Çiya. He found the sight of Diyar sitting for a portrait hilarious, and started ribbing us. I told Diyar I couldn't draw with someone clowning around in front of me; I'd do it later when Çiya wasn't around. Diyar got up and walked off.

I didn't see at first just how disappointed he was, though his irritation was directed at Çiya, not me. I told myself I must find another time to draw him, but I never did.

Another time, Diyar tried to help me wring out my hand-washing in a garden with a working tap. I brushed him off because I was still irritated that Çiya had stopped me having a shower using the hosepipe trailing from the tap up into the branches of a tree – there were YPJ walking around outside. It was a frustrating, tense environment: food and hygiene were rubbish, and I was just randomly irritable some days, despite myself. Diyar was offended, and later, instead of apologising, I just left it. When I left that group I gave Diyar my Swiss Army knife – an expensive one. He was quite moved by the gesture, but I still think a 20-minute drawing and an apology would have been better.

Diyar and Çiya are both dead now. So are Portuguese Kendal and Kendal Kobani, and many other friends of that summer. I try to remember the good times, but moments like those stand out the sharpest. They pain me far more than any memory of battle, and I suppose that's just my punishment.

This roll call of dead friends could run and run.

Gunter Helsten, the little German ex-Legionnaire in his 50s, a peerless soldier and as gentle as a father to the two Canadian and Polish YPJ under his wing.

Tirej, from Shengal. I asked myself many times, how much did the youngsters *really* know the likely end awaiting them? Did some just follow the crowd, either not thinking about it, or paying lip-service to şehid status while secretly believing it wouldn't happen to them?

Certainly not in Tirej's case. He knew.

Reece Harding. Jamie Bright. Dean Evans. Demhat. Heqi. Agît. And more. Every so often, back in my safe London flat with my safe London problems, I get news of another.

Other news is perhaps even more dispiriting, in its way. Some months after my return, a tabloid newspaper exposed Baz as a convicted rapist on the run. The YPG, for him, was a temporary escape. He subsequently returned to Britain and is now in prison. Another guy from that *tabor* is currently incarcerated in Australia, pending murder charges. I choose not to dwell on this side of things but I'd be wrong to omit it altogether.

Peter left a few months after me, and as far as anyone knows has become a ghost – in contact with no one, not a trace of him on the networks we all keep in touch by. I'm not surprised in the least. He ran his own game out there and whatever it was, his contribution on the ground is beyond question.

Over a year after I left, Herdem sent me a photo: the latest in a stream of selfies and emojis. But this photo was of Aso – standing tall and proud in a tight-fitting suit like a Mod, next to a beautiful young woman in a wedding dress. Behind them were white hanging drapes decked with flowers. Aso, grinning from ear to ear. *Bless you, mate*. I can only wonder how he retells the events that forced his exit from the war. With a bit more flash-bang, if I know that guy. But to me he's a hero of the revolution no matter what.

***

In 2017 Jac went on the operation to liberate Raqqa. It was the big one: the effective endgame for the so-called caliphate. I was in London, still on bail under the Terrorism Act, and struggling in various other aspects of day-to-day life. Of course I considered returning for Raqqa; it would have been a push to get there, but I could probably have done it. Why didn't I? The question is as hard to answer as why I went in the first place. The only thing that really matters – I guess – is that I didn't go, and Jac did.

It was Jac's third tour; he'd fought at Tabqa, Man Bij and other places in the interim. By this point he was the last of the original volunteers, possibly the longest-serving westerner out there. Highly proficient in Kurmanji, and now making inroads into Arabic, he led a small sniper team battling from street to street in some of the most intense fighting of the war. The /223 guys had long since gone home, that unit effectively finished – so Jac's new crew took its name.

Jac had changed drastically; ageing from 21 to 24 in a combat environment will do that. Less inclined to giggle and joke around, or to suffer fools around him, he'd developed a directness and *sang-froid*, grown wiser and harder with experience of battle and loss. That steady, dead-serious expression that used to surface occasionally had become his default. He carried himself upright and had acquired the instinct of a fighter, become ingrained to the life. Just before the op I got this message from him:

Mate I swear these new space cadets that I see now.
They bring no kit. Not got a clue where they are or what there doing. Got no admin. No kurdish
They are literally useless lol
They will grow up when their mates get killed and they nearly do.

One fine day in Raqqa, a group of Daesh fought their way to the house Jac's team had taken for a base and set the place on fire. Jac and his comrades escaped the burning building by smashing a hole through the outer wall while some battled to keep the enemy outside at bay. Some days later, in a different location, the enemy actually broke in on them – the Arab guards downstairs had deserted their posts, apparently – and started to fight their way upstairs. Some captured Daesh suicide belts were in an upstairs room and Jac picked one up and threw it out of a window into the street. Seeing the "awesome" result, he threw a second one down the stairwell inside the building. The explosion made everyone blind with dust and smoke for several minutes, and put paid to the enemy intrusion.

One night he did a livestream Facebook video – a Q and A to camera for his many followers, from a darkened basement somewhere in Raqqa city. A generator clattered noisily in the background. His tired, undernourished features looked pale and gaunt in the white halogen torchlight. His eyes and voice were steely and sardonic.

Don't give away your position or the enemy will come and attack you there, counselled some wise internet warrior, on the scrolling comments thread. Reading it, Jac answered, in deadpan tones, "I *want* them to come and attack us. Anyone who doesn't want that shouldn't be here."

Many of Jac's friends, myself included, entreated him repeatedly to come home. No one's luck lasts forever. But he fought on and on, gaining the respect of Kurdish commanders, of covert western

Special Forces, of everyone around him. "He lived and breathed combat," remarked one of his battle buddies. He had more about him than any of us realised, and overtook us all, in terms of the language, the battle experience and just the sheer capacity to endure in that environment. They'd languished for five static months before the Raqqa op, something I'd have found very hard to do, and when on it he spent most of his time tirelessly organising to get his team into the fight – arranging permission, transport, equipment, communications and pretty much everything else.

If I don't do all of that, every single day, he wrote, *we would sit in this building doing nothing until Raqqa is finished*. It was pointless my telling *him* that fighting isn't everything, though I tried to anyway. His answer to that was: *When you're out here it is*.

A few days after Raqqa fell, his team were waiting for the truck that would come and take them away for some well-earned rest. YPG and SDF flags fluttered from the superstructure of Raqqa stadium as the troops picked over the rubble and went about the slow, painstaking work of making the city safe again. By all accounts Jac was done; ready to come home, finally. They decided to give the accommodation a clear-out, to make it safe for civilian returnees. Jac carried a suicide vest down to the street to disarm it, as he'd done numerous times before, telling the others to move back to a safe distance. As he placed it on the ground it blew up, killing him outright.

Two hours later their truck arrived.

I got the call from Joe Akerman that evening, as I was preparing the lessons I had to teach the following week and exercising some restraint with the bottle of red wine on my desk. Joe needed my advice on something, he said, and seemed to have some difficulty getting to the point. When he finally did, it was as though he'd passed on not only the words but also his own difficulty in articulating them, down the line somehow, to me. *Jac's dead.* I went numb and dumb all over. The first friend I ever made out there, and the most painful to lose. We looked into it separately, verified details, exchanged some anguished sentiments. Then we set ourselves to deciding how the family should be told, and who should give them the news (before the press did) that Jac had gone the same way as so many other friends.

EPILOGUE

How this war will be remembered, I don't know. Journalists only capture a fraction, and often it's what they go looking for. The YPG will tell one set of stories, the Peshmerga another, the international volunteers, the academics, the world press and historians and politicos others; the local people (if anyone asks them) others still. When someone tells you, "I've been there," the best answer is probably: "So?"

Dead friends should be honoured, always, and never forgotten. But I decided on my last operation that the living matter more. And maybe that's just one of numerous differences I have with the YPG philosophy.

As for those YPG leaders who wanted to keep the westerners out of the fight – I suppose they knew all along the true nature of things, the true cost. It's a far cry from NATO operations. They don't have what we have. They win by throwing lives, mainly young lives, in their hundreds, their thousands, at the target till it falls. Their objective: to spare future generations the suffering of today's and yesterday's. This has evolved to the point where an individual life seems to have more value *after* it's been sacrificed than before; and they've become a force to be reckoned with as a result.

If I was cynical before I went to Kurdistan, my time there hardly brought me back to idealism. But when I come to reckon it up, I think I can justify it to myself, on balance. I did nothing special – no heroics, no great victories. Maybe I made a tiny difference here and there. But when I see myself in that safe, lucrative job in Saudi, deciding whether to throw it all up or play it safe, I can only see myself making the exact same choice.

As to the inevitable survivor guilt, I've no shortage of that. When I go out for a run, say, I'm quite conscious that Kosta and Bagok can't do that. They won't get their fitness back, like I needed to. Dilsoz won't finish his book. But to fritter my time away any more would just amplify that guilt.

That said, there are still days when it feels like I'm just hanging around, because all the best people have left the party early.

Before my year in Rojava and Shengal, I hadn't just sworn off crusading; I'd become a more withdrawn person in general. Just plodding along, content to keep the world at a distance. Over that extraordinary year I came to feel and realise, finally, the real value of human connection.

I'm still pretty much a loner, however; I haven't changed that much. I'll always regret not making more of the time I shared with people who are gone, now that it's too late. Such friendships are incomplete and fleeting by nature anyway – handfuls of bright moments, like shrapnel shards of some rare, precious metal, scattering through the dark to stick embedded in the heart forever. I'll never be completely alone, as long as I carry those fragments inside me. If I'm proud of anything in that war, it's of having known such people, and of being considered a friend by them. I never thought to gain so much, and so much through irreparable loss. Fighting isn't everything.

The Kurdish phrase *şehid namirin* means "martyrs never die". While the concept of martyrdom isn't an easy one for me, the phrase has become a mantra for Kurd and westerner alike. When I started writing this, the purpose was simply to provide a window into a world most people don't know about, to show *what it's like there*. As things went on, however, I came to see it as a way to keep my friends alive, for myself. If I thought it could bring them to life in the mind's eye of the reader, that would surpass all aspiration. And it would still be nothing, compared to what I owe them.

ACKNOWLEDGEMENTS

It's been a particularly rocky road getting to this point, both for the book and myself. I owe so much to so many people that I'm bound to leave someone out here. Apologies for that in advance; I'll try and get it sorted for future editions.

Firstly, I'd like to thank those who've taught me something about writing at one time or another, most recently Mark Lucas for his insights and patience, and especially Steve Aylett, a true original who will probably get his due one or two centuries from now. Chris Cleave and Suzie Dooré also deserve a nod here, as does Gavin Evans and everyone who ploughed through my early draft manuscripts and gave me feedback. Thanks also to Jo, Paula and Mel from Mirror Books, and to Annabel and Claire at Whitefox.

I should also raise a glass in gratitude to Ali, Joel and Hoss, the dynamic legal trio, for their help over that unfortunate 'terrorism' business (of course, I wasn't worried in the least...). Thanks also to Anne McMurdie.

On a more personal note, there are numerous people whose varied help and support have made a very trying couple of years much more tolerable. Particular stars, in no particular order, are my sister and brother-in-law Abby and Martin, Enrico Ambroso (sorry about the shoe thing), John Billington, Anne and Guy Poffa, Mark Campbell, Ozzy and all at the KCC, Hannah and Stephen, George and Heather, John Bott, Emily Apple, Kader, Kris King, JC Patrick for going easy, the boys at Star Kebab in Homerton and no doubt a bunch of others I'm too thoughtless to remember. It's been genuinely humbling.

Finally, salutations and undying comradeship to Soran, Dersem, Herdem, Khalil, Bucky, Viyan, Qandil, Kamura, Aso, and many, many other hevals, who made this book but who will never see it.

Also by Mirror Books

The Accidental Spy
Sean O'Driscoll

The astonishing, gripping, long-awaited inside story of an ordinary man, who became an extraordinary spy.

After years living in semi-isolation, David Rupert speaks for the first time of how a trucker from New York who liked to holiday in Ireland with his girlfriend, ended up being recruited to the FBI and MI5 at one of the most crucial times in British political history.

Including shock revelations about Rupert's discoveries working within the Real IRA, such as sending bomb parts, hidden inside toys, to a primary school in Donegal. Sean O'Driscoll tells David's incredible story, 'The Big Yank', a 6'7" American tourist, who found himself at the centre of a chilling campaign of terror that targeted civilians, the forces and Prime Minister Tony Blair.

Countless lives have been saved by David Rupert's decision to risk his neck working for years within one of the most brutal and ruthless terrorist organisations in the world. An unprecedented bombing campaign had been planned to destroy any hopes of a peace agreement. Finally, in a trial that rested entirely on the evidence of 'The Big Yank', those plans for ongoing bloodshed and an end to the Good Friday Agreement were brought to a halt.